SRSLY, WTF?'

How to Survive 248 of Life's Worst F*#!-ing Situations EVER

GREGORY BERGMAN, ANTHONY W. HADDAD,
AND JODI MILLER

adamsmedia
AVON, MASSACHUSETTS

Published by
Adams Media, a division of F+W Media, Inc.
57 Littlefield Street, Avon, MA 02322. U.S.A.
www.adamsmedia.com

ISBN 10: 1-4405-2575-7
ISBN 13: 978-1-4405-2575-9
eISBN 10: 1-4405-2578-1
eISBN 13: 978-1-4405-2578-0

Printed in the United States of America.

10   9   8   7   6   5   4   3   2   1

Library of Congress Cataloging-in-Publication Data
is available from the publisher.

SRSLY, WTF? contains material adapted and abridged from:

WTF?, by Gregory Bergman and Anthony W. Haddad, copyright © 2008 by Gregory Bergman and Anthony Haddad, ISBN 10: 1-60550-031-3, ISBN 13: 978-1-6055-0031-7;

WTF? College, by Gregory Bergman and Jodi Miller, copyright © 2009 by Gregory Bergman, ISBN 10: 1-4405-0035-5, ISBN 13: 978-1-4405-0035-0;

WTF? Work, by Gregory Bergman and Jodi Miller, copyright © 2010 by Gregory Bergman, ISBN 10: 1-4405-0322-2, ISBN 13: 978-1-4405-0322-1;

WTF? Women, by Gregory Bergman and Jodi Miller, copyright © 2011 by Gregory Bergman, ISBN 10: 1-4405-0658-2, ISBN 13: 978-1-4405-0658-1.

This book is available at quantity discounts for bulk purchases. For information, please call 1-800-289-0963.

Contents

Introduction: This Time We're F*#!-ing Serious

By Gregory Bergman

Every second of every day someone is facing another absurd situation that makes them say, "What the fuck?" Whether you can't find your keys or you just found out you have to get a testicle removed, there's a WTF moment around every corner. From the mundane to the insane, we are surrounded by shit that makes us scratch our head and wonder what the fuck is going on in this crazy world.

And it's always been a WTF world. Think about all those terrible times in history like the plague—two-thirds of medieval Europe's population decimated. Talk about WTF. And it continues to be a WTF world. Since the release of our outstanding series' first book in 2008, the world has witnessed one WTF moment after another. From the collapse of the global financial system to the popularity of the Snuggie to the invention of smart phones so smart they can now actually blow you, this planet just seems to get stranger and more unpredictable by the day. That's where we come in.

Our mission has always been to teach you how to survive life's worst f*#!-ing situations. It didn't matter whether you were in college or at the office or dealing with the fairer (and far more annoying) sex, our goal has been to provide you with the solutions you need to deal with everything life throws at you. That is our purpose, our passion, and our sacred pledge to mankind.

So join us on the following journey through some of our favorite WTF situations. It's the most comprehensive collection of WTF moments ever. Pulled from *WTF?*, *WTF? College*, *WTF? Work*, and *WTF? Women*, there are so many hysterical WTF situations in this book it will make your fucking head spin.

But don't worry, the WTF? series is far from over, and is in fact just beginning. So long as there are WTF moments to survive, we will always write another WTF? book to help you through them. (Not to mention, writing these books sure as hell beats working. LOL. I know—some guys have all the luck. WTF?)

So seriously, what the fuck are you waiting for? Get reading. WTF?

Chapter 1

WTF?

How to Survive 101 of Life's Worst F*#!-ing Situations

1. You Can't Remember Where You Parked

You've been through this several thousand times before, but you can't seem to learn your lesson. So there you are—again—in the middle of a crowded parking lot without the vaguest idea where you parked. Forgetting you parked in the Orange lot, section G2, Row A is one thing, but not even remembering what floor you're on is incredibly stupid.

Nevertheless, here's what to do:

The WTF Approach to Finding Your F*#!-ing Car

> **OPTION #1: _Think Carefully_**

If you were a 2006 Nissan Maxima, where would you be?

> **OPTION #2: _Report It Stolen_**

Go get a drink and let the cops find it. If they don't, you'll be able to collect the insurance money and get a new one that doesn't have french fries stuck between the seats.

> **OPTION #3: _Wait Until the Place Closes_**

With fewer cars on the lot, you should be able to find yours. This won't work if you misplaced your car at O'Hare.

> **OPTION #4: _Find Someone to Drive You Around_**

The security guy will probably do it, or you could call a cab . . . but you might want to take this opportunity to pick up sympathetic women instead.

➤ OPTION #5: *Make a Spectacle*

Walk around like a jackass with your arm in the air hitting the unlock button on your key and looking for your car's lights to flash. If you don't have one of those electronic keys, your car should be ugly enough to spot.

➤ OPTION #6: *Borrow Another Car*

If there's no security guard and you can't find anyone to drive you around, hotwire another car and borrow it until you find yours.

➤ OPTION #7: *Check your Blackberry*

See if you made a note about where you parked. What good is it to have ridiculously expensive, portable electronic instruments if you don't use them to solve the most ordinary of issues? Maybe you should get one for your kid and make it his job to keep track of your life.

➤ OPTION #8: *Buy the Place*

Close it for renovation. The sole remaining car should be yours.

IN THE FUTURE . . .

Use mnemonic devices. Try to memorize the location of your car based on words you make from the letter and number. If you park in H3, think of three horses. If you park in M16, think of the gun. If you park in F69 . . .

2. Your Dry Cleaner Ruins Your Clothing and Won't Pay for It

If you've ever had a suit or a shirt shrunk down to a miniature version of what it was by an incompetent dry cleaner, you've undoubtedly heard the same bullshit explanation the employee gives everyone: "It was like that already." Sound familiar? Well, now imagine the line is spoken in a thick accent and it will hit home.

The WTF Approach to Getting Some F*#!-ing Money for Your Ruined Clothes

Dry cleaners are some of the biggest liars on the planet and we at WTF have vowed to put an end to their criminal acts. Here's what to do the next time your shirt ends up fit for a Ken doll.

> **STEP #1:** *Get Them to Admit Fault*

Naturally, they're going to deny it the first few times you complain, expecting you to walk away and shrug your shoulders. Don't. Keep complaining. To prove your case, take off the shirt you're wearing and hold it next to the shrunken one. Rhetorically ask, "Did I gain fifty pounds and grow five inches in a week?"

➤ STEP #2: *Protest*

Make a spectacle of yourself and hold up the line. Show the other customers what the cleaner has done. In front of a jury of your peers, with the evidence of the crime, the dry cleaner may give in and offer you credit for more dry cleaning. If you settle for the credit, don't send them anything they haven't cleaned before.

➤ STEP #3: *Sue Them*

A dry cleaner will almost never reimburse you for your loss outside of court. If they did, they'd go out of business. So unless it's worth the hassle, you'll have to forget about it.

IN THE FUTURE . . .

Don't go to discount cleaners. Take your Armani suit to the best dry cleaner in town. If you thought you could just pay $4.50 to get it cleaned properly, think again.

3. You Find a Booger in Your Breakfast Sandwich

Everyone knows that eating at fast food joints is about the worst thing you can do for your body outside of hardcore drugs. And just like when you're about to push a spoonful of H into your veins, when you're about to chow down on some fast food, you don't want to spot a booger in it—even though the booger is probably better for you. Other than the oink, that sausage patty contains whey protein concentrate, water, salt, corn syrup solids, sugar, spices, dextrose, spice extractives, caramel color, BHA and BHT, propyl gallate and citric acid, and monosodium glutamate—which even the Chinese place on the corner stopped using . . . or so they say.

The WTF Approach to Eating F*#!-ing Fast Food

Here's the simplest solution: If you find something suspicious in your sandwich, throw it out and go to a goddamn deli. It's your fault for going there in the first place. *Never return your fast food.*

Fast food restaurants employ the barely employable, and the more you complain, the more bodily fluids they'll try to sneak into your belly.

► OPTION #1: *Eat Food That You Can See Them Make*

You can get a good look at the assembly line at Subway, most Taco Bells, and some burger joints. If you can watch the whole process, you can be pretty sure that it's safe—unless they jerk off in the mayonnaise after hours.

► OPTION #2: *Don't Eat Fast Food*

It doesn't taste that good, it's bad for you, and it makes you fat. If you're in a rush and can't sit down for a good meal, grab an apple or just skip lunch.

Fast-Food Pyramid

Employee's body fluids and hair group:
Use sparingly

Condiment group:
2–3 servings per day

Processed cheese group:
2–4 servings per day

Miscellaneous animal body parts group:
3–5 servings per day

Lard group:
6–11 servings per day

4. A Panhandler Won't Leave You Alone

"**B**rother, can you spare a dime?" It'd be nice if panhandlers were that polite. They might even get a buck or two as a result. But they're not. Usually it's more like this:

HIM: "Got a quarter?"

YOU: "No."

HIM: "Come on. I'm hungry."

YOU: "Sorry."

HIM: "I'm a Vietnam vet."

YOU: "I still don't have any money for you."

HIM: "I have cancer."

YOU: "Yep. Still nothing in my pockets."

HIM: "And AIDS."

YOU: "Still nothing, bro."

HIM: "No? Then f*#! you!"

Still, it's not easy to say no, but you can't give to all of them. If you did, you'd be out of cash in a minute—half a minute in San Francisco, where the homeless population is only rivaled by the homosexual population.

NOTE: Sometimes you'll see people who are both homeless *and* homosexual. You can always tell them apart: They're the ones with the nicest cardboard boxes and the most organized shopping carts filled with crap.

The WTF Approach to Dealing with F*#!-ing Panhandlers

➤ **STEP #1: *Don't Look***

If you do your best to avoid eye contact, then not giving is easier.

➤ **STEP #2: *Lie and Say, "I'm sorry, man."***

Apologize and pretend to look in your pockets as if you would have given him something but you just can't today.

➤ **STEP #3: *Give Him a Lecture on "Personal Responsibility"***

If you have some free time, take out Ralph Waldo Emerson's essay on "Self-Reliance" and read to him. The delicate prose and stirring sentiment will no doubt inspire him—to kill you, probably!

➤ **STEP #4: *Give Some Money—to the Deserving Ones***

If you're like us, every couple of years you wake up and feel generous. But since you can't give to everyone, you have to be choosy. Here's our hierarchy for handing out to the homeless:

THE LEGLESS OR ARMLESS

Give to amputees first, since their lives are the most depressing.

THE REAL VETERANS

There are too many homeless veterans in this country, but how can you tell which ones are lying about serving and which ones are the genuine, f*#!-ed-up article? Ask them. Find out what branch of the armed services he supposedly served in and what company, battalion, etc. If you still suspect him of lying, ask for further proof like dog tags or an old picture of him with a really lame buzz cut.

BLACK OVER WHITE

Given the historical persecution of blacks and minorities, you should give to a black homeless person over a white homeless person, all things being equal. Think of it as affirmative action for losers.

THE TALENTED ONES

Can your homeless person do tricks? If he can dance or do a magic trick, he should be rewarded with a buck or two.

Always Give If You're on a Date

If you are on a date with a girl, always give a panhandler something unless he's really rude or obnoxious. You can never look too nice in front of someone that you want to impress. A buck or so is a small price to pay to get laid. Now, her $14 chocolate martinis, on the other hand . . .

A Bum Story

Match the panhandler's story with the real story.

A. Says he's a Vietnam vet with diabetes.

B. Says he's a former college professor with cancer.

C. Says he's a schizophrenic with no legs.

1. He's really a dumb drunk with cirrhosis.

2. He's a schizophrenic crackhead with no legs.

3. He's really a junkie with diabetes.

Answers: A:3, B:1, C:2

**WHAT THE F*#! IS UP WITH . . .
ASIAN PANHANDLERS**

Why is it that you never see an Asian panhandler in America? Go to Asia and all they do is ask you for shit, but here Asians don't beg for money—apparently they're too busy making it.

---

5. You're at a Red Light . . . at Night . . . for Five Minutes

You're stopped at a light on an empty street. You've already waited three minutes for this thing to change, but it won't. If you go, you risk a ticket, but the thing isn't changing. It might change in a minute. So you wait.

But it doesn't. Now it's been four minutes and you've decided to go, but you see a car in the distance heading your way. It could be a cop. So you wait.

It wasn't. But now you've been there five minutes. Will it ever change? You decide to go for it. You take your foot off the break, hit the gas, and you make it . . . or do you?

The WTF Approach to F*#!-ing Red Lights

➤ STEP #1: *Look Carefully for Cops*

Look in places that you'd hide if you were looking for suckers who'd try to run through a broken light, like behind a bush, in an alley, or in front of a doughnut shop.

➤ STEP #2: *Look for Cameras*

You can usually see them. If you see one, don't go. Wait forever if you have to. Don't worry. The city will get right on the broken light . . . in a week or two.

➤ STEP #3: *Book Through It*

Put the car in gear, close your eyes, and hit the gas. Open your eyes before you get too far though, bozo.

➤ STEP #4: *Complain*

Call the city employees who deal with traffic lights. If you don't know the number, call 911 and they'll direct you. You can also ask their permission to go through the light. Just say that it's an emergency.

6. You Don't Have Any Change for the Meter

We know cities have to make money, but aren't tolls and subway rides and hundreds of different kinds of taxes enough? Do you *really* have to give me a $40 ticket because I didn't have change for my meter? How about making me pay a buck—four times as much as the quarter I didn't have? That would be fair. But $40? The only other times you get this screwed, this fast are when you're late on your credit card payment or need legal advice.

You can beg and cry, but meter maids are as notoriously black-hearted as robber barons, the grim reaper, and teenage boys combined. The best way to fight back is to get a handicapped-parking permit. These little placards will allow you to ignore all but the most serious parking laws—and all you need to do is get an M.D. to vouch for you, limp into your local DMV, and you're set.

Not only can this save you hundreds of dollars a year in parking tickets, you get to park in those conveniently located spaces reserved for, well, you!

Today about 10 percent of drivers in California have handicapped-parking permits. Either there's been a rash of landmine accidents and *Misery*-type assaults or people are wising up.

The WTF Approach to Beating the F*#!-ing Meter System

> **STEP #1:** *Kill the Meter Maid!*

Unfortunately, we cannot endorse or condone, under any circumstances or for any reason, any act of violence—such as the beating, stabbing, stoning, drawing and quartering, running over, shooting, tazering, pepper spraying, drowning, throwing darts at, covering him with gasoline and lighting him on fire, or sticking his face in a George Foreman Grill—on parking-enforcement agents. Just give them a taste of their own medicine instead. Follow the prick home and move *his* car across the street on street-sweeping day.

HOW TO SPOT A METER MAID AS A KID ...

- Starts fires
- Wets the bed
- Is cruel to animals

Or is that list for serial killers?

> **STEP #2:** *Kill the Meter*

Since the first step isn't legal—yet—the next best thing is to take the power away from the machine. Rise up! Don't let some coin-eating piece of metal tell you when you have to leave happy hour. All you need is a business card, some muscle, and a set of *cajones*.

First, fold your business card in half, and then fold it in half again, and then one more time, and then press it down as hard as you can. Now slide your meter-killer into the coin slot as you turn the crank and feed the monster your rigid cardboard square—this is where the muscle comes into play. If you succeed, the crank should twist and an "Out of Order" flag will fly up. *Victory!*

WTFACT: There are approximately 100,000 parking meters in Los Angeles. That's about one for every victim of police brutality.

7. Telemarketers Won't Stop Harassing You

Telemarketers are horrible people. There is no reason to treat them like human beings, let alone nicely. So say whatever you want to them.

The WTF Approach to Handling F*#!-ing Telemarketers

If you want them to stop calling, find out what company the telemarketer is with, the name of the caller, and say, "Never call me again. Take my name out of your database. If you do not, I will sue and file harassment charges against you and the company you work for." Or if you want to have a little fun with them, try one of these:

➤ **OPTION #1:** *Propose*

Ask the telemarketer if she'll marry you. If she says "no," ask her if she's gay.

➤ **OPTION #2:** *Tell Her You're Interested*

But keep putting her on hold.

➤ **OPTION #3:** *Try to Sell Her Something*

Tell her that you have an interesting business proposition for her. Explain that for an investment of just $100,000, she could get in to the lucrative and exciting world of door-to-door dinosaur egg sales.

➤ OPTION #4: *Graphically Explain That You're Busy*

Tell the telemarketer that you're "balls deep in some sweet ass" and to call back when you "ain't f*#!-in'."

➤ OPTION #5: *Sing "Moon River" to Her*

Everyone likes Henry Mancini and Johnny Mercer. Right?

➤ OPTION #6: *Tell Her That Nature Calls*

Tell her that you "gotta shit" and to call back in six hours when you're done.

➤ OPTION #7: *Tell "Yo Momma" Jokes*

Start with this favorite: "Yo' momma's so fat that yo' pops has to roll her in flour to find her wet spot."

➤ OPTION #8: *Ask for a Discount*

Ask her if she has any special deals just for necrophiliacs.

➤ OPTION #9: *Confuse Her*

Tell her that, yes, you are the person she's looking for, but that you no longer live here anymore.

➤ OPTION #10: *Scare the Shit Out of Her*

Introduce yourself as Sheriff McNeil, and tell her that she's just called the scene of a kidnapping. Immediately begin interrogating her as to how she knows the missing person (you). Ask her if she's the kidnapper and to go over her demands. When she starts freaking out and says she's just a telemarketer, tell her that the call has been traced and that the local authorities will be there shortly.

8. You've Been Dieting for Months and Still Haven't Lost Weight

So you've tried eating all meat, no meat, all carbs, no carbs, diet pills, just soup and, maybe once or twice, cocaine—but nothing's helped. Know why? Because diets are bullshit, that's why. Want to drop some pounds? Stop eating like a fat pig and exercise. Simple.

The WTF Approach to Losing Some F*#!-ing Weight

➤ **STEP #1:** *Quit Making Excuses*

Stop with the thyroid problem nonsense or saying that you have really "bad metabolism." You can always lose weight, so just do it!

➤ **STEP #2:** *Never Shop When You're Hungry*

This is the worst thing you can do. Before long your cart will be filled not with healthy vegetables and low-fat food, but with six bags of Cheetos, cookies, doughnuts, and, just because you haven't tried them yet, some disgusting new flavor of potato chips.

➤ **STEP #3:** *Get Some Therapy*

Who knows, you could be eating like a pig because your daddy was mean to you or your mommy didn't give you enough attention. Find out what the hell is wrong with you so you don't have to drown your sorrows in a chocolate milkshake and a banana split.

➤ STEP #4: *Get Another Addiction*

You can take up drinking or smoking or drugs to replace your food addiction. Of course, you might end up dead from an overdose as a fat, pill-popping, cigarette-smoking drunk. Think Elvis.

➤ STEP #5: *Staple Your Stomach*

If you have the dough and you're too lazy to hit the gym, getting your stomach stapled is a fine way to lose weight. Sure it's dangerous, but so is riding a bicycle.

> ### WHAT THE F*#! IS UP WITH . . . FAT AMERICA
>
> This country is by far the fattest in the world. Just look around. This epidemic is a reflection of our gluttonous lifestyle and lack of self-discipline. It's also a reflection of how hard we work. Most employees don't even get a lunch break to eat something leisurely, so they're forced to shove down a sandwich at their desk like an animal trapped in a cage. So file a class action against the man for clogging your arteries, giving you four chins, and making it physically impossible for you to put on your socks. That's the real fat American way.

> ### REMEMBERING RODNEY
>
> "I found there was only one way to look thin, hang out with fat people."
>
> —Rodney Dangerfield

New Diets . . .

As we said, diets don't work, but they help get you started. Here are a few new ones to jumpstart your weight loss.

Bug Diet: Eat bugs. If your house is infested with termites, eat them first. Then check out "Your New House Is Infested with Termites" (Entry #85).

Water Diet: Whenever you're hungry, drink water. Even if you can't keep it up, at least you'll be a fat pig with clear skin.

Hair Diet: Eat your hair. Most cats are sleek and thin for a reason.

Pussy Diet: F*#! it—just eat a cat instead.

9. Your Date Stands You Up

We know what you're thinking: *You're ugly and no one likes you.* Right? Well, *she* certainly thought so when she stood you up. Even if that's true, remember that there is always someone more unattractive and unappealing than you are. So there is a special (or not-so-special) person out there for everyone—even you—and she definitely won't stand you up . . . once you find her.

The WTF Approach to Securing a F*#!-ing Date

➤ **OPTION #1:** *Lower Your Standards*

If your standards are too high, you don't deserve to get laid. If you're 5'6", bald, and work at Kinko's, you're not going to be pulling in too many supermodels unless you're hung like a horse. If you are, make a photocopy of it and keep it in your wallet at all times.

➤ **OPTION #2:** *Get Help*

Maybe you could use a little makeover. Call one of those shows like *Queer Eye for the Straight Guy* that specialize in making unattractive people look good. Or better yet, just become queer yourself. Gay guys can always get laid no matter how vile they are.

➤ OPTION #3: *Make a Good-Looking Friend*

Go out on the town with a cool guy that gets chicks so, by proxy, maybe you can, too. Feed off the scraps like the dog that you are.

➤ OPTION #4: *Join* **Match.com**

Maybe you met your first date on the site—but she stood you up. News flash: You probably weren't using the site right. Make sure to put your income level at $150,000 plus and never, ever say you're shorter than 5'10".

For you girls, just try not to look too smart—brains are icky to most guys. Think about it, would *you* fuck a brain?

➤ OPTION #5: *Try Speed Dating*

With this idea, you may get turned down by multiple women in five minutes, but they're at least showing up. Dating is a numbers game anyway, so speed dating is to your benefit. If you meet a million girls, one of them will let you in between her legs.

Remember, though: First impressions are lasting impressions. And, when you only have a couple of minutes, you've got to get their attention quickly.

So say this:

"Hi, I'm [fill in name here]. I'm rich, well educated, and hung like a horse."

If you *are* hung like a horse, whip it out. Make sure to smile—women love a guy with a great smile.

➤OPTION #6: *Date a Blind Chick*

Not only can she not see you, the idea is kind of hot.

➤OPTION #7: *Join Sex Addicts Anonymous*

You might feel out of your league, but these floozies won't stand anyone up.

for the ladies . . .

For you gals, getting a date isn't as difficult—but getting stood up is just as painful. Maybe you're getting too old? In which case, you should be knitting a sweater and playing with one of your ten cats instead of being out on the prowl.

➤OPTION #8: *Go to Thailand*

Just go, pussy will find *you*.

➤OPTION #9: *Give Up*

Maybe you were stood up for a reason. Join a monastery and become celibate. If you can't get laid, you might as well fool around with God and gardening.

10. You Finish Your Cigarette and There's No Ashtray in Sight

L ife is tough enough for smokers. They die earlier, they spend extra cash on their habit, and they smell like shit. So why make it harder for them by implementing fines when they toss their cigarette on the sidewalk or out of a car on the highway? There's no excuse for such nonsense. That's why if you are a smoker and you can't find an ashtray, we at WTF give you permission to toss your cigarette butt on the ground wherever you are—your in-laws' house included.

But for those of you who are environmentally conscious, here are some other options:

The WTF Approach to Ashing Out Your F*#!-ing Butt

▶ **OPTION #1:** *Put It Out on Your Hand*

Come on, tough guy, show your stuff and impress your lady friend by putting out a lit cigarette on the palm of your hand. The trick is to keep the cigarette in motion the whole time. Try it at home first—please!

▶ **OPTION #2:** *Use Your Tongue*

If you are *really* cool, put it out on your tongue. Even cooler? Put it out in your f*#!-ing eye.

➤ OPTION #3: *Eat It*

Tobacco is natural—it was put here by God for our consumption. So if you like organic food, chop up the cigarette and shove it down your throat.

➤ OPTION #4: *F*#! It*

Yeah, we know this is weird and hard to do, but try anyway. It will definitely be hot.

Cement Isn't **That** *Flammable*

News flash for morons: There is no need to step on a burning cigarette butt on the sidewalk. You are not saving anyone's life; you are just pissing people off. Sidewalks are made out of cement, jackass, not papier mâché. Get a grip and get a life. You're not a vigilante; you're just an obnoxious asshole.

And another thing: Nothing ruins an ecosystem more than cementing it over. So what f*#!-ing difference does it make if you toss a butt on the ground? Come on!

WHAT SIDE ARE YOU ON?

FAMOUS SMOKERS

Winston Churchill

Albert Einstein

Gunter Grass

John F. Kennedy

George Orwell

Franklin Delano Roosevelt

Jean Paul Sartre

Vincent Van Gogh

Oscar Wilde

FAMOUS NONSMOKERS

Adolf Hitler

Think about that the next time you light or *don't* light up.

11. The Salt Cap Wasn't Screwed On and You Dump It on Your Meal

Salt is essential for human survival. It's a preservative and a flavor enhancer. It's in almost everything that's good: chips, soda, ham, milk, and, of course, in true WTF fashion: cum. Roman soldiers used to be paid in salt (sometimes, cum). But that doesn't mean you want a cup of it on your dinner (neither salt nor cum). When someone forgets, even if it's you, to screw the top of a saltshaker on properly, it can ruin a meal. That is, unless you're armed with a thorough knowledge of WTF.

The WTF Approach to F*#!-ing Salt-Covered Food

➤ **OPTION #1:** *Return It*

If you're at a restaurant, they'll probably make you a new order, even though it's not really their fault. Just ask nicely. If they refuse, you could always try to pay in salt (and you can certainly tip in salt).

➤ **OPTION #2:** *Give It Away*

Give it to the homeless guy who's always begging on your block. That'll shut him up.

➤ OPTION #3: *Serve It to the Fam'*

If it happens while you're cooking and are tired of always making dinner, serve it up anyway with a nice parsley garnish and glass of fine merlot. If they ask why it's so salty, ask, "It's salty?" You'll be off the hook forever.

➤ OPTION #4: *Take It to the Track*

Go to the racetrack and give it to nine horses. Bet on the tenth.

IN THE FUTURE . . .

Be careful. Hindsight is 20/20—next time you reach for the saltshaker, check the f*#!-ing top.

➤ OPTION #5: *Give the Gift of Salt*

If you have horrible neighbors, leave it on their doorstep as a gift.

➤ OPTION #6: *Teach a Lesson*

If your wife is neglecting your needs, serve it to her while telling the story of Abraham's wife Sarah, who was turned into a pillar of salt by God as punishment for her disobedience.

➤ OPTION #7: *Try Your Luck*

If you're down on your luck, throw the dish over your left shoulder. That should be good for 1,000 years of good luck.

Finally, if you find your food covered in salt, be sure to take it with a grain of salt.

12. You Can't Pull Down Your Pants to Crap Because Someone Peed on the Floor

That burrito you had for lunch is talking to you. And it's getting louder by the minute. Finally, you find a restroom, just to see that some animal pissed all over the floor, making it a hazard to pull down your pants. If you can hold it until you find a clean bathroom, feel free. If you can't, try this.

The WTF Approach to Shitting in a F*#!-ing Piss-Ridden Stall

➤ STEP #1: *Roll 'em Up*

If you're wearing jeans, you might be able to keep them off the floor. Slacks are a different story, as they are flimsier and harder to keep in place. You can try rolling them up, but they might not stay that way.

➤ STEP #2: *Soak It Up*

Use the paper towels (if there are none, use toilet seat covers) on the floor to soak up the urine and protect your pants. You could also use toilet paper, if there's enough. Keep in mind that toilet paper is much thinner, and you'll need more of it.

➤ STEP #3: *Hang 'em Up*

If there are neither paper towels nor toilet seat covers, but there's a dispenser for either of those things, take off your pants and hang them on the empty dispenser. If there is no such dispenser, you can place your pants on the sink, but proceed with caution. The sinks in public restrooms are often as filthy as the toilets.

➤ STEP #4: *Tie 'em Up*

If you can't find a clean place to put your pants, you can tie the legs around your neck. Be sure to empty your pockets beforehand. If you're into asphyxiophilia, kill two birds with one stone—tie them tight and jerk off while you're at it.

➤ STEP #5: *Shit in the Sink*

If you're worried about wrinkling your pants and the sink is too dirty to place your pants on, then shit in the sink. It's filthy anyway. Also, legs dangling, your pants are protected from the bathroom floor. Make sure there is adequate space between your asshole and the sink. You don't want to shit all over yourself. If you do, turn the faucet on lukewarm and enjoy a makeshift bidet. Once you shit this way, *mon ami*, you'll never use the toilet again.

13. Your Favorite TV Show Is Canceled

It's often sad when a show ends, but when a show is canceled prematurely it can be traumatic. You'll never learn what happens to your favorite characters and you'll have nothing to do on Thursday nights. But just because television executives pulled the plug doesn't mean you have to wallow in your loss forever. You can either learn to let go or learn to fight back.

The WTF Approach to Handling the Cancellation of Your Favorite F*#!-ing Show

➤OPTION #1: *Get Active*

Start a letter-writing campaign to get your show back. Create a website that encourages other fans to write to the studio and everyone involved in the production.

➤OPTION #1.5: *Get* **Really** *Active*

Take it further by banding together with other diehards and picketing outside the studio. If successful, consider using these organizing skills for a cause that's not insanely stupid.

➤ OPTION #2: *Get a New Favorite Show*

Whatever your favorite show was, there's probably a comparable show you haven't yet seen, whether it's new or old. If you liked *Star Trek*, watch one of the half-dozen reincarnations of the franchise or *Battle Star Galactica*. If you liked *The Office*, watch the other *The Office*. If you liked *Beverly Hills 90210*, you're a moron.

➤ OPTION #3: *Watch Old Episodes Over and Over*

If the series is long enough, you can probably watch it several times before you get tired of it— wasting weeks of your life.

➤ OPTION #4: *Write Fan Fiction*

If you are truly sick, reading and writing fan fiction is another option. You can even write yourself in. You can help your heroes keep New York City's streets safe by locking up murderers, travel the

universe in an intergalactic space ship, and help save lives by solving very complex and mysterious medical cases. Plus, you can have yourself sleep with the main character just like you've imagined so many times before.

14. Some Loudmouth at the Movies Won't Shut Up

Everyone loves the movies. There's nothing like the smell of the popcorn, the cool chill of the theatre, and the possibility—however remote—that your date will give you some action if you nudge her enough. But there's one thing that always looms over a potentially wonderful movie: the chance that some schmuck will spoil the escapist experience and waste your ten bucks by opening his stupid fat mouth and blabbering. And all you can think is: Seriously, WTF?

Doesn't he know the three laws of movie etiquette?

THREE LAWS OF MOVIE ETIQUETTE

1. Shut the f*#! up and watch the film, schmuck.

2. Shut the f*#! up and watch the film, schmuck.

3. Shut the f*#! up and watch the film, schmuck.

The WTF Approach to Shutting Him the F*#! Up

For those of you who aren't schmucks, here's a step-by-step method for dealing with one:

➤ **STEP #1: *The Shh!***

Shh! the schmuck without looking at him—no reason to reveal your identity at first.

➤ **STEP #2: *The Turn and Shh!***

Shh! again, but this time turn to the schmuck, thus revealing your identity. This tells the schmuck that he does not live in a vacuum. The average movie schmuck will stop after this second step, as the "turn and *shh!*" produces a certain embarrassment and shame—even for schmucks.

➤ **STEP #3: *The Polite Request***

Turn and look the schmuck square in the eye. Pause for a second and stare so he knows you mean business. Then, in a polite yet noticeably restrained tone, ask the schmuck to, "Please be quiet."

➤ **STEP #4: *The Command***

If step three doesn't work, then it's official: You are dealing with a real f*#!-ing schmuck here. This means you've got to step it up in order to save your movie experience, not to mention the experience of your fellow non-schmucks trying to watch the film, too. Don't let them or yourself down. Stand up and say exactly what you meant all along: "Shut the f*#! up and watch the picture, schmuck!"

NOTE: While *schmuck* is used here for the purposes of consistency, you may substitute whichever insult you choose. However, we don't condone the use of any derogatory slurs regarding race, ethnicity, gender, or sexual orientation in Step #4 . . . that's Step #5.

Consider your options . . .

1. Small popcorn-small drink combination for $6.00

2. The medium for $6.25, which is substantially bigger than the small

3. Extra-large disgusting bucket of popcorn that—not that you would ever need one—comes with free refills, for $6.50

If you were hungry, the third option would be the obvious choice. What a deal! But since you're just thirsty, you'll just have a soda. So you look up at the prices again, only to see that the small soda by itself is $5.75, just a quarter less than the small popcorn/small drink combo, which is only fifty cents less than the big popcorn/big drink supersize vomit special.

What a scam. Oh well, looks like you'll have to take the large combo, fat ass. After all, they *made* you, right?

Factors to Consider Before Telling the Schmuck Off

Let's face it. Some people are just too scary for us to tell off. Sometimes we've got to bite our tongue, not out of courtesy, but out of self-preservation. Here are a few things to check before you push the prick too far:

- Height, weight, and muscle density of the schmuck

- Number of schmucks with the schmuck

- Location of the theater—safe or not-so-safe neighborhood

- Clothing of the schmuck—look out for blue or red outfits that may suggest gang affiliation

15. Finally, a Hot Girl Hits On You . . . but She's a Hooker

A real hottie comes up to you at a bar and starts chatting you up. She's laughing at your jokes, touching you when she talks, looking at you deeply. You ask if she wants to go back to your place, when she spills the beans—the hooker beans. Sure, you could always say "No, thank you," but this isn't a guide on how to be a good little boy or girl.

Most hookers you'll see on the streets probably aren't for you. They're toothless or legless or have a fat schlong under their skirt. But every once in a while, a really hot-looking hooker will want to do you for a couple hundred bucks. This is when WTF comes in, oh, so handy.

The WTF Approach to Scoring with a F*#!-ing Hooker

➤ **STEP #1:** *Stay Local*

If your date wants to drive out to the middle of the Mojave Desert, you better pass. Sure, maybe she'll blow you on the way there and during your drive back to town. But then again, she could also just as easily take your wallet and car and leave you stranded bare-ass in the middle of nowhere.

➤ STEP #2: *Get a Room*

The last thing you need is to go to jail on a laundry list of baloney laws. If you're going to splurge, you might as well pay for a room at the Motel 6, too.

➤ STEP #3: *Question Her*

Before you talk about money, ask her if she's a cop. If she says "no," ask her to grab your junk. This shows both of you that the other isn't a policeman. If she does that, you can be pretty sure she's not there to protect and serve—just to serve.

WTFACT: In Sweden, selling sex isn't a crime, but buying it is a crime. The Swedes view hookers as exploited victims. Suckers. • In the United States, prostitution is legal in parts of Nevada and in parts of Rhode Island. • In Hungary, prostitutes are unionized. This gives a whole new meaning to "Union Job." • In the Sudan, you can get the death penalty for prostitution. Then again, when you live in Darfur, you can get the death penalty for pretty much anything.

➤ STEP #4: *Remember—No Glove, No Love*

If you're going to get nasty with a girl that does it for money, you better rock a rubber. There are more than twenty-five STDs floating around these days, and none of them gives you super powers.

WHAT THE F*#! IS UP WITH . . . GLAMORIZED PROSTITUTION

After *Pretty Woman* glamorized prostitution, too many young girls started believing that if they could just go to Hollywood and become a whore, everything would turn up roses. But that ain't the truth. The chances of a street hooker riding off into the sunset in a white limousine with Richard Gere are slim. There's a better chance she'll wind up hacked into pieces and tossed in the back of a pickup truck.

16. A Really Drunk Girl Hits On You

Yes, it was *her* choice to drink. Yes, she did hit on *you*. And yes, who's to say whether or not she would have hit on you if she was sober.

You can find a way to rationalize anything. That's what human beings do, and why we are capable of such terrible things. But even though it was her choice to drink and even though you aren't doing anything illegal, taking advantage of a drunk girl who's about to pass out and vomit all over the place is probably wrong. Yes, it's hard to say no to sex—and even harder when you are feeling tipsy, too.

The WTF Approach to F*#!-ing Figuring Out if She's Too Drunk to F*#!

➤ **STEP #1:** *Determine Her Level of Sobriety*

While you don't have to go so far as carrying a breathalyzer in your pocket (though that's actually a really good idea), there are other ways to determine the girl's level of drunkenness. Walking the line, standing on one leg, and following a flashlight with your eyes have all long been used by the police to determine the level of alcohol consumption, so try one of those tests. If she passes them, thumbs up. If she doesn't pass, get her a cup of coffee, and try again in a half hour.

➤ STEP #2: *Drink More*

So she's passed your field sobriety test, but she's still way more wasted than you. While the question of taking advantage of a *really* drunk girl is answered—you're not, she's passed the tests—you are still way too sober for any entertaining sex. (Sober sex with a drunk girl is like poking a dead jellyfish—where's the excitement?)

If you match her to the point where you are equally drunk, it'll make things a lot more interesting. So, drink up.

➤ STEP #3: *FUI*

Now that you're both well lubricated, it's time for some f*#!-ing under the influence. Take your cue from middle school multiplication, a drunk f*#!-ing a drunk equals a positive experience.

And just like middle school multiplication, you won't remember it.

17. All Geared Up to Party, but You Can't Get in Da' Club

Yeah, son. This club is poppin', yo. There's mad fly honeys everywhere. You got your new gear on, mad loot in your pocket, and you brought your best game. If only you could get in the doors. Instead you're stuck outside, and it doesn't look like they lettin' you in. What to do, foo'?

The WTF Approach to Getting in Da' F*#!-ing Club

➤ OPTION #1: *Find Women*

Find a group of eight scantily clad, hot women to walk in with. But then again, if you can get eight hot chicks at will, you'd already be on the list.

➤ OPTION #2: *Slip the Bouncer Some Cash*

If you want to know how much to give the bouncer, use this formula:

(Number of men in line x 2) + (number of women in line ÷ 3) + (cover charge x 1.5) = the necessary amount of loot

If you can't do this in your head, you should probably stay home and brush up on your algebra.

➤ OPTION #3: *Go Back to the Pub*

It's almost as good as being surrounded by beautiful women at the hottest club in town. Strike up a good chat with Mickey the barkeep. If you're lucky, he'll tell you the story about the time when he caught the marlin mounted on the wall, or how he lost his right hand in 'Nam. Make sure to play Billy Joel's "Piano Man" on the jukebox and think about all your shattered dreams. End the night dancing with a fat college chick to "Livin' on a Prayer," which, apparently, you are.

WHAT THE F*#! IS UP WITH . . . BOUNCERS

Hey, bouncers! Just because you decide who is cool enough to get in doesn't mean you're cool. You're doormen, not celebrities. Get over yourselves. You make twelve bucks an hour, for crying out loud . . . plus the tips people like us have to dish out.

➤ OPTION #4: *Leave Your Neighborhood*

You might not be cool enough for the East Village, but you'll probably fit in nicely in Jersey. Or better yet, relocate someplace where they think that even Jersey is cool.

➤ OPTION #5: *Ditch Your Friend*

It might not be you. It could be your friend. Sure, he's nice, but ever since you started hanging out with him, you've gotten half the chicks you used to and you can't get in anywhere cool. Hang out with him Tuesday afternoons, not Saturday nights. Replace him with someone better for the weekends. But be careful not to find someone too much better or you'll wind up alone on Tuesday afternoons—and Saturday nights.

18. You're Out on a Date and You Run Into an Ex

Boy, you're into this girl. She's cute, fun, and seems like she'll be great in the sack. So, you take her out for a night on the town, dinner at your favorite place, dancing at the coolest bar, and then, with a little luck and a lot of tequila, wild sex all night.

You pick her up from her place, and she's as hot as can be. The conversation is good, and she seems way into you—you start to hope she suggests skipping the dancing altogether. But as you pull in to the Denny's down the street from your place, you see a very familiar Jetta parked in the lot.

Once inside, you see a girl you used to go out with, and before you can suggest another restaurant, you've got a glass of ice water in your face.

The WTF Approach to Not Running into Your F*#!-ing Exes

> **OPTION #1: *Expand Your Playing Field***

If you've spent five years bagging the women that live within a two-mile radius of your house, you can't be that surprised if you run into them. Expanding your stomping ground means more new girls and a lot less exes.

WTFACT: Los Angeles has a population density of 8,205 per square mile. If you don't travel outside of a two-mile radius from your house, you have about 100,000 people in your world. Half are women, giving us 50,000. Seven and a half percent are within five years of your age, making our number 3,750. Ten percent are gay (3,375). A third are married or have a boyfriend (2,230). Some 15 percent are overweight (1,900), and half of them are ugly (950). Of those thousand girls, half have serious emotional issues, and of the 475 girls that remain, only a handful would ever go out with you. Now, expand that to ten miles and you have 2.5 million people, giving you a total of 11,875 girls in your possible dating pool (twice that if you don't mind psychos). Now isn't that a much sexier number?

> **OPTION #2: *Go Upscale***

Chances are, the girls you date don't do fine dining. If you're too lazy to drive across town, pay up and go upscale.

> **OPTION #3: *Make Staying in Cooler***

Get a pool table, a fully stocked bar, a 100" plasma television, a chef, a butler, a maid, etc., so that there's no longer any reason to leave your place. If you have problems with exes stopping by, get a Doberman or a shotgun.

This option is also great because, if the level of service you offer at home is better than she can get anywhere else, she'll let you on top of her for as long as you want.

19. You Get Asked Out on a Date and Are Expected to Pay

A first date is a tryout. You don't know each other, and you've gotten together to discover if there's potential. So why should you alone be expected to foot the bill—especially if she was the one who did the asking? If you choose to, good for you. But it isn't fair that she gets to go out for free over and over again. Here's how to avoid paying without ruining your chances to score.

The WTF Approach to F*#!-ing Paying Less

➤ OPTION #1: *Disappear Before the Check Arrives*

When you see the waiter approaching with the bill, go to the bathroom. Stay in there for a little while. With luck, when you come back, she'll have her card on the table and at least offer to pay half.

➤ OPTION #2: *Be Up Front*

Let her know that you never pay for first dates. Even if she thinks you're cheap, you have the remainder of the dinner to redeem yourself. This is much better than surprising her at the end. In fact, this setup can alter the natural dynamic and work in your favor. You've established from the very start that it isn't just your job to impress her; it's also her job to impress you. Who does she think she is, anyway?

➤ OPTION #3: *Cut and Run*

If you don't like her, don't pay for the whole date. Wait until she goes to the bathroom, drop your share on the table, and leave. If she's *really* awful, just leave.

First Dates for Cheapskates

Taco Bell: Everybody likes burritos, and you definitely can foot the bill. But should you, really?

Picnic in the park: Find the cheapest brie in the store, strawberries, and a bottle of André and put it in a backpack. Now you're not cheap, you're romantic.

Rollerskating rink: It'll show that you're young at heart, and if she fits into your ex-girlfriend's roller skates, you'll make out like a bandit.

A hike: It shows you're athletic, and the most you'll be expected to buy is a bottle of water.

The beach: If you live by a beach, you should take her to one. If not, go to the lake. If you don't live by a beach or a lake, you should move.

Three Dates and You're Out

If you *are* going to be the sole financier of this dating trial period, your investment should start paying dividends by the third date. If she doesn't give it up by then, look elsewhere. It's a global marketplace.

IN THE FUTURE

If you get stuck with the bill, don't go out with her again. Unless "going out" means coming over to play hide the salami.

20. Your Best Friend's Girl Hits On You

She's always flirted with you. She touches your leg when she talks to you. She laughs at all your jokes. When she hugs you, she holds on a little too long. And, most importantly, she just *looks* like she's easy. It was all in fun until the night she whispered in your ear that she wanted you . . . *badly*. What to do, what to do?

Before you act, think of the age-old adage, "bros before hos." But this can be misleading. In some situations, what seems like the wrong thing might be the right thing to do.

The WTF Approach to Handling Your Buddy's F*#!-ing Cock-Hungry Girl

➤ **OPTION #1: *Bang Her and Tell Him***

The first benefit of this is obvious. You get to bang her. The other benefit is less obvious, however. By telling him, you're doing him a world of good. He has a right to know that he's dating an unfaithful and untrustworthy girl. As a true friend, it is your job to get to the bottom of things, to investigate. You've got to make sure that she's the nasty slut you think she is. It's your obligation to find out and to let him know. After all, what kind of friend would you be if you didn't?

➤ OPTION #2: *Bang Her and Don't Tell Him*

On the other hand, there's no reason to hurt his feelings. It's best to not tell him. He likes the girl and they have a good relationship. So she needs a little dick on the side—big deal. Better you than some random guy she picks up at a club who could have God knows what kind of diseases. Do you really want to put your friend in danger like that? Be a true friend and protect him by having sex with his girl over and over again. Give it to her so hard, so fast, and so often that she won't have the energy to look elsewhere. After all, what kind of friend would you be if you didn't?

➤ OPTION #3: *Don't Bang Her and Tell Him*

What's the matter with you? You can't bang your friend's girl. Do the right thing by keeping your dick in your pants. Now go and tell him like a true friend, so he knows the kind of person he's intimately involved with. After all, what kind of friend would you be if you didn't?

➤ OPTION #4: *Don't Bang Her and Don't Tell Him*

On the other hand . . . it's best not to get involved. It's none of your business and it's not your place to pry into their relationship. Also, he may not believe you, and instead accuse you of trying break up him and his girl. Do the right thing and keep your mouth shut. After all, what kind of friend would you be if you didn't?

NOTE: As you see, you can justify any action you take. So, the real question and determining factor is: Is she *hot*, or not?

21. Your Girlfriend Takes You to the Farmers' Market, Again

WTF is *so* great about a grocery store outside? Shopping for food is a chore, not entertainment. Even clothes shopping, though all straight guys hate it, is better than food shopping. People in this country work more than fifty hours a week and then have to spend the majority of their free time doing stupid chores like grocery shopping. Come the weekend, the one time when maybe, just maybe, you don't have to bust your ass with monotonous shit, you spend it picking out tomatoes on the street sold by a bunch of hicks from out of town? No, thank you. Eating at a nice restaurant and heavy boozing to forget about yet another horrible week of work sounds much more fun.

The WTF Approach to Getting Out of the F*#!-ing Market Trip

➤ OPTION #1: *Tell Her You're Sick*

You haven't been feeling well since last Saturday, when as usual, you went to another farmers' market.

➤ OPTION #2: *Make the Farmers' Market Too Expensive*

If you buy $500 worth of candy apples, organic corn on a stick, and giant green beans, maybe you can convince her that the farmers' market just isn't in the budget. Instead, suggest one of your favorite upscale steakhouses and an exclusive VIP gentleman's club to save money.

➤ OPTION #3: *Starve Yourself for a Day and Go Pig Out*

Fifteen-dollar organic cauliflower never tasted so good.

OTHER THINGS TO DO AT A FARMERS' MARKET . . .

- Make chitchat with hick farmers
- Haggle over the price of an avocado
- Pretend you're having a good time with your girlfriend, chit-chatting with hick farmers, and haggling over the price of an avocado.

The Whole Third World Is a Farmers' Market

For all you farmers' market fans, why don't you pack up your shit and head to a Third World country? Locals there shop outside every day (if they're lucky). Know why? Because they don't have f*#!-ing grocery stores.

22. You Just Got a Drink and Some Klutz Knocks It Over

It's exactly where you want to be. It's crowded, it's loud, and the chances of organizing a gangbang look promising. It's your favorite spot and tonight is going great. Then, just when you've forgotten how boring your life is and are actually having fun, some klutz knocks over your drink.

How to react to such a situation depends on your point of view. If you consider your martini glass to be half empty, you might just shrug your shoulders and say, as you usually do, "Oh well, life sucks" and not take action. If you're an upbeat kind of person and see the drink half full, then you've got no other choice then to make the klutz pay up.

The WTF Approach to Dealing with a F*#!-ing Klutz

> **STEP #1: *Act Immediately***

Don't waste any time. The klutz might disappear in the crowd. Confront the klutz and tell him what he has done.

> **STEP #2: *Make Demands***

Chances are, the klutz will not offer to get you another drink, so demand it right away.

➤ STEP #3: *Knock Over the Klutz's Drink*

Sometimes it's best to follow the Old Testament principle of, "an eye for an eye." Knock the klutz's drink all over him. If he gets mad and threatens you, you now have the green light to take Step #4.

WHAT YOUR DRINK SAYS ABOUT HOW YOU'RE GOING TO REACT

Jack Daniel's straight up: If you were really a true Jack lover, you'd probably have hit the klutz *before* he knocked over your drink.

Margarita: Man, you're just there to, like, have a totally good time and, you know, chill out and talk to your buddies and stuff. You don't want to, like, start anything, but that was totally f*#!-ed up, dude.

Martini: You don't really care about the drink. You have money to buy another one. If you do anything, it's to show off.

Pabst Blue Ribbon: You're already broke, so either you get him to buy you a new one or you're going home.

Midori Sour: You couldn't hurt a fly, but you think the klutz's kinda cute . . .

for the ladies . . .

If the klutz is someone you are attracted to, then you may want to be more diplomatic—at least at first. Getting the klutz to compensate for his mistake by buying you a drink should be easy—just bat your eyes and wiggle your hips. Then again, if getting a free drink at a bar is an issue for you, you are very ugly and should do yourself, the klutz, and everyone else a favor and just *go home*.

➤ STEP #4: *Aim Low*

If the klutz gets nasty and denies it, threaten him. If this doesn't work, you know you've got to take physical action. *Do not* let the klutz off the hook, no matter what. The best way to win a fight with a klutz is to attack his weakness— balance. Trip the klutz and watch him fall. Then, take the klutz's wallet and buy drinks for you and all your friends.

23. You Get Pulled Over After a Couple Drinks

It could never happen to you, right? Wrong, you fool. Unless you're a teetotaler or you just have a bus pass, you'll eventually get stopped by the cops after a night on the town.

The WTF Approach to Being F*#!-ing Pulled Over

➤ **STEP #1:** *Swish and Swallow*

Keep mouthwash in your glove box. Some cops won't notice you've had anything to drink if you don't smell like a friggin' sailor.

➤ **STEP #2:** *Decline the Field Sobriety Test*

If you admit that you're drunk, that's proof in itself. If you deny it, the burden of proof is on them. If they ask you to take a field sobriety test, decline it. The alphabet backward? Alternating bringing each index finger up to the tip of your nose? Putting one foot in front of the other and walking a straight line? Admit it—you'd have trouble doing this without the added performance anxiety.

➤ **STEP #3:** *The Breathalyzer*

The cop's next move will be to give you a breathalyzer. If you've only had a couple drinks you'll be fine and on your way. However, if you think you might fail, decline.

NOTE: In some jurisdictions the penalty for declining a breathalyzer is a mandatory suspension of your license. But WTF do you think they'll do when they find out you're over the limit? They'll do that and more.

> **STEP #4:** *The Blood Test*

At this point, the cop will bring you to the station for a blood test. By that time, your blood alcohol level may drop if it was just above the limit.

What Not to Do When You Get Pulled Over

Take cocaine: It makes the alcohol less noticeable—by drawing attention to your powdered nostril and dilated pupils.

Offer a bribe: Your bills can be coke free, or not, depending on how "down" the cop looks.

Hit the gas: You won't get very far, it's a waste of gas, but it does add a dramatic flair.

REMEMBERING RODNEY

"I drink too much. The last time I gave a urine sample it had an olive in it. "

—Rodney Dangerfield

Don't Be MADD, It's Your Fault

Sure, you want to blame the fact that you couldn't find adequate public transportation or the fact that women don't seem to want to have sex with you unless you get them and yourself drunk, but don't be pissed. Since 1980 (the year Mothers Against Drunk Driving was founded), alcohol-related traffic fatalities have decreased by about 44 percent, and MADD has helped save more than 300,000 lives.

WTFACT: About three in every ten Americans will be involved in an alcohol-related crash at some time in their lives. Buckle up.

IN THE FUTURE . . .

Make friends with nerds. Everyone should have at least one friend who is a nerd and doesn't drink—and will drive. Yes, only nerds and ex-alcoholics don't drink.

24. You Meet the Girl of Your Dreams but She's Not Into You

You could always spend more time at the gym, make more money, or develop a personality, but there's an easier way to impress your dream girl: Lie.

Dishonesty is the best policy if you want the hottest women. Plus, chicks lie all the time. They put on makeup, stuff their bras, and say they like a guy with a sense of humor. It's time to get back.

The WTF Approach to Getting the Girl Who's Way Out of Your F*#!-ing League

➤ **STEP #1: *Lie About Your Job***

While a novice liar might think he should just pick a job that pays a lot of money, this isn't the best idea. Cater your lie to the venue. If you're at a rock concert and you see a girl you want to impress, be a music producer. If you're at a ball game, be a sports agent. If you're at a Goth club, be a gravedigger. And, if you're at the local Irish bar, be an out-of-work machinist. However, for a lie that will work anywhere, with anyone, being a doctor is best. Everybody respects a doctor.

➤ STEP #2: *Lie About Your Family*

You don't have one. Be the lone stranger who doesn't need anyone to thrive. Be a widower, an orphan, or tell a tragic story about the loss of your first and only child. Your perseverance and show of strength will draw her to you.

➤ STEP #3: *Lie About Your Politics*

Find out what political stance she takes and take the opposite view. If she's pro-choice, be pro-life. If she's for free trade, be a protectionist. If she's against slavery, be for it. This will get her fired up, and hopefully that fire will continue to the bedroom.

Study Your Prey

If you want to take it to the next level, you need to understand exactly who it is you're lying to. Depending on the girl, you'll have to customize your lies to turn you into Mr. Right.

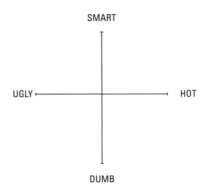

After determining which quadrant she's in, you'll need to create a persona that fits. Here are some examples:

Hot/Dumb

To impress her, tell her you have a job that pays a lot (she's going to have to rely on someone). Show her that you're smarter than her, but don't intimidate her. Make sure to smile a lot and laugh at every stupid thing she says.

EXAMPLES OF HOT/DUMB INCLUDE:

- Paris Hilton

- Jessica Simpson

- Carmen Electra

Ugly/Dumb

Tell her whatever you want. It doesn't matter anyway. She's just grateful you're talking to her.

EXAMPLES OF UGLY/DUMB INCLUDE:

- There are no Ugly/Dumb celebrities. Hollywood has some standards.

- Wait . . . Sarah Jessica Parker

Hot/Smart

To impress her, you'll have to tread carefully. She's no dummy, so don't tell her you're an astronaut if she works for NASA. Make sure all your lies are in areas she's not too familiar with. She can't know everything.

EXAMPLES OF HOT/SMART INCLUDE:

- Sharon Stone

- Cate Blanchett

- George Clooney

Ugly/Smart

These are the keepers. This is wife material, so don't mess this up. Ugly/Smart women will take care of *you* instead of running off with the gardener—no matter what. After all, what hot young gardener would have her?

EXAMPLES OF UGLY/SMART INCLUDE:

- Barbra Streisand

- Whoopi Goldberg

- Hillary Clinton

25. You're Too Short to Be Noticed by Girls

If you're 6' or taller, this entry isn't for you—unless you happen to be visiting the Netherlands. This fun-loving nation of giants boasts an average male height of 6'1", compared to 5'10" for American males. The reason? Our scientific theory goes like this:

Marijuana use = the "munchies" = food consumption = growth

Others point to a high dairy diet and a relatively even distribution of wealth, leading us to a new, less scientific theory about the benefits of Gouda and socialism. However, some critics argue the experiment was conducted unfairly, with many Dutchman were measured while still wearing their clogs.

Nevertheless, if you've been passed over for being too short, or been shot down because you didn't meet her height requirement, and you need some help holding your own in a bar full of giants—in Holland or in your hometown—here are some ways to stand out from the crowd (clogs are optional).

The WTF Approach to Being F*#!-ing Vertically Challenged

➤ **OPTION #1:** *Disco Fever*

In case you haven't noticed, the '70s have been back for a while. Shag haircuts and tight jeans could be just the beginning. Be the first person to bring back platform shoes for men . . . *please*!

➤ **OPTION #2:** *Be Really Tough and Good Looking*

Go to the gym and get ripped and, if necessary, get plastic surgery. If you look really, really good, women might notice you among the giants—particularly if you shove a few of those big shots out of your way!

➤ **OPTION #3:** *Inconspicuously Stand on Your Tippy Toes*

This is a great way to catch a lady's attention if you're short—and one of our personal favorites.

Stand by the wall on your tippy toes and rest your heels comfortably on the wall. Instead of being an average-looking short guy, you're now tall and average. The difference is enough to get you laid.

➤ **OPTION #4:** *Date Shorter Chicks*

Go out with a tiny girl and you'll feel tall in comparison. Also, your penis will look bigger. Win/win for both parties.

WTFACT: The Danes are the second tallest nation, averaging about 6' for males. America, which was the tallest nation for many years, now ranks below many Western European nations. Now Europeans can *literally* look down on us.

26. You're Having a Nice Dinner Out but the Waiter Is a Dick

For some of you, complaining to the manager about a nasty, lazy, or just plain stupid waiter comes naturally. But not everyone is born to complain. If you find yourself biting your tongue when you should be standing up for your rights as a customer, follow the WTF approach instead.

The WTF Approach to Dealing with a F*#!-ing Prick Waiter

➤ STEP #1: *Remember Who's Boss*

Don't let a snappy attitude or an aura of self-importance alter the dynamic between you and your waiter. Remember that you are in control here—he is here to serve *you*. Think of your waiter as your personal food servant. You wouldn't let a servant tell you what's what, would you? You paid him good money, so you're the boss—act like one.

➤ STEP #2: *Talk to Him*

At WTF, we're all for diplomacy. If you're having a problem with your waiter, the first thing to do is address him—there's no need to go to his boss right away. If he's being a prick, tell him so. If he takes ten minutes to refill your drink, tell him that what he is doing is unacceptable.

►STEP #3: *Demand the Manager*

If the nasty waiter doesn't change his ways, you need to speak to his manager. This is the point at which you need to shine. Make sure you tell the boss that you "always come here" and that you have "never been treated like this before."

If the manager knows you aren't a regular, you can also say that, "you own five restaurants" and that, "you have never seen anything like this in all your years in the business." This is a good way to embarrass the manager and get the prick waiter fired—plus, it might just mean the difference between a complimentary meal and a $150 check.

Attention All Servants

Lose the f*#!-ing attitude. We don't care whether you work at the fanciest restaurant in Beverly Hills or a stinky diner off Route 66, you are a servant and you should act accordingly. It's your job to serve your customers well and smile wide as you do it.

And yes, it's clear that this is only your "job," not your career. You're a great actor in "real life." But until you actually become the next Daniel Day Lewis, you don't work for MGM—you work for tips. Now go fetch me another goddamn Diet Coke already!

WHAT THE F*#! IS UP WITH . . . BEING AFRAID THEY'RE GOING TO SPIT IN YOUR FOOD

Some people shy away from complaining about bad service because they're scared the waitstaff's going to hock a loogie in their food as an act of revenge. This fear is both cowardly and ridiculous. The chances of this happening are minimal—and near impossible in a quality restaurant. Not to mention that considering the unknown hormones and crap in your two-ton cheeseburger, a little spit should be the least of your concerns.

27. You're in the 10 Items-or-Less Line and the Jerk in Front of You Has 11 Items

If it was a Sunday and you had nothing to do, maybe you would let it slide. But it's a weekday during rush hour and you're just trying to get a few things. You're not in the mood to let some schmuck cut corners—even if he's only trying to sneak in one extra item.

Rules are rules, and this jerk better follow them . . .

The WTF Approach to Getting Some F*#!-ing Grocery Store Justice

➤ **STEP #1:** *Don't Ever Let Anyone Get Away with It*

Do what it takes. If alerting the grocery bagger doesn't work, demand to speak to a manager. As a last resort, reach into the violator's cart and begin tossing items over your shoulder until only ten items remain. If the violator looks a lot tougher than you, you can also try slamming your shopping cart into his leg. Make sure to get a running start from aisle 5.

WTF: UP CLOSE AND PERSONAL

At WTF, we practice what we preach. One morning before work, I was patiently waiting in the express line at the grocery store to buy bagels for the office (I'm just that kind of guy) when I witnessed someone trying to get away with eleven items instead of the clearly defined maximum of ten. That's right, under a big sign that read "10 Items or Less" this rule-breaking anarchist tried to get away scot-free. To be sure, I counted again. Four cans of cat food, two bags of eucalyptus mints, a box of Cream of Wheat, pickled beets, Ovaltine, prune juice, and mint jelly. *Eleven.* So what did I do? I alerted the cashier, of course. I told him of the violation of the store's policy and the following ensued:

"What is he talking about?" the violator said as she turned to me, pretending she didn't know.

ONE WORD OF ADVICE: PLASTIC

Grocery baggers have yet to stop asking customers if they want "paper or plastic?" despite the fact that no one *ever* chooses paper, which is less malleable and harder to carry. Why keep asking? For the *one* person who is so environmentally conscious that she is willing to put up with a little personal inconvenience to help the planet? Ridiculous.

"I'm talking about the fact that the sign says '10 Items or Less' and you have more than the allotted amount, more than what you are permitted to have," I said. "That's cheating, and cheating is wrong."

The cashier just stood there. "Come on, give her a break," said some giant red-haired fool at the back of the line. I turned to him. "Why should I give her a break? Rules are rules."

"She's an old woman."

But why should her age matter? I was not about to let this rule breaker—whatever her age, race, creed, color, sex, sexual orientation, gender identity, national origin, religion, disability, or familial status—get away with blatant disregard for the rule of law and order. I stood my ground.

"I demand that she goes to another line or forfeits one item of her choice," I commanded. "I want to talk to a supervisor."

It didn't come to that. The rule breaker decided to go to another line, rather than give up one of her items. The cashier and the others in line just stared at me, as if it were *my* fault.

"How could you do that to an old lady?" the red-haired fool repeated.

I just shook my head and laughed. *Old*, I thought. *Yeah, old like a fox.*

—GB

WHAT THE F*#! IS UP WITH . . .
PEOPLE STILL USING CHECKS

Seriously. Unless you're an eighteen year old who just got his first checkbook, writing a check for groceries is embarrassing and takes time. But if you are going to do it, at the very least have the store name, date, and your signature filled out. Don't be surprised, dummy, you always have to put those parts on there. And for those of you who actually ask the cashier who to make the check out to: Well, rack that empty head of yours and take a good f*#!-ing guess!

28. You've Gone to the Bathroom and Realize There's No TP

Many people find going number two to be a very relaxing experience. You can read, think, or practice telekinesis—time on the toilet is good clean (well, not *so* clean) fun. Nothing lasts forever, however, and after the deed is done, it's time to clean up and join the rest of the world.

But wait, what if you find that there is nothing there for you to clean up with? And what if you find yourself *alone*—in a house or worse, a public bathroom—without toilet paper? WTF are you going to do? Here are some tips to help guide you through one of the shittiest situations in this book, literally.

The WTF Approach to Being Caught Without F*#!-ing Toilet Paper

➤ **OPTION #1:** *Stare at the Holder*

Sometimes staring at the empty holder where toilet paper should be and shaking your head can help you.

➤ **OPTION #2:** *Use a Substitute*

First, go to the obvious choice, such as paper towels, which are unfortunately a little out of reach from the toilet in most public restrooms. That's okay. Hobble there quickly, grab some, and sit back down.

If you aren't lucky enough to have paper towels within a hobble's reach, look to the trash can. Be careful and exercise caution before taking something out to wipe your ass. Look for used pieces of paper towel, and then smell them to make sure they're wet with water, not urine.

If you can't find paper towels or a trash can, you're going to have to rough it and use the cardboard toilet paper roll, which is often left on the toilet paper spinner. You might get lucky and there'll even be a little piece of paper stuck to the roll that you can use. Before wiping, make sure to wet half of the cardboard roll in order to make it more malleable, less abrasive, and a more effective shit cleaner. Be sure to keep from running half under the water so you can wipe dry your now-wet ass cheeks. You may also want to break the dry half into smaller pieces so you can go back for a second or third sweep—you don't want to take the chance of wiping your ass in one fell swoop only to find that you're not fully clean—that's just gross.

➤ **OPTION #3:** *Shower*

If you're in the comfort of your own bathroom, just get your stinky ass up and turn on the shower. Think of it as a giant bidet.

➤ **OPTION #4:** *Shit Splash*

If you're in a public bathroom, however, and there is no paper or cardboard around, you've got to get creative.

Stand up and waddle to the sink, turn the faucet on warm (but not hot) and, if you're lucky enough to have access to that pink soap, lather up your hands and then turn around.

Next, hop up on the counter and stick your ass right in the sink. This not only brings you closer to the faucet, it prevents any runoff from getting on your underwear and pants that lie on the floor around your ankles.

NOTE: If this is a one-too-many-bean-burrito kind of bathroom trip, you might want to remove your pants and underwear completely before attempting this method of water wiping.

With your ass in the sink, you can now perform the "shit splash" by taking your soapy hand and splashing water between your cheeks. Again, be careful not to spill. You'll still be wet, but with water, not with shit.

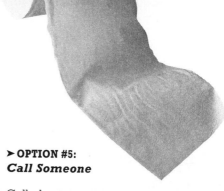

➤ OPTION #5:
Call Someone

Cell phones were invented for *just* this type of emergency. Call a friend and get him to bring you some toilet paper.

If you're at someone else's house, it's her fault that you have no toilet paper. So just yell through the door and make her get you some. Who knows, she might feel bad and offer to wipe your ass.

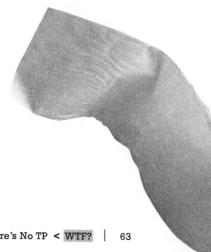

29. On Your Lunch Break the Soda Machine Eats Your Change

It's your lunch break. The first half of your day's been rough. You're dying for a soda. And if you don't get one, you're liable to scream at your assistant, start smoking again, or even hit the bottle. You slide your buck into the slot, press the button, the machine makes a whole lot of noise, and then . . . nothing comes out. Don't despair, WTF is here.

The WTF Approach to Getting Your F*#!-ing Soda

➤ STEP #1: *Call the Company*

On most vending machines, you'll find a telephone number somewhere near the dollar slot. Call it, and demand that they immediately bring you a soda.

➤ STEP #2: *Call the Cops*

If you walked into a convenience store, grabbed a soda, and walked out, you'd be a thief. If you walked in, gave the guy a dollar and he took the dollar and the soda, he'd be a thief. In this case, the machine is a thief and the authorities must be alerted for the safety of other people whose only crime was the desire to quench their thirst with, say, a nice refreshing Coke, which is the best cola product on Earth.

> **NOTE:** Coke did not pay for this product placement. But we'll certainly solicit them for our next book.

➤ **STEP #3:** *Get Even*

If no one cares about the machine stealing your money, then they shouldn't care about what you do to it next.

Gather your coworkers and move the soda machine into your office. Leave a note explaining that you'll be happy to return it upon receipt of your hard-earned buck.

TRY OUT THESE NEW DRINKS!

- **Mountain Dick:** With a big dose of caffeine and aphrodisiacs, it won't just keep you up, it will keep your girlfriend up, too.

- **Sprite Lemon:** We took the lime out. It was a huge breakthrough.

- **Frat-paccino:** This drink is a unique blend of Colombian coffee, cocaine, Cheetos, and lukewarm beer.

30. Your New Boss Is Out to Get You

Your new boss is gunning for you and you don't know why. You work hard—or at least you *think* you do. And you're nice to him. So what is his deal? When this happens there is only one thing to do: go over his head. He ain't the King—he's just another putz with a tie. Whether that means to *his* boss, the government, or the IRS, there's always something you can do to let him know that he's not the only one playing for keeps.

The WTF Approach to Beating Your New Boss at His Own F*#!-ing Game

➤ STEP #1: *Look for Dirt*

Check his trash can, his phone log, and if you can, his e-mails. See if he's banging anyone he shouldn't be, if he's embezzling money, or if he's cheating on his taxes. If he's like most of us, he's probably doing *something* wrong.

➤ STEP #2: *Hire a Private Investigator*

If you know his every move, you can get the real dirt. You might be able to blackmail him into letting you become an independent outside advisor, which means you keep your pay and don't work—at least until the board of directors catches on.

➤STEP #3: *Get Him in Trouble* with His *Boss*

This is a last resort. File a complaint outlining how he has been harassing you. Feel free to include details about all his shortfalls. In addition, be sure to explain how hesitant you are to do this and how rarely you complain about anything.

Or . . .

➤STEP #3: *Get the Government Involved*

If your boss is the owner, it may seem like there's no one else to complain to, but there is. Is there an inappropriately placed trash can? Tell OSHA. Are there 1099 workers that should be on payroll? Tell the IRS. And, be sure to let your boss know that you've done so. If he's stupid enough to can you after that, it's considered retaliation for "whistleblowing," which isn't a legal reason to fire someone.

> **IN THE FUTURE . . .**
>
> Be your own boss. Start your own business so you never have to deal with a boss again. If you aren't talented enough to be successful, become a consultant, because if you're incapable of being part of a solution, you can always make money prolonging a problem.

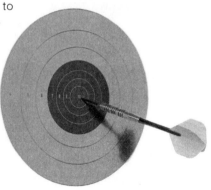

31. A New Coworker Is Driving You Insane

Just as there are different strains of the flu, there are different types of annoying coworkers. You'll find the ass kissers, the sloths, the bullies, and the know-it-alls. But whichever kind of annoying coworker you face, there's one thing you, sadly, can't do—throw him out the f*#!-ing window.

You've been trucking along at your job for a while now, and on a good day enjoy your work. Well, as much as anyone can enjoy work. But this new disease is driving you nuts. He's incompetent, annoying, and his repulsive hyena-pitched laugh bounces off the office walls. You just can't take it anymore. Here's what to do:

The WTF Approach to Handling a Toxic F*#!-ing Coworker

➤ STEP #1: *Make Concessions*

The first thing you must do is try to accommodate his annoying habit by making slight adjustments to your rituals that won't upset your well-being. If the jerk smacks gum, put on headphones, or steal his pack when he isn't looking.

➤ STEP #2: *Befriend Him to Change Him*

If you're friendly, you might be able to get him to change to be more cool and less annoying. Then again it's not easy to make someone change. Your ex-girlfriend tried that with you, remember?

➤ STEP #3: *If You Can't Beat Him, Join Him*

If that doesn't work, try to do exactly what he's doing. If he's skating by without doing a shred of work because he's a kiss ass, become one too. It's going to take some practice to get it right. The first couple of times you compliment your boss on his new suit, he'll probably raise an eyebrow and think you're being sarcastic. But keep at it. It's about time you put

those four college drama classes to use.

➤ STEP #4: *Get His Ass Fired*

If nothing works with this prick, it's time to get serious. Get him fired. A little innocent sabotage goes a long way. Leaving illegal drugs on his desk or rerouting his home page to a porn site might do the trick.

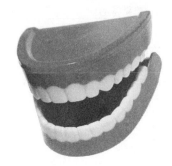

32. You're Out of Personal Days, but Have Tickets to Opening Day

"You can't use sick days for non-health-related issues," says your goody-two-shoes coworker. No shit—being at the park for the first pitch of the season is a matter of life or death. Just call in sick and follow these rules.

The WTF Approach to Getting Out of F*#!-ing Work

➤ STEP #1: *Lie*

No matter how cool your boss is, how cool you think he is, or how much you've talked ball with him in the past, *never* tell him the truth about those box seats. *Always* lie. See Options #1 and #2 for possible excuses.

➤ OPTION #1: *Call in Sick*

The truth is that you *are* sick. Or would be if you missed this opportunity. Every kind of sickness can only get worse. And that's why you call out, in order to make sure you get better and not worse and not miss more work. If you have a cold, you call out and stay home from work to avoid turning it into pneumonia. If you have opening day tickets, you call out and go to the game to avoid sinking into a deep depression after you find out you could've been at the game where your team rallied in the bottom of the ninth with a bases-loaded, two out, 3-2 count grand slam.

➤ **OPTION #2:** *Other Lies*

If you've been "sick" too often and you don't want to arouse suspicion, come up with a more clever excuse, like:

- You woke up to find a horse's head in your bed.

- You had to answer some tough questions by some nasty Spanish priests.

- You woke up to find that you had turned into an insect.

Making Bad Lies Good

There is a whole list of standard excuses people use such as:

1. Got the flu

2. Grandmother passed away

3. Car broke down/won't start

On the surface, these are typical lies that should be avoided. But, with a little bit of tweaking, they're okay. The trick is to make your excuse both specific and more grandiose.

The previous list of common lies should be converted to these:

1. **Got AIDS.** Instead of the common flu, you now have a fatal disease. This is a good lie for two reasons. First, due to the stigma that still unfortunately surrounds the disease, your boss would *never* think anyone would lie about something like that. Second, and on a related point, it is that very social stigma that would scare your boss into giving you not only the benefit of the doubt in the future, but also special treatment, for fear of some kind of legal action. Finally, having AIDS gives you a green light to use the "flu excuse" whenever you want. After all, you've got to be extra careful not to get *really* sick.

2. **Mom died.** Almost every adult has dealt with the death of a grandmother. No big deal. That's why the "grandmother died" excuse is all too common. But if you say that your mom died instead, you have one of the best excuses for missing work or anything else in the world. You get immediately credibility. After all, what kind of a sick f*#! would lie about his mom dying?

3. **Car is possessed.** Having your car break down is not enough. Getting to work is *your* responsibility, not your boss's. Also, if you say you were in a wreck, you're going to have to show proof that your car was hit. It's best to avoid any excuse relating to your automobile. However, if you're bent on using an auto-related excuse, say that your car, nicknamed "Carrie," has become possessed and is terrorizing the neighborhood. If you say it convincingly, the boss might not believe you, but he will think that you're insane and need treatment. Again, fear of legal action will prevent him from firing you over your mental illness. He'll probably just encourage you to get professional help, which, quite frankly, you might need.

33. Your Computer Crashes and You Lose Your Big Presentation

This is the big one, the one that can take your career to the next level. The one that can get you out of your cubicle and into the corner office. But your computer decided to get an e-STD and shit out on you the night before the big day—losing everything. Maybe it was the spam, maybe it was a virus, or maybe it was all the porn. Don't worry, though, there's always a way to scoot by.

The WTF Approach to Handling a Ruined F*#!-ing Presentation

➤ **OPTION #1:** *Rear-End Someone on the Highway*

Pretend you have whiplash, and take a ride in an ambulance to the hospital. Have a nurse leave a message with your boss.

➤ **OPTION #2:** *Call in a Bomb Threat*

The good old "bomb in the building" trick always wastes an hour or two. The federal government sees this gag as actual terrorism, so either don't do it or don't get caught.

➤ OPTION #3: *Make Yourself Sick*

First, eat about five hotdogs with lots of ketchup. Then go to your boss's office before the meeting and let him know that you're feeling sick. He'll probably suggest you try to give the presentation anyway. Right before you enter the boardroom, take a swig of ipecac syrup. When the urge to puke hits you, don't resist. Try to make eye contact with him, open your mouth, and let it go. Your colleagues may hate you, but at least you can sue if you're fired.

➤ OPTION #4: *Wing It*

You're never going to make it in the corporate world by wimping out. Computer issues or not, go balls to the wall and do what you do best—bullshit. Here are some things to mention if you decide to wing it:

- Say "synergy" a lot. Just throw the word in wherever. Everyone thinks it's an important concept, even though no one fully understands what it means.

- Talk about the need to increase profit margins and marketshare. Companies like these things.

- Always end with your future plans to enter the Chinese market.

34. Your Ugly Boss Wants to Jump Your Bones

You've caught her staring at your ass. She's bumped against you in the elevator. She calls you into her office just to hand you junk mail. She repeatedly asks to meet outside the office to discuss upcoming projects. Basically, she wants to f*#!.

The WTF Approach to Handling Your F*#!-ing Ugly Boss

➤ OPTION #1: *Get Drunk and Do It*

You'll f*#! anything after a couple of drinks, so why not someone who can better your career? After all, the reason you have a job is to make money so you can get with girls. By getting with this one, you're setting yourself up for even more money, more sex, and more drama—just the way you like it.

➤ OPTION #2: *Bring a Horny Friend*

It might not be you. Your boss might just be hard up. Throw your friend at her to solve the problem. This tactic also gives you an excuse next time she hits on you. Just say you don't date people your friends have dated.

➤OPTION #3: *Sue Her Ass*

If she crosses the line, sue her. If she hasn't yet, provoke her by wearing tighter pants.

for the ladies . . .

I'll give you the same advice I gave the guys: Close your eyes and do it. You've shagged nastier guys for no good reason. Comparatively, doing it for a promotion is a step up.

UGLY SCALE		BONUS TO MAKE IT WORTH IT
Rosie O'Donnell➤	10	$5.12 million
Barbara Walters➤	9	$2.56 million
Heather Mills ➤	8	$1.28 million
Brooke Hogan ➤	7	$640,000
Janice Dickenson ➤	6	$320,000
Kathy Griffin➤	5	$160,000
Fergie➤	4	$80,000
Madonna➤	3	$40,000
Lauren Conrad➤	2	$20,000
Jessica Biel➤	1	$10,000

35. You Blew the Company Softball Game

It's the bottom of the ninth. The bases are loaded. You're down by one. All you have to do is get a hit and your office team will win. You'll be the hero, and coworkers will tell stories about you at the water cooler until next year's big game. Strike one. Strike two. Strike three. You're a f*#!-ing loser. Now what?

The WTF Approach to Not F*#!-ing Blowing It

➤ STEP #1: *Convert*

Your God just isn't working out for you.
Try another one.

➤ STEP #2: *Practice for Next Year's Game*

Practice may not make perfect, but it might save you from being the office schmuck. Learn how to get a f*#!-ing grip: Hold the bat like a bat, not like a dick.

➤ STEP #3: *Sit It Out*

In key situations, ask to sit on the bench. If you need to fake an injury, do it. You'll never be the hero, but anything's better than being the villain.

➤ STEP #4: *Change Jobs*

If finding another job in the United States doesn't create enough distance between you and your folly, get a job in China. They like ping pong anyway.

IN THE FUTURE . . .

Fake a seizure. If there's a chance you're going to screw up in a key situation, start twitching and fake a seizure. People will assume that a malady of some sort caused it. By the time the ambulance shows up, they'll pray for God to save your life, not to take it. This way, you'll never have a chance to mess up in the first place. This tactic will also work if you are about to screw up an important presentation or even if you're late for work.

36. You're Taking a Business Trip and Your Wife Wants to Go

One of the few perks of corporate life is occasionally getting to travel. While St. Louis might not be Paris, at least it enables you to take a break from the stress of domestic responsibility and enjoy a little time for yourself. But what if that domestic stress travels with you? Here's how to make sure your wife doesn't want to come along.

The WTF Approach to Ditching the F*#!-ing Mrs.

➤ **STEP #1:** *Lie About Where You're Going*

Tell your wife you are going to places that she would never want to go. Dangerous places are the best. If you are taking an international trip, tell her you're going to Iraq. If you are taking a domestic trip, tell her you are going to Detroit. In fact, no matter where you are going, always say Detroit.

➤ **STEP #2:** *Induce a Terrible Fear of Flying*

Make her scared of flying. In the weeks before your trip, bring up any news story that has to do with plane crashes (or just make some shit up). You can also start watching movies that will freak her out about flying, like *Airport*, *Alive*, *Fearless*, or *Die Hard 2*, and make sure she's really on edge.

> **STEP #3:** *Bore the Shit Out of Her*

Tell her every single detail of your trip, including all the meetings you'll be going to and the characteristics of all the boring people who will be there. Most important, go over your boring presentation a thousand times. Just think about all the boring things you normally tell her about your work and multiply it by a factor of ten.

37. Your Assistant Is Making a Play for Your Job

Sometimes ambitious coworkers get a little *too* ambitious and want to move up at your expense. While getting them fired might be an option, it's not always the best choice for your department or the company. And besides, there are other ways to deal with this delicate situation. Of course, you could just do your job well. If you're on top of your game, you won't have to worry about being replaced. Nah, follow these rules instead.

The WTF Approach to Squashing a F*#!-ing Underling

➤ **STEP #1:** *Put Him in His Place*

Make a clear distinction between who's the boss and who's not. This should help to keep the usurper in his place.

➤ **STEP #2:** *No Exceptions*

Don't let him park in a manager's space, even when he comes in for overtime work on Christmas Day. Those spots are for managers, not assistants. Rules apply 24/7, 365 days a year.

➤ **STEP #3: *Don't Socialize***

Don't fraternize with him outside the office. He's your bitch, not your buddy.

➤ **STEP #4: *Put Him Down***

If he makes a mistake, let him—along with the rest of the office, his girlfriend, and his mom—know.

➤ **STEP #5: *Keep It Formal***

Don't let him call you by your first name. You're "Sir," "Boss," or "Master."

➤ **STEP #6: *Humble Him***

Whenever you have an important visitor, call him in to take your lunch order.

➤ **STEP #7: *Take Away His Toys***

Replace his Mac with an Etch-a-Sketch and demand the same quality work.

When It's Serious

If it's gotten to the point where it's either you or him and you suspect the big bosses might choose him, do whatever it takes to get him out of there, including:

- Plant drugs in his office and call the feds.

- Masturbate on his desk. Make sure that you haven't jerked off in a few days so you can get as much as possible on his possessions.

- Change his home page from Yahoo.com to Blowjob.com.

- Slash his tires every morning, and complain that he's always late.

- Put rotten food and insects in his desk drawer.

- Have sex with his wife (just because).

38. You Overdraw Your Account by 25¢ and Get Charged $25

Most banks like nothing more than to kick you when you're down. When you cut it close, they're just waiting for you to make the slightest miscalculation so they can charge you twenty-five bucks. This is particularly irritating when you put a sandwich on your card, add a tip, and get nailed twenty-five bucks for each charge. The grand total for the sandwich is now $56. And you thought it was a waste at six bucks. In cases like this, there's only one thing to do:

The WTF Approach to F*#!-ing Overdrafting

The best way to handle this situation is by *rep surfing*. Rep surfing is when you call customer service until you get a rep who gives in to your demands. With a click of a button, a rep can save you a load of cash by bending the rules a tiny little bit. Follow these steps:

➤ **STEP #1: *Call in the Middle of the Night***

If the rep ain't got shit to do, he might hear you out.

➤ **STEP #2: *Give Him a Sob Story***

Gain the service rep's sympathy and he'll be putty in your hands.

➤ STEP #3: *Remember—It's Not His Fault*

Even though you want to tell him he's a dipshit, don't. He's not the one fining you; it's the bank.

➤ STEP #4: *Remind Him of Your Loyalty*

Don't let him forget how many years you've been a customer of the bank. While the rep certainly doesn't give a shit, it'll make it easier for him to justify helping you out.

➤ STEP #5: *Ask What He Can Do*

Now that you've reminded him of your customer loyalty, ask him nicely if he can do anything for you. This makes losers like him feel special and powerful, and he just might bend company policy to help you out.

NOTE: The lunatic method in which you start screaming and carrying on works best at a branch office. But word to the wise—keep an eye on the security guard.

39. Your Ex Charges Up Your Credit Cards as a Goodbye Present

It's easy to overspend with a credit card—and even easier for a bitter ex. Unless you're Larry King and can easily pay an ex-wife's spiteful shopping spree, you're liable to pay up the hefty sum.

The WTF Approach to Dealing with F*#!-ing Debt

➤ STEP #1: *Blame Her*

Not that the card company will care about your bitter battle. As long as she had authorization to use your card before her meltdown, you're liable for her charges. The chance of this happening is almost worth not just tossing your next girl the plastic when she begs you to go shopping with her.

➤ STEP #2: *Max Out Your Cards*

Chances are your sob story isn't going to work. So if you're already screwed with your credit card company and don't see any light at the end of the tunnel, royally screw yourself. F*#! it. Go out and have a good time.

➤STEP #3: *Disappear*

Change your address. Change your phone number. Change your name. They're going to try to hunt you down after you've maxed out your cards. You have to be ready to run *Fugitive*-style. But instead of hunting down your wife's killer, you might consider hunting down your credit card charging ex and killing her.

Welcome to the Real World

When someone lends you money, the reason they charge you high interest is because of the risk involved. For the credit card companies, they're making an investment in you, which didn't pay off. That's life. A world where every investment paid off would be a perfect one: one where violence, drugs, and sexually transmitted diseases didn't exist. But we don't live in that world. We live in a WTF kind of world. A world where you find a field of pot growing in your backyard, a world where your

home gets infested with termites, and a world where your favorite television show is canceled. In this world, not every investment pays off.

Credit Contracts

You obviously have never read a credit card contract, or else you wouldn't have a credit card. You may be surprised that being able to jack up your interest rate at will is just the beginning. If you miss a payment the credit card company can:

- Turn your guest room into a collection call center.

- Take your kids on that trip to Disney World you've been promising them for years but couldn't because you've been neck-deep in credit card debt. Why would they do this? Because credit card companies are vicious, mean, and have an appreciation of the ironic.

- Nail your wife.

40. You're at the Grocery Store but Forgot Your Wallet

Stealing is wrong. While few will debate this cornerstone of civilization, there is a gray area. *Sometimes* stealing is acceptable—like when you're starving and left your wallet at home. While in some countries they lop off your hand if you're caught stealing, in America we'll probably give you a slap across the wrists. So if you need to bend the rules to fill your stomach, there are guidelines to save yourself from a wrist-slapping—or hand-chopping as the case may be.

The WTF Approach to Feeding Your Face Without a F*#!-ing Dime

➤STEP #1: *Clear That Conscience*

Nothing says, "I'm guilty" more than a guilty conscience.

➤STEP #2: *Clean Yourself Up*

If you look like a vagrant, they'll be watching you. Then again, if you didn't look like a vagrant, you wouldn't be stealing food.

➤STEP #3: *Keep It Cheap*

Don't steal high-priced items like lox, caviar, or truffles. Steal bread, hotdogs, or SPAM.

NOTE: Stay away from the liquor. We know you're thirsty, but go out and earn that shit by begging like every other dumb drunk.

➤ STEP #4: *Don't Worry About Getting Caught*

The cops will feed you in the jail house, and if you've been reduced to stealing hot dogs, you probably don't have anywhere better to be.

Scam Time

If you're adept at lying, you might be able to skip the stealing and go right to scamming your way to a decent meal. If you think you're up to it, try one of these:

The Fast Food Scam: Don't tell anyone we told you this, but fast-food restaurants are easy to scam. Grab a bag with their logo on it out of the trash from their parking lot. Pick one or two items that you'd like to eat. Now, drive up to the window and tell them they forgot to put those items in your bag. Tell them that you were there just thirty minutes ago and that it was a big order, so they must remember. They'll likely fork those items over no questions asked. If they do ask you anything, just come up with a believable story. If a fast-food worker can catch you in a lie, it may be better that you starve.

The Grocery Store Scam: In a grocery store parking lot there are receipts galore. Pick one up, and choose the food of your choice from the list. Go inside and complain that the item wasn't included. Be sure to ask for a manager and act confident. This will not work with a Thanksgiving Day Turkey or a watermelon.

The Pizza Scam: Order a pizza with a bunch of toppings. When the delivery arrives, check the pizza and immediately complain that it's missing a topping. Call up the shop and speak to the manager and complain. Tell him that you will not pay for it because it's not the pizza you ordered. If he offers to send another one, tell him to forget it because you're starving. They might take the pizza back, but they'll probably leave it for you. If it doesn't work, try another pizza shop.

41. Your Roommate Skips Out the Day Before Rent Is Due

It's the first of the month and, as usual, you can barely come up with your half of the rent—let alone your roomie's half. You had a feeling that you couldn't trust that guy. Shit! You can try to reason with your landlord, but he is probably a heartless bastard. So, what can you do? In pornographic movies, the landlord takes sex as payment for rent. In the real world, this is less common. Sure, your landlord may want to tap that ass, but he's got bills, too.

Still, there's always something that can be done when it's the first of the month and you're short on funds, and with WTF, you might just be able to keep a roof over your head.

The WTF Approach to Making Your F*#!-ing Rent

► **OPTION #1: *Sell Your Junk***

You can probably sell a lot of things lying around your apartment. CDs, DVDs, and video games should be sold off first. If you're really short, start selling jewelry and appliances. Hit up eBay or similar auction sites to hock your wares, but avoid pawnshops, since they give you a bad rate, and you'll never come up with the money to get your stuff back anyway.

➤ OPTION #2: *Sell Your Body*

If you're decent looking and have lax morals, get a job at a strip club. If you're not so cute, get a job at a shitty strip club. You can also go on craigslist and sell whatever services you have to offer, even if they don't seem like much. Willing to give nude massages, light spankings, or let strangers take a dump on your stomach? There's a market for your services.

➤ OPTION #3: *Sell Your Children*

When worse comes to worst, you can sell off your children to science, the circus, or possibly a high-profile celebrity with an adoption addiction—think Angelina Jolie. At least these people will be able to afford to keep a roof over your kids' heads.

➤ OPTION #4: *Borrow Money*

If you haven't already used up your credit line with your friends and family, go ahead and borrow a little from them. They know you're not good for it, so don't feel too bad about not paying them back.

If everyone in your personal life knows what a no-good slacker you are and won't float you a few bucks, max out your credit cards, get a couple payday loans, take whatever credit any moron will give you, and then change your phone number. Don't borrow from the mob, though—you'll end up renting a hospital bed or spot in the nearest river if you do.

➤ OPTION #5: *Get a New Roommate*

So what if you think you prefer to live alone. You'd also prefer to fly first class, drive a Mercedes, and spend your summers in the Hamptons, but you can't even make your rent. Just think of it as college, except you're thirty. If you're a post grad at your local university, choose wisely; your new roomie might have tons of sexy, co-ed friends that love older guys.

➤ OPTION #6: *Change the Locks*

Buy some time before they break down the door. In the meantime, try to come up with the cash or start packing. If you can't move in with your parents and have no friends, find a codependent lover to move in with.

➤ OPTION #7: *Move*

You could always follow the lead of your prick roommate and bounce before your landlord has a chance to evict you. Granted, your new living arrangements will be a little different from your current situation.

Old Place:

1200sf home, 2BR 2BA, with a big backyard shaded by two huge beautiful maple trees. Gleaming hardwood floors, spacious kitchen with huge range/oven and updated cabinets, fireplace, central heating and air conditioning. Very large living room with big windows looking out on the great backyard. Each bedroom has its own full bath.

New Place:

Chevy Blazer, '87, 2 door, V6, power windows, 4 × 4, clean interior, clean engine, runs good, stereo, A/C needs to be recharged.

42. You Got Laid Off and Now You're Broke

In this economy, every paycheck could be your last. If you find yourself out of work, out of cash, and out of luck, you can try these options.

The WTF Approach to Living without a F*#!-ing Income

▶ **OPTION #1:** *Beg for Money*

A classic way of obtaining cash for drugs is begging for change on the street. This is a difficult game, however, and with so much competition out there (you're not the only loser, you know) you've got to get creative to survive. Here are some great ideas for panhandling angles:

- **Be Specific.** The key to any good sympathetic story is specificity. Be specific about how much you need. Ask for a quarter to use a payphone or $1.50 to catch the bus. The more money, the more specific you need to be.

- **Be a Fish-Out-of-Water.** Everyone loves a story about a fish out of water. Think of Jon Voight down on his luck in the Big Apple in *Midnight Cowboy*. If you're doing the "I'm stranded and I want to go back home to my nice dumb town" routine, again ask for something specific, like $17 for a Greyhound ticket. This is a lot of money for panhandling, but if you come across the right kind of compassionate fool, you just might succeed.

- **Be Crippled.** If you are crippled, that's great for panhandling, though admittedly not great for much else. If you're not, do the old Eddie Murphy no legs routine from *Trading Places*. Who knows, you might be living like a fat cat in no time.

- **Be a Vet.** If you actually are a vet, good for you, and we humbly thank you for your service. Now get the f*#! off the street! If you aren't a vet, hit up the Army Surplus store and invest in your future.

- **Be Earnest.** Some beggars choose to be blatantly honest, betting on people's appreciation of the truth and sense of

humor to make them give. Put up a sign that reads something like "Fired by The Man" or "The Economy Sucks" and see how people respond.

➤ OPTION #2: *Steal*

Stealing is a classic way to get quick cash. Now, while we don't condone stealing, if you are going down this road anyway, at least steal from corporations rather than directly from individuals. It's simply not as bad to steal a watch from Bloomingdale's as it is to steal the neighbor kid's brand new red bicycle. Though it might make a good getaway vehicle if you don't already have one.

➤ OPTION #3: *Sell Yourself*

Becoming a prostitute is also a great way to earn quick cash. If you're any good at it, you just found yourself employed in a recession-proof profession.

43. You Owe a Lot of Money to the IRS

First of all, while it might seem cool to owe money to bad guys—all that danger, intrigue, and other bullshit—we're talking the IRS here. They make Tony Soprano look like a pussy. Bad guys can threaten you with a swim in the East River. The IRS promises poverty, humiliation, and a trip up the river. Here are tips for when Uncle Sam's cronies come knocking.

The WTF Approach to Handling a Debt with the F*#!-ing Government

➤ OPTION #1: *Pay 'Em*

Don't be a cheapskate. If you've got the dough, cough it up. It's better to be broke than to be locked up. Well, unless you're *really* broke.

➤ OPTION #2: *Grow a Beard and Work Out*

This is a great way to naturally disguise your appearance while you plan a potential getaway. If you don't have this kind of time before the IRS comes looking for you, try the old Groucho Marx nose and glasses routine. Fair warning: These guys are not as dumb as you think.

> **OPTION #3:** *Move*

Sometimes just leaving town is enough to keep you safe. At least for a little while. Just remember to learn your lesson and pay your f*#!-ing taxes. If you don't learn your lesson, you'll run out of places to hide. And they will find you, sooner or later.

> **OPTION #4:** *Gamble For Your Freedom*

Take your last few coins to the casino and go for it. Maybe you'll win big enough to pay off your debt. Maybe you'll lose it all. The little cash you have left won't matter much when you're your cell-mate's bitch.

Geographical Hierarchy of "Bad" Guys

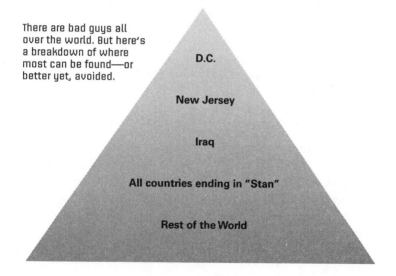

There are bad guys all over the world. But here's a breakdown of where most can be found—or better yet, avoided.

D.C.

New Jersey

Iraq

All countries ending in "Stan"

Rest of the World

44. Your Stock Portfolio Takes a Sudden Dive

You wake up in the morning, grab a bagel and an orange juice, and read the paper. It's your usual routine, checking the *Wall Street Journal* to see your stocks and those little plus signs next to the company you invested in so heavily. All's well—nothing can keep you from riches that will soon be pouring in. Then you turn on the television to find that every channel is breaking in with the report that the company's bankrupt and your stocks are in the dumps. It's over—no more little plus signs.

The WTF Approach to F*#!-ing Sunken Stocks

➤ STEP #1: *Sell Your Hummer*

This was the first thing you bought when your stocks started to soar. We know, it looks cool—but you're poor now and can't afford the gas. If driving a tank compensated for your small penis, we'd say keep it. But it doesn't.

➤ STEP #2: *Start Suing*

Go after everyone you can think of, for reasons that don't even have to really make sense, and see what sticks. It's the American way.

➤ STEP #3: *Get Back to Work*

Early retirement was boring, anyway. Did you really want to sell your condo in New Jersey and travel on a luxurious yacht?

Or . . .

➤ STEP #3: *Defenestration*

Like they did in the 1920s when people lost fortunes, you could jump out a window. But if you're not above the fourth floor, don't bother. You'll just get another bill.

It's Time to Sell When . . .

Here are some signals that may make you want to dump your position as shareholder.

- Pauly Shore is appointed CEO.

- Your company announces a new drug to cure cancer—but it's in the furniture business.

- The latest earnings conference call was cut short because the company didn't pay the bill.

IN THE FUTURE . . .

Learn your lesson. If you ever get money again, stop investing in speculative stocks because your brother says he knows a guy who knows a guy who says it's going to go up. Pick a safe bet like oil or gold. The dollar will continue to fall forever (generally, making gold more valuable). And don't worry about alternative energy. We won't get serious about that until every last drop of oil is sucked from the earth.

- You call customer service and the CEO answers.

- They're headquartered in Vancouver. Trust us, look it up.

NOTE: WTF is not registered as an investment advisor in any jurisdiction whatsoever—not even Vancouver.

45. You Have to Spend Your Vacation Fund on a Root Canal

All year, you've been slaving away, saving up, looking forward to the little time your employer gives you off. But when the time finally comes, you're inevitably short on cash.

Now, you could always just do nothing. Who really cares about Mount Rushmore, Machu Picchu, or the French? The world is full of boring shit, bugs, and disease, and by staying home, you'll have plenty of time to catch up on daytime television, those books you bought in the '90s, and masturbating.

But if you really need a getaway and don't have any loot, here's what to do.

The WTF Approach to F*#!-ing Vacationing on the Cheap

➤ **OPTION #1: *Turn Your Apartment into an Exotic Locale***

Get blowup palm trees and some margarita mix, toss some dirt on the floor, and hang a crucifix on the wall. Now you could be in one of dozens of Latin American countries. If you live in L.A., just go outside for the same effect. Also, tell your colleagues you're going somewhere exotic to do something you like to do, for example:

Alaska for fishing, Australia for surfing, or Cambodia for sex with prepubescent girls. While you're holed up at home, be sure to read up on your supposed destination, including travel memoirs of people who aren't losers and could afford to actually go. This material will give you stories to share once your vacation ends and everyone asks you about your trip.

➤ OPTION #2: *Charge It*

If you haven't yet loaded up all your credit cards, you're one of the few Americans who can still charge it. Join the crowd, load up your cards, and worry about it when you get home. Be sure to get some of those pricey cash advances because in the Third World, whether that is New Delhi or New Orleans, they only take cash.

➤ OPTION #3: *Travel on the Cheap*

Stay local instead of going to some distant place. Sleep in your car or a tent instead of a hotel. Eat at Taco Bell instead of the Cheesecake Factory. Pick up women with your good looks and charm instead of hiring hookers.

You can also try to hop a freighter ship. While it might be slightly less comfortable than a cruise, at least the deck won't be swarming with boozed-up retirees.

Top Travel Destinations for Losers and Cheapskates

Las Vegas: Flights there are relatively cheap and there's always a hotel deal somewhere. If you stay away from gambling, strippers, and shows, Vegas can be a bargain. But if you stay away from gambling, strippers, and shows, why the hell would you go to the desert?

Camp Anywhere: Without exception, every place in America is only an hour or two from some kind of mediocre nature park. Also without exception, every person in America has a buddy who owns a tent he bought when trying to shag some dirty hippie.

Mexico: About 25 percent of Americans live less than a day's drive from Mexico. Go there. Avoid pricey tourist traps and you'll feel like a king. Plus, you can bring back pharmaceuticals, cheap tequila, or even Mexicans to finance your trip. You should focus on the pharmaceuticals, however, as they are easier to carry and fetch a far higher price.

HOW PEOPLE SPEND VACATION	
Having fun:	5%
Trying to have fun:	10%
Hung over from trying to have fun:	15%
Worrying about having fun:	70%

46. You're Lost Abroad and Need to Find the Train Station

First of all, what the f*#! are you doing in Timbuktu? And why can't they speak English? It's not your fault *at all* that you're traveling around unprepared and uneducated, now lost and without the slightest idea of how to get to the train station for your 11:30 departure. Weren't the British bringing civilization, the English language, and tea to every corner of the world? Well, they were, but the Spanish and French were out there, too—and they had better food. But now you're lost with your thumb up your ass like some dumb American.

The WTF Approach to Not Knowing the F*#!-ing Language

➤ OPTION #1: *Find a Translator*

Your best bet is to hire a local or make a local language–speaking friend. There's always some hot, desperate, English-speaking NGO moron trying to save the world. Ask her.

➤ OPTION #2: *Gesture*

You should be able to use universal gestures for basic directions. Find a local who looks like he can handle a rousing game of charades. Raise both hands and shrug to signal you have a question.

Then try to simulate a movement or two that will relate you're looking for a train station. Maybe break out a few moves from the opening of *Soul Train*. You'll either end up getting to the station or in some underground club with flashing lights, lots of bass, and a smoke machine. Either way, you win.

NOTE: If you're lost in an oppressive country, be careful asking for help using hand gestures; one wrong move could be fatal. In some countries, they'll not only respond by moving their index finger across your neck to simulate cutting your throat—they'll actually do it.

➤ **OPTION #3: *Go to an Irish Pub***

There's one in every corner of the world. Ask for Seamus. He'll either give you directions to the station, or get you drunk enough not to care where you are.

➤ **OPTION #4: *Enjoy Yourself***

Forget about getting home. Immerse yourself in the culture. Who knows, you just might find it more interesting than Cleveland. *Hmm*, maybe not.

Traveling Checklist for Visiting Another Country

Before you head out, save yourself some trouble and ask yourself these questions about your intended destination:

❏ Has the civil war calmed down?

❏ Can you go without getting a vaccination?

❏ Can you walk around at night without a police escort?

❏ Can you find a good piece of cheesecake?

❏ Are they still lenient regarding prostitution (not that you're interested or anything, you just prefer liberal governments)?

❏ Can you actually speak the f*#!-ing language?

If you did not answer yes to all of the above questions, go to Florida . . . again.

47. You're Arrested in the Third World for No Good Reason

You thought you were obeying the rules, but maybe you should have done a little more research about what was legal and what wasn't before you traveled to your Third World destination. You might have found out that many of these shit holes share one law in common: A law that makes it illegal to be white and look like you have money. Of course, they'll say they pulled you over for speeding on your motorbike, but really they just want to shake you down for a few bucks.

While going to jail in the United States isn't a walk in the park, being locked up in Laos will make a stint in Rikers Island feel like a day at the beach. Trust us. Now, we're not going to lie to you. In this situation, even with WTF, you're pretty much f*#!-ed.

The WTF Approach to Surviving a F*#!-ing Third-World Jail

➤ **STEP #1:** *Get Used to Eating Rodents and Insects*

They'll be running around everywhere, and they taste better and are more nutritious than the shit they'll feed you.

➤ **STEP #2:** *Convert*

Start believing whatever religion they believe in. Everyone loves a convict that turned to God, as long as it's their God.

➤ **STEP #3:** *Try to Avoid Drinking the Water*

Until it dries up, drink your own piss. Do not drink piss from other inmates, however tempting. Even the water is better than that.

➤ **STEP #4:** *Don't Get F*#!-ed in the Ass*

Just like at home, you don't want to get f*#!-ed in the ass by a prisoner. Sure, it may hurt less in Bangkok than in Pelican Bay, but the chances of getting AIDS are moderately higher.

➤ **STEP #5:** *Bribe Them*

The good thing about a corrupt system is that it's corrupt. They may put you away for twenty years for stealing a pack of gum, but they also might take $20 to let you go on a homicide charge. Pay up and get out.

48. A Hurricane Ruins Your Honeymoon

You survived the wedding, the family, and bridezilla herself. Now you want to spend a little time on the beach, tanning, recovering, and sipping fruity drinks. But, the ocean doesn't give a shit about your petty problems. It's more interested in evaporation, condensation, and one mother-f*#!-ing monstrous storm.

The WTF Approach to Dealing with a Rainy F*#!-ing Honeymoon

➤ OPTION #1: *Get Out*

If you're scared of a little water, we don't blame you. Buy the first plane ticket out of town and watch the destruction on CNN from your safe little living room. Expect to pay big bucks for those tickets. The airline has bills to pay, too.

➤ OPTION #2: *Stay In*

Luckily, it's easy to find cardboard in third-world places like Louisiana, Mexico, and Florida. Tape it to your hotel window, and have your honeymoon where you ought to have it—in the bedroom. Scuba diving, massages, and the beach are all just foreplay anyway.

➤ OPTION #3: *Go Out*

If you can't afford to get out, and the prospect of anymore nookie with bridezilla makes you sick, go surfing. Think Brody from *Point Break*. The good part of this is: you're either stupid and dead or stupid and awesome.

IN THE FUTURE . . .

Don't go to hurricane territory during hurricane season. We know that it was a good deal. That's because it's f*#!-ing hurricane season!

WTF: UP CLOSE AND PERSONAL

Shortly after I was married, my new wife and I honeymooned in Cancun. It happened to be in the middle of hurricane season, but I went online and learned that hurricanes don't go there every year, no big deal. Plus, the airfare and hotel were so cheap that I would have booked it even if it looked like a meteor was going to hit there. The day before the trip, we heard about a hurricane forming. We were kind of excited, a little scared, but after the wedding we needed that goddamn trip. For several days, we watched the monster approach, both on CNN and out the window of the hotel. Then, it turned, destroying Belize. It was kind of disappointing.

—AWH

49. Everyone Else Is Going 90 MPH but You Get Pulled Over

Everybody speeds. That's good for cops. It's their bread and butter. Nabbing a crook is an expense for the state with all the court and jailing costs; nailing someone going ten miles over the limit is easy money. So next time you're minding your business, speeding along with everyone else, and the blue lights start flashing—blame capitalism.

The WTF Approach to Getting Out of a F*#!-ing Ticket

If you get pulled over, don't let the uniform, the boots, and the gun intimidate you. He's not going to shoot you if he catches you in a lie. Instead, remember back to when you were a kid, when lying to authorities was not only no big deal, but good fun, too.

➤ **OPTION #1: *Hospital Emergency***

Say that you were rushing to the hospital. Just don't be cliché. Don't say your wife or your mother is in trouble; that's too standard. Say your mother's cousin or your stepsister. The obscure specificity will lay the groundwork for him to believe you.

➤OPTION #2: *You Left the Oven On*

While this isn't as emotionally evocative, it can't be disproved with a phone call.

➤OPTION #3: *You're Late for a Meeting*

This opens up a dialogue between you and the cop, which could lead to him letting you off the hook if you get along. When the cop asks you what you do, don't pick something you know he'll hate or have disdain for, like a stockbroker, a lawyer, or a drug dealer. Say you're something he can either relate to or is universally liked, like a fireman or a doctor.

➤OPTION #4: *You're About to Crap Your Pants*

With clenched teeth and a grimacing face, explain to the police officer that you have a serious case of colitis and you just finished the world's largest burrito. If you can, let a wet one rip. You'll

probably ruin a pair of underwear, but you'll save yourself a ticket. Even Robocop would pity you.

➤OPTION #5: *You're Being Followed*

Say you're sure you're being chased. Be sure to describe the car's color and model and give one or two numbers in the license plate. There's a fine line between being convincing and sounding like a paranoid lunatic. Depending how well you do, he'll either put out an APB and let your ticket slide, or he'll take you in for suspicion of drug use.

---

for the ladies . . .

If you're an attractive woman, you don't need a stepsister in the hospital, you don't need to be a firewoman, and you don't even need the threat of soiling yourself. Just smile while you toss your hair. If that doesn't work and you like him, offer to toss his salad, too.

---

50. A Detour Takes You Through a Bad Part of Town

With all the news and films about violence in America's inner cities, you might be nervous about going through certain parts. But sometimes construction or a car wreck sends you to some very sketchy neighborhoods. Here are some very basic rules you can follow to increase your chances of ever getting out.

The WTF Approach to Taking a F*#!-ing Detour

➤ **STEP #1:** *Avoid Driving Through at Night*

If the detoured drive can wait until it's light out, wait. While you can get jacked in the daytime, the darkness of night is every criminal's favorite cover.

➤ **STEP #2:** *Watch What You Wear*

Avoid wearing gang colors. (Red and blues are out.) If you're a guy, don't wear anything that makes you look gay. And if your sunglasses are aviators, take them off—people may take you for a cop, which would be bad news. Your best bet is to get down to boots, jeans, and a T-shirt if possible. If not, good luck.

► STEP #3: *Turn Down Your Music*

A car with a nice sound system just screams, "Steal me!" Remember, you're trying *not* to draw attention.

► STEP #4: *Don't Make Any Stops*

If you're thirsty, low on gas, or out of smokes, it can probably wait. The only acceptable reason to stop is a red light or a stop sign. Even then, keep your eyes peeled. Better to make an unnecessary right-hand turn than get your car stolen.

Inner Cities Can Be Fun

Inner cities may be dirtier and more dangerous, but they're also more fun. Think of Rio de Janeiro—one of the world's most visited places, but also one of the most dangerous. Danger is fun; getting killed is not. Unfortunately, where there's a lot of danger, fools get shot.

REMEMBERING RODNEY

"I came from a real tough neighborhood. I put my hand in some cement and felt another hand."

—Rodney Dangerfield

IN THE FUTURE . . .

Use the buddy system. Next time you know a detour will be taking you through a shady part of town, talk a friend into going with you. At least then you won't die alone.

51. You Need to Go but You Can't Find a Bathroom

It's happened to all of us, even those who have tremendous control over our bodily functions. You're out of your house with no public restrooms in sight, and all of a sudden you've got to piss like a racehorse. Where are you supposed to go? Not just anyplace will do—or will it?

The WTF Approach to Not Having a Bathroom in F*#!-ing Sight

➤ **OPTION #1: *Go in an Alley***

But be sure not to accidentally piss too close to a bum. If you do, toss him a couple bucks for messing up his crib.

➤ **OPTION #2: *Hit Up the Gas Station***

They usually have a bathroom, and they're usually lenient about letting people use it. That's why they're so f*#!-ing filthy.

➤ **OPTION #3: *Shit in the Street***

If you have to take a shit, hold yourself up between two parked cars for leverage and let it drop. For toilet paper, use foliage, trash, or, if you can't find anything, rub your ass on the side of the vehicle.

➤ OPTION #4: *Pick a Nice Place*

The fancier the restaurant, the more likely they are to let you use the bathroom without eating there. Because they're not inundated with these requests like the less ritzy places, they're likely to make an exception. Unless, of course, you look like a bum. But if you are a bum, you already know where to go. Next stop, the ritzy parking lot.

➤ OPTION #5: *Use Someone's House*

If you're nowhere near home or a friend's house, and you have a phobia about public bathrooms— and you're not about to shit on the street—there's only one option: Put on the necktie you keep in your trunk and impersonate a Jehovah's Witness. If people don't slam the door on you, kindly ask to use their bathroom. Don't worry, if you get into a conversation about the faith, the only thing you need to remember is that they hate birthdays.

> IN THE FUTURE . . .
>
> Always keep a Super Big Gulp cup in your car. They're obviously made to shit in—no one wants that much Mountain Dew.

52. The Person Next to You on the Plane Won't Shut Up

You don't know how it happened, but somehow a couple of cordial hellos turned into his life story. Now the putz won't shut his mouth.

The WTF Approach to Dealing with a Noisy F*#!-ing Seatmate

➤ **STEP #1: *Avoid Eye Contact***

This should signal that you're not interested in chatting.

➤ **STEP #2: *Keep It Short***

Answer questions with simple yeses and nos. With luck, he'll take the hint.

➤ **STEP #3: *Get Busy***

Engage yourself with a book or some paperwork. This tactic might show him that the conversation is over. If you're dealing with a real pain in the ass, he'll probably ask you about your book or your papers, opening up a whole new can of worms.

➤ **STEP #4: *Get Up***

Break up the conversation by going to the restroom. No matter how deep you are in conversation, you can always excuse yourself to pee. Bring a blanket when you return to your seat. Close your eyes and lean back, signaling to him that you're going to sleep.

➤ STEP #5: *Tell Him to Shut Up*

If he still won't shut his trap, tell him that you enjoyed speaking to him, but you really must get some sleep. Say it politely, but make it very clear. This should shut up 99 percent of airplane nuisances.

IN THE FUTURE . . .

Don't forget your iPod—it'll help you block him out.

Or . . .

Take four Tylenol PMs and have a beer before you get on the plane. Worst case, you stay asleep . . . forever.

➤ STEP #6: *Get Serious*

For the 1 percent who are still talking, you'll have to take serious action. Look for an empty seat and move there, unless it's next to a kid or a really fat person. If there isn't an empty seat, tell the flight attendant to find someone to switch seats with you. If there's a noisy kid on the plane without his parents, have him sit in your seat. That way, the two most obnoxious creatures onboard can enjoy each other's company.

➤ STEP #7: *Get Even*

If you can't switch seats, order a cocktail and spill it on him when you hit turbulence. Then order milk and do the same thing. If that doesn't work, order a cup of coffee.

Best New Airline Deals

It's no secret that the airline industry is suffering. These companies will do anything now to get your ass onboard. Some new initiatives:

- If an engine goes out, get a free shitty cabernet.

- Fly ten times a year and get a complimentary pilot's license.

- Take a layover Saturday night and spend it with a flight attendant of your choice.

- If the landing gear doesn't come down, you get a free Salisbury steak.

53. Some Jerk Cuts You Off in Traffic

Traffic. The worst of all contemporary ills. It's where most of us commuters spend hours a day, and it's where the most mild-mannered person can turn into a raving, raging lunatic. But just because we're all susceptible to road rage doesn't make it right to cut people off and drive like a selfish, dangerous prick. There are rules of the road, just like in life. And when someone breaks them, here's what to do.

The WTF Approach to Handling Being F*#!-ing Cut Off

➤ **STEP #1: *Give Him the Bird***

People don't flip people off enough. There should be more silent *f*#! yous* on the road, not fewer.

➤ **STEP #2: *Cut in Front of Him Repeatedly***

Torture the bastard by cutting in front of him and hitting the brakes. See how he likes it.

➤ STEP #3: *Hit the Oil Slick Button*

If you're an international spy or you just happen to have the cash, get a real cool James Bond–type automobile and hit the oil-slick button. Watch the prick spin out of control.

➤ STEP #4: *Follow Him Home and Kill Him*

This only applies to sick f*#!s in creepy places where people often go insane—like California. (There was a famous case in Los Angeles in which a driver, angered that he was honked at, followed the honker home and killed him, his wife, and his two kids. Now *that's* road rage!)

The Great Equalizer

They used to call the gun the "great equalizer" because it enables a small, weak person to kill just as easily as a big, tough one. You just need to be strong enough to pull the trigger.

The automobile is also a great equalizer, which is why you get cut off every day by some snot-nosed teenager driving like an idiot. In their car, everyone feels like a tough guy. If you really are a tough guy, you've got to get out of your car when the traffic stops, smash his window with your elbow, and drag him out onto the street.

54. You're Stuck Behind a Slow Driver on a Windy Mountain Road

Depending on where you live, this situation can be a common occurrence or something that you can't even imagine. "Why would there be a road in a mountain?" an urbanite may ask, in between hocking up a lungful of smog.

Nevertheless, if you ever leave your city, you'll probably find a Sunday driver taking his sweet time driving up an interminably long, windy road, and for some reason that prick won't let you pass.

The WTF Approach to Dealing with a F*#!-ing Sunday Driver

> **OPTION #1: *Use Your Cell Phone***

Call friends and family members who you wouldn't normally call. Don't tell them the only reason you're calling is because you're bored off your ass.

> **OPTION #2: *Enjoy the Scenery***

Pull over and take a short walk. Clear your mind, get some exercise, and give the bozo driving 30 MPH a head start. It's been ten years since you've been outside Detroit, so you might as well soak it all in.

➤ OPTION #3: *Go Nuts*

Lean on your horn and start swerving. If he thinks you might follow him to his next stop to kick his ass, he might let you pass.

Road Rules in the Country

Unless you can see the driver, use this guide to determine what type of person is in the vehicle. Be careful who you piss off.

- **RV:** Old retired person. May have army-issued handgun but probably won't use it unless you resemble a Viet Cong.

- **Prius:** Some environmentally conscious yuppie scum taking a drive through the countryside. All they've got to protect themselves are a pair of sculpted legs from yoga class and a lukewarm latte.

- **Black Cadillac:** You may think it's an old person, but it could be a couple of goodfellas. They're probably just as scared of the country as you are, but they've got the guns to kill you and the shovels to hide the evidence.

- **Big dirty truck:** This is what you need to watch out for. These hillbillies have been waiting all week to find a city slicker like you to shoot. And that may be the least of your problems. Think *Deliverance*.

- **Small dirty truck:** You might see one of two kinds of people driving: a day laborer or a hot country girl. You'll know the difference by whether they're blasting mariachi or Shania Twain.

55. You Are Asked to Speak at a Funeral

Speaking in public is nerve-racking enough, but speaking at a funeral is the worst. Fact is, you're not a poet—you work in real estate. But that doesn't mean you should decline. Just prepare with a big dose of WTF.

The WTF Approach to F*#!-ing Eulogies

➤ **OPTION #1: *Pay Someone***

Put an ad on craigslist for a writer. Give details about the deceased's life, his strengths, his accomplishments, and the nuances of your relationship with him. Give specifics, like the way his scruffy beard felt when he kissed you, how he loved Cuban cigars, or how he used to let you pick which switch on the tree to get beaten with.

➤ **OPTION #2: *Rip One Off***

Take a famous eulogy and swap out the details. For instance, Jawaharlal Nehru had a great one for Gandhi. Keep all the stuff about "divine fire" and "great soul," but cut all the references to India.

➤ **OPTION #3: *Fake a Breakdown***

Go up to the podium with several sheets of paper and, after reading a line or two, pause and start crying uncontrollably, occasionally muttering words as if you're trying to speak. Not only is this intensely evocative, but it doesn't require a gift for words.

Option #4: Fill in the Blanks

If you really have nothing to say, use the WTF *Prêt-à-Dire* Eulogy:

_____ was a great (man/woman). (He/She) will always be
[Name]

remembered and will always be in our hearts. In the _____
[number]

years I've known (him/her), (he/she) has always been _____,
[adjective]

_____, and _____. (He/She) was not only my
[adjective]   [adjective]

_____ but also my friend. Every _____, we went to
[relation]   [timeframe]

_____ together, and I will never in my life forget those times.
[place]

I'm sure we all remember the time (he/she) _____. Afterward
[action]

(he/she) told me _____. And I'll never forget those words. In this
[saying or cliché]

world, there are _____ people, and there are _____
[adjective]   [opposite adjective]

people, and I can tell you that _____ was the _____
[Name]   [superlative of adjective]

person I ever met. I will never forget _____, and I will miss (him/
[Name]

her) for the rest of my life. There will never be another _____.
[Name]

SUGGESTED ADJECTIVES

fair, loving, helpful, compassionate, intelligent

56. Your In-Laws Hate You for No Good Reason

Of course they think you're a loser. That's their job. Sure, maybe you're in a band and work at Costco, or maybe you're a writer and you tell dirty jokes in silly little books, but you could also be a brain surgeon. But the facts don't matter—you're just not good enough for Daddy's Little Girl. However, there are ways to win over her parents. Whether it's a dinner at their house or a night out on the town, if you're at your best, you just might be able to make them think you're not a total scumbag.

The WTF Approach to Impressing the F*#!-ing In-Laws

➤ STEP #1: *Know Thy Enemy*

Find out what her father is into and learn enough to listen and ask questions. No need to tell stories or give your opinion unless it's asked for. You get to screw his daughter, so he gets to talk.

➤ STEP #2: *Wear a Tie*

No matter the occasion. You might feel like a schmuck wearing a tie at Applebee's, but that's the point. This shows them that you're willing to look like a schmuck for them.

➤ STEP #3: *Come Bearing Gifts*

This is, after all, how you won their daughter over—it wasn't your abs, that's for sure. Get the dad a ship in a bottle. Every older guy likes dumb shit like that.

➤ STEP #4: *Pay for Dinner*

Insist that you pay for dinner, even if it's cooked at home.

➤ STEP #5: *Do the Dishes*

Nah, *nothing* is worth doing dishes.

---

for the ladies . . .

"He's not who you think." If you have the kind of parents who don't approve of your husband for who he is, then lie a little. If he's a janitor, confess to them that he really works for the CIA, and is undercover at the local junior high to expose a plot to overthrow the educational system in the United States. Make sure to swear them to secrecy because you can't put him—or them—in danger.

Guess Who's Coming to Dinner

Just like in the movie, parents who don't initially approve of a son-in-law can change their minds. Of course, if her parents don't approve of your relationship based on the color of your skin, you better step up your game and be a pretty damn good match in every other way. It's easier for her bigoted parents to get over their racism when you're acting like Sidney Poitier, and admittedly less so when you're going by "C-note."

Things You Shouldn't Do Around Your Father-In-Law

- Escort your wife by her neck
- Fiddle with his model ships
- Point and laugh at the crucifix on the wall
- Slap your wife's ass
- Slap her mom's ass
- Ask if they swing

57. You Find a Bong in Your Son's Room

Normal, well-adjusted teenage boys share a natural curiosity about three things: sex, drugs, and sports. So if you find a bong in your son's room, don't be too alarmed. Nothing could be more natural (the curiosity—not the weed).

That said, while beer is the *real* gateway drug, pot is illegal, and smoking too much of it will slow him down and result in poor clothing choices. Also, you don't want him to move on to more serious addictions that are a direct result of marijuana such as eating cookies, listening to Pink Floyd, and taking a hacky sack wherever he goes.

The WTF Approach to Stopping Your Kid from Smoking F*#!-ing Weed

▶ **OPTION #1: *Tell Him Where Drugs Come From***

If your son gives you that "it's natural" and "God gave him the plant" crap, tell him that he's an idiot. Almost every drug comes from a natural source—heroine from poppies and cocaine from coco leaves. On second thought, if you tell him this, it might not scare him, but make him curious about growing other drugs. And before you know it he'll have green thumbs—not just green bud.

➤ OPTION #2: *Pretend to Call a Cop*

If you really want to nip his weed addiction in the "bud," wait until he is really high and then have a friend come over dressed as a cop. Let him in, and have him tell your kid that, using his new thought-reading machine, he knows he's high on pot. Let him add that he has a hidden camera following your son to watch his every move. This will scare the shit out of your boy. By the time he figures out it's a joke, he'll be so petrified that drugs will be the last thing on his mind.

➤ OPTION #3: *Join Him*

Sometimes kids do things to rebel against their parents. If you join your son and smoke with him, he'll be so annoyed he'll quit toking the reefer before he can say, "marijuana." If there's any hesitation, make sure to invite all his friends over and hang out with them.

HOW YOUR KID SPENDS HIS WEEKEND		
Activity	*Before Pot*	*After Pot*
Sleeping	30%	30%
Eating	5%	30%
Jerking off	65%	30%
Researching New Weed	0%	10%

With or without pot, your kid's a moron. At least with it, he wastes his time more evenly.

58. You Find Out That You're Adopted

Imagining that the parents who raised you are not your real parents after all might put a smile on your face, but what if it were really true? What would you do if you found out that you were actually adopted? For those of you in this predicament, consider these rules before you start searching for your real mommy and daddy—you know, the ones who didn't want you in the first place.

The WTF Approach to Dealing with Being F*#!-ing Adopted

➤ STEP #1: *Get Therapy*

Everyone who finds out they're adopted has issues—namely abandonment issues. A therapist can help you work through this by talking about your emotional problems. Don't worry about the cost; your adoptive parents who love and adore you will feel guilty and foot the bill.

➤ STEP #2: *Don't Look for Your Birth Parents*

They gave you up for a reason. They *hated* you.

Or . . .

➤ STEP #2: *Track Down Your Birth Parents*

. . . But only if you plan to systematically destroy their lives, cripple them with guilt, and wind up with a fat check in your hand for all your emotional pain and suffering.

➤ STEP #3: *Love Your Adoptive Parents*

Put the past behind you and be happy with the parents you have. They raised you, so don't be an ungrateful little bastard. Of course, technically, you *are* a bastard.

YOU'RE NOT MY DADDY

Too many adopted kids think they can stay out late and do whatever they want after they find out that their adopted parents aren't their birth parents. Just because you didn't come from your dad's sperm and your mother's egg doesn't mean that they are not your parents. They are. But that doesn't mean you have to listen to them. No one listens to their parents.

WHAT THE F*#! IS UP WITH . . . "KID-CRAZY" CELEBRITIES

Some people make fun of Angelina Jolie because she adopts a lot of kids, as if she were "kid crazy" or something. But what she does is great. Imagine these kids living in a Third World country rather than having a wholesome childhood in Hollywood with a superstar mom who traverses the globe looking for another child to cheer her up. What could be a better, more normal childhood than that?

How to Tell If You're Adopted

If you suspect you are adopted but aren't sure, here are warning signs:

❏ You're black and your parents are from Wales.

❏ Your dad has a substantially bigger penis than you.

❏ You have no baby pictures.

❏ You have two mommies.

❏ You are ugly and your parents are hot.

59. You Find Out You're Cut Out of Your Parents' Will

It's happened to many an heir apparent, Tori Spelling and Baron Hilton famously among them. Your parents decide to cut you out of their will or to leave you a tiny percentage of their wealth. Those animals! You've put up with their nagging, their boring stories, and their pitiful expressions of love for years, and for what? To be left out in the cold, just as you saw the bright, shimmering light at the end of the tunnel—at the same time they did, no less.

The WTF Approach to Getting Your F*#!-ing Slice of the Pie

> **OPTION #1: *Pull an Anna Nicole***

Take your parent's estate to court. Be sure to fabricate proof of you and your parent's loving relationship. For example, crayon drawings of you and mommy, soaked in tea to authenticate their age.

> **OPTION #2: *Pay Off a Nurse***

Have a nurse testify that your deceased parents requested that the will be changed on their death bed to leave you everything.

➤ OPTION #3: *Discredit Your Siblings*

Start gathering evidence to make the case that you deserve your siblings' shares. Point to the You-Tube video of your sister in New Orleans on Mardi Gras working it for beads.

➤ OPTION #4: *Guard Fluffy*

In the instance that your parents have left everything to a pet, be sure to establish yourself as the most appropriate guardian for the mutt. Then, promptly help the mongrel write a will, complete with pawprint. Afterward, run over Fluffy in your new Bentley.

➤ OPTION #5: *Blackmail the Poor*

When the poor impoverish you, get back your money. If your selfish parents gave everything to charity, blackmail is your best option. Assure the charity that you will keep them in court for the next decade unless they pay you handsomely to be their spokesperson.

When All Else Fails . . .

So none of the above worked in your favor and now you're on the verge of being broke—take one of these last-ditch efforts:

- If your parents were in the public eye, write a book outing your father as a homosexual or sell the movie rights to your life story, complete with child abuse charges (no one's left to refute them!).

- Start a business helping other would-be heirs protect their future assets.

- Blow the rest of your money on coke and whores. If you're going to be broke anyway, you might as well go out in style.

- Get a job. Work. Just friggin' work, you spoiled brat!

60. Your Preteen Kids Ask You About Sex

You've been dreading this conversation since you saw the sonogram. And now the little brats beat you to it. Instead of waiting for you to have a well-thought-out speech prepared, they start asking you questions. Your kiddies keep hearing about penises and vaginas in school and they start asking you questions like: "Where do babies come from?" "Why does mommy scream at night?" and "What brand of lubrication is best for anal?" How to deal? Try this:

The WTF Approach to F*#!-ing Impromptu Sex-Ed

➤ OPTION #1: *Lie*

If you think you can get away with it, lie to your kids and stick to stories about storks and other nonsense. After all, you've already lied to them about Santa Claus, so why stop now?

➤ OPTION #2: *Use Clever Metaphors*

Saying daddy drives his choo-choo train into mommy's love tunnel might sound better than saying that daddy shoves his fat cock into mommy's little pussy.

➤ OPTION #3: *Make Sex Sound Icky*

The other way to go about explaining sex—particularly if your kids are too old and too savvy for the "choo-choo" routine—is to explain in medical detail what actually happens during intercourse. It would turn anyone off.

➤ OPTION #4: *Let Them Watch You Have Sex*

If watching you and the old lady go at it all night like depraved animals won't answer their questions once and for all about sex and turn them off from it, nothing will.

NOTE: WTF is not responsible for the thousands of dollars in therapy it's going to take to correct your kids after letting them watch you and your wife. That's your own damn fault.

REMEMBERING RODNEY

"What a kid I got, I told him about the birds and the bees and he told me about the butcher and my wife."

—Rodney Dangerfield

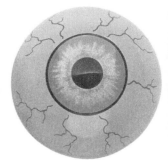

61. You Find Out Your Teenage Daughter Is Having Sex

Unprotected teenage sex is not the problem it used to be in the United States. Safe sex and abstinence programs have significantly decreased the number of adolescent mishaps. But that doesn't do you much good if you find out that your daughter is one of those girls getting an early start. Here's what to do if you want to avoid being a very, very pissed off grandparent:

The WTF Approach to Handling Your F*#!-ing Sexually Active Daughter

► STEP #1: *Blame Each Other*

When your child does anything wrong or unwise, it is best to vent your frustration by blaming your spouse or ex-spouse for teaching her bad habits and being a bad influence. This is much easier than facing up to the problem at hand and dealing with it like the adults that you claim to be.

> **STEP #2:** *Beat the Living Shit Out of Her Boyfriend*

It won't help the situation any and your daughter will hate you for it, but it might make you feel better.

> **STEP #3:** *Disown Her*

She has tainted herself and the family's good name. God be with her. She is going to need all the help she can get. Just not from you.

Teenagers Like Sex

Kids get bored and have intercourse. It's always been that way and it always will be. So don't beat yourself up about it happening. The only way to stop your daughter from having sex is to instill in her the fear that she will burn for eternity in hell if she does so. Even then, this threat will only work until she's sick of giving blowjobs.

YOUR DAUGHTER MIGHT BE HAVING SEX IF . . .

- She dyes her hair different colors

- She wears makeup

- She likes pop music

- She likes to dance

- She's always on the phone

- She wants a car

- She likes reality TV

- You're not as close as you used to be

- She's a slut and you *know* it

62. You Realize You're Going Bald . . . at Twenty-Five

Like your father and his father before him, you knew this day would come—only a few pathetic strands remain from your once thick, glorious mane. But before your thirtieth birthday? *Really*? Though you've tried Rogaine, Propecia, and similar products, utter baldness is inevitable. Try the following alternatives instead.

The WTF Approach to Tackling F*#!-ing Baldness

> **OPTION #1:** *The Comb-Over*

Sweep your hair from the good side all the way across your bald head. This is a fantastic, timeless hair style and absolutely conceals any male pattern baldness without arousing any suspicion. Use an entire bottle of hairspray and pray for no wind.

> **OPTION #2:** *Use Spray-on-Hair*

This only works with dark hair, and even then not well. Avoid rain.

> **OPTION #3:** *Wear More Hats*

You can pay homage to some of your favorite heroes, such as Davy Crocket, Abe Lincoln, or Otto von Bismarck. Or you can become a cowboy, a nineteenth-century gentleman, a 1930s businessman, or even wear a turban and say you're a sultan. However, if you decide to rock the turban, you should probably wear a baseball cap when you fly.

➤ OPTION #4: *Convert to Judaism*

If you choose to become an Orthodox Jew, you'll have to cover your head at all times in public due to a strict dress code. While the religion's strict rules will successfully hide your hair loss, the downside is that you'll need to be circumcised. If you already are, you might even have to have more taken off.

NOTE: The rare double circumcision is only practiced by extremist and abnormally well-hung Jewish sects—think Ron Jeremy dressed as a rabbi . . . without pants.

➤ OPTION #5: *Become Amish*

In addition to the hat, Amish women don't judge men by the thickness of their hair, but on how fast they can raise a barn.

➤ OPTION #6: *Bic Your Head and Work Out*

If you're African American, going bald is no big deal. There are countless bald black sex symbols—and you've got that "well endowed" thing going for you anyway.

It's a little tougher for white guys to pull it off, but it's not impossible. Notable bald, sexy white men include Bruce Willis, Mr. Clean, and the guy from *Kojak*.

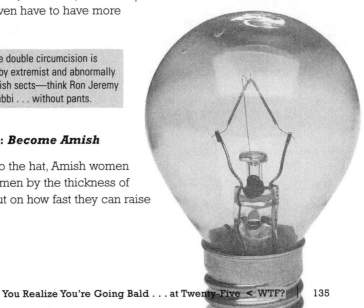

➤ OPTION #7: *Get New Friends*

If you hang out with only fat guys, even if you're bald, you'll look better. Unless, of course, you're both fat and bald.

➤ OPTION #8: *Ride a Bike Everywhere*

This will do two things. It will get you in shape and improve your overall appearance, and it will give you a reason to never take off your helmet. This is a great way to hide your growing bald spot, as long as your bike is nearby.

for the ladies . . .

All isn't lost if you're starting to lose your hair. Sinead O'Connor, Britney Spears, and Sigourney Weaver in *Alien III* all made being bald sexy. Nevertheless, you better be able to make up for it in the bedroom.

➤ OPTION #9: *Get Wacky*

Glue feathers to your head and tell anyone who asks that you're undergoing a metamorphosis that will eventually turn you into a turkey. After all, becoming a giant bird is better than being just another bald guy.

*WTF*ACT: The Vikings tried an odd hair loss remedy—rubbing goose crap all over the scalp. It didn't work. Why do you think they wore such ridiculous hats?

63. You Find Your Thirteen-Year-Old Sister's Ass on MySpace

The Internet is dangerous. Not only does it allow children easy access to porn, but with a few clicks, your little baby sis might just broadcast her own. Soon pedophiles from all over the world are messaging her about how "booty-licious" she is, how they enjoy the "junk in her trunk," and how much they'd like to "tap dat ass."

The WTF Approach to Stopping a F*#!-ing e-Lolita

> **STEP #1: *Don't Believe Her***

Refuse to accept anything she says as the truth. Not a single word. Only one in 100,000 teenage girls ever speaks the truth.

> **STEP #2: *Limit Her Private Time***

Put her computer in the living room so you can see whether she's writing a report on cross-cultural communication or browsing interracial porn.

> **STEP #3: *Refuse to Allow Her to Have a Webcam***

Keeping a webcam off the computer not only reduces the chances that your kid sister's ass will show up on MySpace or a video of her dancing around will make it onto YouTube, it also reduces the chance she'll wind up on PornSpace or YouPorn—at least anytime soon.

64. You Wake Up Next to a "10 at 2:00, 2 at 10:00"

If you wake up after a night of drinking and debauchery next to a surprisingly ugly bedmate, you've already broken the cardinal rule of drunk sex: *Never* spend the night with someone you brought home while in a drunken stupor. If it's your place, kick her out. If it's her place, catch a cab. Either way, the minute you've climaxed, get free of this person immediately. Because no matter how sober you think you are, there's a good chance that what seemed like a "10 at 2 A.M." will end up being a "2 at 10 A.M."

For those of you who need the cuddling as much as the sex, here's what to do if you find yourself entangled with a monster after what seemed like a fabulous night.

The WTF Approach to Escaping This F*#!-ing Nightmare

If you're at her place . . .

➤ OPTION #1: *Leave Quietly*

If you wake up in a stranger's bed and the animal is still sound asleep, get your shit and get the hell out as fast as you can. If you feel guilty about this, leave an apple by her pillow as a token of your appreciation and respect.

If she's really, really ugly, feel free to poison the apple for revenge.

➤ OPTION #2: *Stay with Her*

If you stay with the same person long enough, chances are, there will come a point when you're going to have to be drunk to have sex with her anyway. Stick it out and get to know each other.

➤ OPTION #3: *The Quick Excuse and Run*

Here are some good excuses to shout over your shoulder as you leave the beast's lair:

- Late for work (yes, doctors work on Sunday)

- Family member in the hospital

- Late for church

- Reservations at exclusive brunch (wish you could come, but they're totally booked)

- Cable guy's coming

If She's at Your Place . . .

➤ OPTION #1: *Emergency!*

"Oh my God! I'm so sorry. Wake up, please! Sorry, gorgeous, but you're going to have to leave. I hate to do this (*wink, wink*) but my mother just called and she's in town for a surprise visit. I'm sorry, but you have to leave."

► OPTION #2: *Say You're Married*

If you *are* married, you're a schmuck and you get what you deserve. If you're not, tell the "2" you are. After you get lectured, she'll be on her way. If the "2" chooses to stay, then, even though she's ugly, you have to admit it's kind of hot that she doesn't care about things like that.

► OPTION #3: *Play Dead*

If you're a real coward, play dead. Don't move and barely breathe. When she goes to call 911, make a run for it. You could get lucky. If she's a real romantic, she might kill herself like in *Romeo and Juliet*, leaving you off the hook for good.

> ### IN THE FUTURE . . .
>
> Stop drinking so much. Learn your lesson, and don't hit the bottle so hard. Make yet another pledge to only bang chicks you've seen before you put on your beer goggles.

65. You Realize That You Are Gay

The consensus now is that if you're gay, you were born that way. Nothing you can do about it. Sure, you can join the priesthood and try to suppress it (we've seen how successful that plan is), but chances are, you'll eventually be living life as a homosexual no matter how much you fight it. It's what you were destined to do.

The WTF Approach to Coming Out of the F*#!-ing Closet

➤ **STEP #1:** *Cancel Your Fishing Trip*

Unless you're fishing for cock or hunting for dick, you're no longer obligated to fish or hunt.

➤ **STEP #2:** *Get a Decent Haircut*

Now that you're officially gay, you're not going to be able to go to Super Cuts for your next 'do.

You're probably going to have to get a new wardrobe, and throw out the wagon-wheel coffee table as well. You don't want to be an embarrassment to your new community.

➤ **STEP #3:** *Come Out in Style*

There's no reason why coming out of the closet and announcing your gay lifestyle has to be a grim, serious affair. Try to make it fun. Take your dad to a baseball game and have it announced on the scoreboard in front of thousands of fans and millions watching at home. He'd appreciate the effort.

➤ STEP #4: *Spill the Beans, Save the Franks*

Coming out of the closet isn't easy. It's got to be one of the hardest things to do. (Not that we would know. We don't want readers to get the wrong idea. We're not gay. Not that there's anything wrong with it. To each his own, you know. We're just not gay, so please don't get that idea just because we're writing about it. Not that there's anything wrong with that!)

WTFACT: Approximately one in every ten people is homosexual. You are not alone!

Gay Family Values

An argument propagated by conservatives against the legalization of gay marriage is that it would corrode the institution and lead to a further decay of "family values." Really? Well, here is some information for you bozos: Massachusetts was the first state to allow gay marriage and it also consistently ranks among the top states for the lowest divorce rate. It's true, and the Bible Belt states—whose political leaders constantly taunt "family values"—have the highest divorce rates.

YOU MIGHT BE A HOMOSEXUAL IF . . .

❏ You went to boarding school in England.

❏ You cook a lot and you're not Italian or French.

❏ You're white and you can dance.

❏ You have a flair for fashion.

❏ You want to have sex with men . . . *a lot.*

66. You're About to Have Sex and Find Out You're Out of Condoms

Unless you're a virgin, in which case you're probably not reading this book (you know the phrase, "old enough to read, old enough to . . ."), you've been in a situation where you're about to get your groove on only to find out that you're fresh out of condoms.

Being hard up for a rubber in the heat of the moment is quite possibly one of the worst things you can experience (though not getting an opportunity to use a condom is worse). Nevertheless, if you're about to ride bareback on a new pony, you better think twice: It might just save your life.

The WTF Approach to Not Having Any F*#!-ing Condoms

➤ **STEP #1:** *Just Say No!*

If it helps, think of Nancy Reagan saying it—spread eagle wearing nothing—nothing but wrinkles, that is.

➤ **STEP #2:** *Remember: There Is No Substitute*

Saran Wrap, plastic baggies, and aluminum foil don't work. Trust us. It's not worth even trying.

➤ STEP #2.5: *When It's Worth Trying*

If she's really, *really* hot and doesn't *look* like she has an STD—double-bag it and secure it with a rubberband or a twisty-tie.

> **NOTE:** If you're desperate enough to try this out, WTF applauds your creativity but will not pay for any hospital bills. We will, however, suggest ironic baby names like Ziploc, Glad, and Hefty.

➤ STEP #3: *Know What Not to Do*

- Use that old lambskin condom. Stay away from lambskin condoms! First of all, they don't stop diseases, and second of all, they're made from baby sheep intestines and smell like a farm, which shouldn't be sexy—except to a sheep. Hmm . . .

- Opt for the pull-out method. If venereal disease isn't scary enough for you, consider having a baby with that barfly you took home. Yikes.

- Let *her* bang *you*.

Location, Location, Location

If you're in Africa, Asia, or certain parts of Florida, you might find that the locals don't even know what condoms are, let alone endorse their use. Some tribal cultures even believe that using a condom is a sin because it separates a man from his partner.

Good luck trying that one with the chick from *Match.com*.

> **IN THE FUTURE . . .**
>
> Live by the Boy Scout motto: Always be prepared. Jogging half a mile to the store with a hard on is not an option. (Though every Boy Scout has played that game . . . right?) And, depending on your particular proclivities, you may want to keep several sizes on hand.

67. Your New Girlfriend Giggles at Your Penis

You knew you weren't big. You never thought you'd be a porn star. But laughable? WTF?

The WTF Approach to Working with What You're F*#!-ing Packing

> **OPTION #1:** *Learn Cunnilingus*

If you think this is a foreign language, your sex knowledge obviously needs some work. Either rent some girl-on-girl porn and practice on the back of your hand, or find an older woman. She'll turn you into a pro.

> **OPTION #2:** *Date a Dwarf Instead*

If you aren't big enough for her, try an Asian dwarf.

> **OPTION #3:** *Shave Your Pubic Hair*

This will make your penis at least appear bigger. You can also try applying some light foundation down the middle of your shaft, making your penis appear longer. However, it will also make your penis look thinner. So, if girth is your problem, use horizontally striped condoms and practice gyrating in giant circles.

➤ OPTION #4: *Get a Big Truck*

This always compensates for a small penis. After all, how could a guy with such a big truck and such big wheels have a small dick?

➤ OPTION #5: *Make More Money*

Nobody's perfect. Since you've got no bulge in the front of your pants, make sure that in the back there's a fat wallet stuffed with $100 bills. Many women will find you irresistible. There are a lot more gold-diggers than size queens out there anyway.

➤ OPTION #6: *Get a Dildo*

Nowadays, sex toys are far better than a real penis. The only thing they don't do yet is cuddle her. So practice your spooning because that's all you're good for.

➤ OPTION #7: *Five Rubbers*

You might not feel shit, but at least she will.

➤ OPTION #8: *Become a Priest*

If you live up to your vows, you won't use it anyway.

68. Your Girlfriend Starts Getting Too Kinky in Bed

Most guys complain that their girlfriends aren't kinky enough. "You want to put what *where*?" she flinches. "You want to do *what* with another girl?" she asks—though this time, she can't help but be a little curious. But what if you're one of the few guys whose girlfriend isn't just kinky, but *too* kinky?

Crazy, kinky sex can be a slippery slope. At first it was enough to cover each other with whipped cream. Then, before you know it, twin midget transsexuals are living in your closet. Be careful—before you know it, she'll be turning the kink up to eleven. Follow our approach if you don't want things to get out of hand.

The WTF Approach to Curbing the F*#!-ing Kink

➤ OPTION #1: *Have Less Sex*

The only way to make normal, "vanilla" sex exciting—or even worth doing—is to do it less often. Go on a trip, get sick, or just tell her that you have a headache. This will make her want sex more and appreciate *any* kind—even the boring kind that you're capable of giving. However, there's a risk with this strategy. She might feel that you are less interested in her, and therefore spend more time trying to seduce you in extra-kinky ways, such as lying on the coffee table spread eagle when you get home—with a bald eagle on her lap.

➤ OPTION #2: *Give Her to the Gardener*

If you really can't satisfy her appetite for wacky sex, find someone who can. Make the gardener or the pool boy or your driver screw her silly. You might as well pay people to handle *all* your chores.

➤ OPTION #3: *Develop a Disgusting Fetish*

One way to bring her kink down to a manageable level is to become too kinky yourself, thus scaring her into regular sex. If you are unseemly hairy or fat, wearing a simple lace teddy will turn down her kink in a heartbeat.

REMEMBERING RODNEY

" I'm a bad lover. I once caught a peeping tom booing me. "

—Rodney Dangerfield

Here are some other kinky fetishes that are sure to turn her off:

- Ask her for a blumpkin—if you don't know what this is . . . google it!

- Wear diapers and a bib like a fat baby, suck on your thumb, and make her change you.

- Shave your pubic hair, roll it into a ball, and eat it like a cat.

➤ **OPTION #4:** *Talk to Her*

It's the last thing you want to do and it's one hell of a chore. But sometimes, if you speak really slow and look her in the eye, you can actually communicate with her. She might even listen—though it's doubtful.

KINK SCALE

1. Missionary position only

2. Doggy style, oral, and the occasional 69

3. Light spanking and hair pulling

4. Anal, rim jobs, and facials

5. Dildos, butt plugs, and sex with a porno on the flat screen

6. Threesomes, sex in public, and fisting

7. Heavy bondage

8. Cunnilingus during menstruation after a jog on a hot summer day

9. Fecalfelia, golden showers, and bestiality

10. Necrophilia

11. Necro-bestiality in public on a hot summer day—or fucking a dead donkey in the middle of the mall

69. Your Girlfriend Gives You Herpes

The news is in. Those itchy little bumps on your penis aren't a temporary rash you got from eating shellfish. You've got herpes, dipshit, and all signs point to your girlfriend. Before you start screaming at her, follow these rules.

The WTF Approach to Dealing with Your F*#!-ing STD-Giving Girlfriend

➤ STEP #1: *Resent Her*

Say that you understand and forgive her, but secretly resent her for the rest of your life. You know you're going to anyway.

➤ STEP #2: *Guilt Her When Appropriate*

Whenever you want something to go your way, just remind her of the scorching sores on your penis. That should make her feel guilty enough to give in.

➤ STEP #3: *Determine if She Knew She Had Them*

Check her medicine cabinet. If there are no clues, call her doctor and ask to renew a prescription for herpes medication. If you can, use a female friend to make the call. As a last resort, break into her gynecologist's office to find her files. If you get caught, tell them that your herpes outbreak drove you temporarily insane.

If you find out she knew beforehand . . .

➤ STEP #4: *Get Retested*

Herpes might be the least of your problems. Get tested . . . for *everything*.

➤ STEP #5: *Leave Her and Join* **PositiveSingles.com**

This is an extensive website for hip young singles covered in sores. (Yes, this is a real website.)

WTFACT: About one in five Americans have herpes, but 80 percent of these people are unaware of it. Pull down your pants and check . . . *now*!

➤ STEP #6: *Audition for a Herpes Medication Commercial*

You'll be able to claim that you're not just a paid actor, but an actual user of the product. This may offer you the break you need to take over the entertainment industry.

WTF ABOUT TOWN

We recently interviewed a particularly vocal herpe about his hopes, dreams, and plans for the future.

WTF: Can you please state your name for the record?

Herpe: Herpes Simplex 2.

WTF: What's the difference between you and those Simplex 1 characters?

Herpe: They're an embarrassment. They hang out on the mouth, usually on the outside, and can even be mistaken for a pimple. Those ain't herpes, they're cold sores. They're afraid to go down and do the dirty work where the sun don't shine.

WTF: What do you say to people with herpes who complain about the itchiness and pain you guys cause?

Herpe: Life's tough. You think that I chose this lifestyle? Do you think if I could choose my destiny, this would be it?

WTF: If you could pop up anywhere, where would you choose?

Herpe: I'd choose Angelina Jolie's lips . . . either pair.

70. Your Lover Answers the Phone During Sex

You're so close, and you think she is too (not that you ever know for sure if she can—with you). Then the phone rings. Once, twice, and, before the third ring she's off of you and chatting away. WTF?

Nothing is more annoying than being interrupted during the heights of passion—at least for *you*. What do you do when your lover answers the phone during sex in order to make sure it doesn't happen again?

The WTF Approach to F*#!-ing Intercourse Hangups

> **OPTION #1:** *Determine the Importance of the Call*

If your lover's a doctor, you're going to have to deal. Your orgasm may be important, but the life of a five-year-old kid hovering between life and death takes precedence . . . unless it's been a really, really long time.

So it better be a matter of life or death if she can't wait the two minutes it takes to have sex in order to call back.

> **OPTION #2:** *Count to Sixty Then Finish Yourself Off*

There's no reason to wait for your lover to get off. Teach your lover a lesson and do it yourself. After all, there's no touch more skilled than your own.

➤ OPTION #3: *Make a Phone Call*

Two can play at that game. Stay on the phone long after she hangs up. When your lover tries to get back to business, tell her to wait. You're on the phone, for Christ's sake.

➤ OPTION #4: *Turn It into a Sex Game*

Just because she has to answer the phone doesn't mean the sex has to stop. Continue pleasuring her while she tries to maintain a conversation. If you want to get really kinky, don't hold back and let the person on the line join the fun. If they're down with it, maybe he'll start talking dirty. Who knows? This could turn into a regular thing. But tread carefully. If it gets too wacky, the next time you call her, she could be at his place.

IN THE FUTURE . . .

Secretly put the phone on silent before you start. This way, there will be no calls and you can continue uninterrupted. When she goes to the bathroom, turn her ringer back on. With luck, the phone will ring so you can relax.

71. Your Mom Catches You Masturbating

If you have ever been caught spanking your monkey by your mom, you understand what true horror is: the image of your mother's mortified face forever etched in your memory. If you find yourself in this sticky situation, here's what to do.

The WTF Approach to Being F*#!-ing Caught by Your Mom

> **OPTION #1: *Wash Up and Apologize***

This particular option is best if your mom happens to be very conservative or religious. Apologize to her and promise that you will never do it again. Tell her that Satan took hold of your hand and, through the power of his evil genius, forced you to do it.

> **OPTION #2: *Flip the Switch***

Try turning it around on her. Blame her for her lack of respect for your privacy. She should have knocked. You can also scold her for not letting you bring home a girl to have sex with, thus forcing you to masturbate. Reinforce that she has no right to tell you what to do with your body, and that masturbation is normal, healthy, and a good way to pass the time.

> **OPTION #3: *Pretend Nothing Happened***

If you just pretend nothing happened and never bring it up,

your mom will do the same. She probably wants the image of you stroking yourself out of her head—desperately.

►OPTION #4: *Quit Masturbating*

Yeah . . . right.

The WTF Approach to What Not to Do

Do not ask for help: Even if the particular bathroom where you're jerking off happens to be in the Deep South, asking your mom to help you climax is *not* okay—even if you just want her to watch and cheer you on. Now, a stepsister— that's a different story altogether.

Do not continue: No matter how close you are to finishing, the minute your mom sees your erect penis pointed toward the sky, you should discontinue your masturbatory session immediately, as a show of decency and respect to the woman who gave you life. Once she splits, game on.

Do not deny it: No matter how gullible your mother is, there is no way you can convince her that you had an itch. She gets itches too, and when she does, she scratches them, she doesn't yank them.

Do not feel ashamed: If your mother tries to make you feel guilty, don't let her. Who brought you into this world, a stork?

Do You Masturbate Too Much?

Yes, it is possible. If you answer yes to one of these questions, you might have a problem:

- ❑ When you cum, does smoke come out?

- ❑ Is there a palmprint on your penis?

- ❑ Are the ends of your pubes singed?

- ❑ Instead of a cum-rag, do you use a Q-tip?

- ❑ Are your balls flat?

72. The Ladies Call You the "One-Minute Man"

What are you, thirteen? This has to stop. If you can't keep it going long enough for a lady to be interested in another test drive, it's time to learn what's up.

The WTF Approach to Avoiding an Early F*#!-ing Release

➤ OPTION #1: *Take Meds*

You'd be surprised what kind of medications are available nowadays. They have pills not only to get your dick up, but also to stop it from going down too quickly. But beware of the side effects, especially with some of those ancient Chinese herbs.

➤ OPTION #2: *Wear a Condom*

This is a pretty good advice anyway. It can save a life, stop you from being a parent, and significantly decrease your sexual pleasure. Using a condom will work if your problem is that you have an extra-sensitive pee pee, but not if the problem is all in your head.

➤ OPTION #3: *Don't Go Out with a Loaded Gun*

If lasting more than a minute requires that you jerk it thirty times beforehand, do it.

➤ OPTION #4: *Think About Baseball*

If you think about something that doesn't turn you on, this will take your mind off your problem. If the sport itself isn't enough, picture the baseball team naked. This will work, unless you get turned on by sweaty guys in tight pants swinging large bats. In this case, think of women's volleyball players instead. A sport people of all sexual orientations can think of is women's basketball.

➤ OPTION #5: *Get an Uglier Girlfriend*

Maybe she's just too hot for you and your penis, so try downgrading. If you're not sure you want to ditch your lady before you test out your theory, hang out at WNBA games and chat up the girls. Don't worry about breaking her heart—at this rate, she'll be walking out on you soon anyway.

73. After a Night of Drinking You Wet the Bed

Many kids wet the bed at night, turning their clean bedsheets into a pool of piss. It's relatively normal. But as an adult, you're up shit (or rather piss) creek.

Wetting the bed after a night of drinking can cost adults relationships, friends, and a ton of laundry soap. The obvious thing to do is to stop drinking and see if you can now go to bed piss free. But we at WTF would never encourage you to be a teetotaler, so here are steps you can take:

The WTF Approach to Avoiding a Wet F*#!-ing Bed

➤ **OPTION #1: *Wear Diapers***

The obvious thing to do is to wear diapers when you sleep. After all, you're a big friggin' baby anyway, so you might as well act like one.

➤ **OPTION #2: *Sleep in the Bathtub***

Invest in a Jacuzzi and enjoy a good, clean night's sleep.

➤ OPTION #3: *Get a Giant Litter Box*

You can build one yourself, or you can try to purchase one from a lion tamer.

WTFACT: Approximately 1 in 100 adults wet the bed—drink or no drink. Eww.

➤ OPTION #4: *Dream of the Desert*

Listening to waterfalls and streams flowing is a common tool to help lull many an insomniac to sleep, but it's the last thing you want to do. You could look for a tape of sounds of the desert instead. Common sounds of the desert are rattlesnakes, sandstorm winds, and, in some regions, violent Anti-American rhetoric.

Date Someone Who Can Help

You might be able to find assistance and support from a special someone:

- **Date a nurse.** Try shacking up with her. She might find your repulsive habit cute and child-like. Plus, she's used to people pissing themselves like animals anyway.

- **Date a laundress.** Finally, someone who doesn't mind washing sheets over and over again.

- **Date a pervert.** There are a surprising number of people out there with a urine fetish of some sort. Date one of these perverts and she'll enjoy the surprise wet spot.

74. You Suspect Your Partner Is Cheating

Something's not right. She's changed. There's a bounce in her step and you didn't put it there. Not only that, but she's out of town five days a week.

The WTF Approach to Catching a Possible F*#!-ing Adulterer

➤ **STEP #1:** *Do Some Investigating Yourself*

Check her phone. Check her car. Look for unfamiliar hairs on her jacket, blouse, and panties.

➤ **STEP #2:** *Hire a Sleuth*

Make sure to get her on tape. In most states, this will be the difference between her getting everything you've worked so hard for, and her only getting half.

➤ **STEP #3:** *Get Creative*

Anonymously send her flowers and see if she tells you about them.

> *REMEMBERING RODNEY*
>
> "I have good-looking kids. Thank goodness my wife cheats on me."
>
> —Rodney Dangerfield

➤ **STEP #4:** *Flip the Switch*

Start having an affair. If she begins to suspect you of having an affair, chances are she's not having one. Otherwise, wrapped up in her own infidelity, she's unlikely to notice. She'll be too busy trying to cover for herself. Of course, this could also mean that you're cheating when she's not, but you just *have* to find out.

➤ **STEP #5:** *Get Even*

If your detective work proves she's a cheating whore, send any incriminating e-mails that you find to everyone from her ninety-five-year-old grandmother to the mailman to Anderson Cooper.

REASONS TO EXPECT YOUR
PARTNER IS CHEATING

● She left the house smelling like Chanel No. 5, and came home smelling like cum.

● Her hair looks like she's been driving around in a convertible all day, but she drives an SUV.

● Every time she has to "work late," she comes home and showers immediately.

● You find a box of extra-large condoms in her bag, and, well, those aren't yours.

● She keeps getting "wrong number" calls.

● When she does want to have sex with you, it's a lot kinkier.

● . . . Or conversely, she looks even more bored.

75. You Discover the Girl You're Dating Is a Dude

You've kissed her, you've felt her up, but you and your new sexy lady have yet to go all the way. There's a reason for this and it's not that she's waiting for the "right" time like she says. But you can't wait any longer. So you try and spice things up by jumping into the shower with her. You open the curtains and . . . bam! Your chick's got a dick. Now what?

The WTF Approach to Dating a F*#!-ing Tranny

➤ **OPTION #1: Call Jerry Springer**

Finally you can be a guest on your favorite show. Call *The Jerry Springer Show* and tell them your story. If you get picked as a guest, you can share your folly with the whole world, including your parents and close friends. Make sure to act surprised when your "girlfriend" confesses that she's a dude. Then, as is customary on the show, hit her until the bodyguards drag you off.

➤ **OPTION #2: Make Her Go All the Way**

For decades, science has been able to successfully transform a penis into a fully functional vagina.

In fact, using the most sensitive parts of the penis, doctors can create a clitoris that's just as good—if not better—than the genuine article. Studies suggest that these new girls on the block have less trouble having an orgasm than their natural sisters.

➤ OPTION #3: *Find a Real Chick*

Finding a chick without a dick that is just as bitchy and annoying shouldn't be difficult.

➤ OPTION #4: *Ignore It*

You like the girl. She's smart, she's sexy, she's sweet. So, she has a dick. Nobody's perfect.

WTF: UP CLOSE AND PERSONAL

For those of you macho men who are confident that you would never mistake a guy for a girl, I can assure you that anything is possible. I once felt the same way. Until, on a mild spring day in Manhattan, I was proven wrong.

During the annual Puerto Rican Day parade in 1999, I came across one of the most beautiful women I had ever seen. She was exotic, elegant, and had the kind of body that made me drop to my knees and thank God I'm a man. Unfortunately, after a romantic afternoon of flirting, kissing, and some mild touching, she confessed to me that so was she! But beggars can't be choosers . . .

—GB

76. You Can't Get Control of the Remote Control

After sex, kids, and money, control over the television is one of the most heavily disputed subjects in every household. You want to watch the ballgame, and she wants to watch some *Lifetime* movie about a teenage mother with breast cancer.

The WTF Approach to the F*#!-ing Remote Battle

➤ STEP #1: *Give Middle-of-the-Road Channels a Shot*

Don't go for the black and white of ESPN versus Lifetime. Instead try out the History Channel, Home & Garden TV, and VH1. You'll be surprised how much you might like shows about fixing up houses to sell them for more money, or how riveting news about Britney Spears's latest spectacle can be. The same goes for you, ladies. Before you know it, thirteenth-century European battle formations will be your favorite topic—after Britney Spears, of course.

➤ STEP #2: *Get Another Television*

Prerequisites for any successful marriage are two TVs, two cars, and two bank accounts (make sure that you have your name on both, though, just in case). Also, try to splurge enough to get the exact same size and quality TV as your primary one. If you can't afford that, make a schedule to alternate who gets to use which TV to avoid any further disputes.

> **STEP #3:** *Throw Out the TV*

If you can't afford two TVs, you might just want to sell the one you have and live without it. Who knows, you might read and have sex a lot more.

> **STEP #4:** *Get Divorced*

If the infighting over the remote doesn't stop, get a divorce or break up and move out. (Make sure you get that f*#!-ing TV in the settlement!)

WHERE THE F*#! IS THE UNIVERSAL, UNIVERSAL REMOTE?

We're not asking for something fancy to control time like in the movie *Click*, just something of manageable size that you can use for your television, your DVD player, your stereo, your thermostat, your microwave oven, the lights, and, of course, to bone your wife.

77. You Find Out Your Girl-friend Is a Stripper

She works late, she's hot, and she knows how to dance really, really sexy. Sometimes she'll see a stop sign when you're walking around town and start twirling around it and dry humping it. But she *says* she's a waitress at a nightclub. Then, one day your friend calls you and thanks you for the lap dance. "Your girlfriend was really good at sitting on my dick and moving around. You didn't tell me she's a stripper."

What now?

The WTF Approach to Dealing with a F*#!-ing Stripper Girlfriend

➤ STEP #1: *Visit Her at Work—Incognito*

If you don't mind the fact that she's a stripper but just want to know whether or not she's actually a hooker too (this may be shocking news, but some strippers are not "just dancing to put themselves through med school"), dress in disguise and visit her place of "business." Buy a lap dance or two and talk in a funny accent. Let her take you to the VIP room and see just how "very important" she makes you feel for a couple hundred bucks.

And then . . .

► OPTION #1: *Break Up with Her*

If you just can't handle that your girlfriend takes off her clothes and sits on stranger's laps until they orgasm—if you are just *that* old-fashioned—you're going to have to break it off. Make sure to at least get a complimentary lap dance for you and all your friends before you call it quits.

► OPTION #2: *Marry Her*

Imagine the possibilities. You could spend the rest of your life having sex with not only her but all her stripper friends—and maybe at the same time. Your so-called marriage will be just one long bachelor party! Plus, when was the last time a stripper *really* wanted you?

► OPTION #3: *Enjoy It While It Lasts*

Chances are good that within a month or two she'll be living at some other guy's house in some other city. Strippers are always on the move. Think of them as naked gypsies that pop a lot of pills and suck a lot of dick.

YOUR GIRLFRIEND MIGHT BE A STRIPPER IF . . .

- She has a tattoo of an arrow pointing to her vagina that says "Pay Here."

- She has a lot of money but it's all in singles.

- She does more coke than Robert Downey Jr.

- She does coke *with* Robert Downey Jr.

What Her Stripper Name Says About Her

- **Candy:** She has an oral fixation and likes to be babied.

- **Danni:** She likes hip-hop, being spanked, and muff diving.

- **Star:** She reads a lot of Stephen Hawking and does a lot of anal.

78. You Forgot Your Girlfriend's Birthday

She seemed a little bitchier than normal, but you chalked it up to PMS. Then she suspiciously asks you the date, but you don't know. You look at the stupid kitty calendar she put up on your wall, and then it hits you in the face. The balloons, the hearts, and the stars covering that little square tell a pretty clear story. But you read the words anyway: "Don't forget my birthday again, or you're a dead man!" You could dump her, admit that you forgot, or tell her that you're now a Jehovah's Witness, but none of these options will help facilitate you getting laid. So here's the plan:

The WTF Approach to Covering Up Forgetting Her F*#!-ing Birthday

➤ STEP #1: *Don't Flinch*

Tell her the date, go back to the couch, and keep watching television. While you're watching, try to remember her favorite restaurant and what the hell she might want.

➤ STEP #2: *Make Moves*

Excuse yourself to the bathroom for a shower and bring your cell. While the water is running, call the restaurant and make a reservation.

Also, it's time to call in a favor with someone to get a present and flowers delivered there.

➤ STEP #3: *Put Your Plan in Action*

When you get out of the shower, tell her that you're hungry and you want to get a bite to eat. Hopefully, your buddy won't flake.

➤ STEP #4: *Execute*

At the restaurant say, "Happy Birthday." She'll probably be surprised that you remembered. Women love surprises.

IN THE FUTURE . . .

Dump your girlfriends a week or two before their birthdays, Valentine's Day, or Christmas. However much you like her, it's probably going to end soon anyway, so save yourself some money in the process.

If you're not willing to do that, keep a wrapped bottle of fancy chick perfume, a frozen cake, and some champagne in your house. You might as well stock up on tampons, potpourri, Summer's Eve, and Lean Cuisines while you're at it.

79. You Misplaced Your Wedding Ring

As ridiculous and arcane as the tradition of marriage might be, equally ridiculous is the age-old tradition of wearing a wedding ring. Nevertheless, you got married and got a ring. And however you feel about it, if you lose your wedding ring, you better have a damn good excuse.

The WTF Approach to Dealing with a F*#!-ing Misplaced Ring

➤ OPTION #1: *Buy a Replica*

If you've got the cash and you're unlike most married men—in that your wife doesn't go over every single friggin' purchase with a magnifying glass—just cough up the dough and buy another.

➤ OPTION #2: *Cut Off Your Finger*

Though painful, it might pale in comparison to hearing your wife yell at you for what a careless dumbass you are. You can choose to be a real man and just cut it off with a dull knife, or you can get it amputated by a back-alley doctor for a few bucks.

Either way, instead of being yelled at and made to feel guilty and forced to console her, she'll be babying you. Until, of course, she remembers the wedding ring. "Why didn't you find the wedding ring?" she'll say. "If you loved me, you would have made sure to grab it no matter what happened." Women.

➤ OPTION #3: *Cut Off Your Hand*

If you've got a really suspicious wife, then cut off your whole hand. Luckily, it's the left hand—unless, of course, you're unfortunate enough to be left-handed—so it won't hurt your ability to masturbate, which, being married and all, you're definitely going to need.

➤ OPTION #4: *Flip the Switch*

When she asks what happened to your ring, tell her you don't wear it anymore. When she asks why not, just say that you'll start wearing a wedding ring when she starts acting like a wife. After an initial shock, she'll spend the next few weeks wondering what she's done wrong and how to make it up to you. Women.

➤ OPTION #5: *Remove Her Wedding Ring*

Before she notices, remove her wedding ring when she's sleeping. No, don't cut off her hand—that will wake her up. Wait until she's in a deep sleep and rub butter on her finger and slowly slide it off. When she wakes up, she'll probably notice and wonder what happened. At that moment, look down at your hand and say, "Oh my God, mine is gone, too!" This way, you can blame some wedding ring thief that goes into people's houses and steals them.

On the other hand, she might be convinced that your whole marriage was just a dream—or a nightmare.

80. Your Girlfriend Wants to Get Exclusive

This day was bound to come. Where did you think you were, Mars? Who did you think you were, the one guy who can go out with a chick for months and avoid it? Ever been out with a girl before? Did you really think she was just going to go out with you until you were ready to make the next move? Think again, because the time for "the talk" has come. What will your answer be?

The WTF Approach to the F*#!-ing Talk

> **OPTION #1: *Tell Her You Want to Keep It Open***

If you're not sure whether you want to get serious, nothing will put things in perspective more than the knowledge that she'd be going out with (meaning banging) other guys. If this drives you crazy, then you probably like her and you'll ask *her* to get exclusive.

> **OPTION #2: *Say, "Okay"—but Keep Playing the Field***

The truth of the matter is you never signed up for this, and it's unfair that she alone defines the dynamics of your relationship. You may like her the best out of the women you're dating, but you need more time to see if you want to get exclusive. Make sure you memorize all phone numbers and take frequent showers.

➤ OPTION #3: *Break It Off*

If you're not *that* into her, break it off now before you cause any more damage. Sure, you'd like to sleep with her for a few more weeks, but bandages are best pulled off quickly. She'll inevitably accuse you of leading her on. Say goodbye and that you're sorry. (Even though you know that in your heart of hearts, you did nothing wrong. You liked her, you went out with her, and you would've liked to keep liking her and going out with her. So WTF is with this woman?)

EVEN IF YOU HAVEN'T HAD "THE TALK," SHE MIGHT THINK YOU'RE EXCLUSIVE IF:

- You go out with her every Saturday night.

- You've met her family more than once.

- She keeps a lot of her crap at your house.

- You've been dating more than a month.

- You pick her up and/or drop her off at the airport.

- You've taken her on more than one weekend trip.

- You've helped her move.

NOTE: While none of these things constitutes an implicit exclusive dating agreement, a few together may. However, if she keeps a box of tampons in your bathroom cabinet, you've definitely got a girlfriend. And before you know it, a wife, too.

81. You Are Accosted by Proselytizers

Most religious groups try to woo new members. It's just the way it is. And their intentions are usually good. They are, after all, trying to save your soul. But while the motives may be admirable, these pushy proselytizers can be a bit annoying, especially when you've just laid down to take a nap after a long day at work and they keep ringing your doorbell like some cheap door-to-door salespeople. And then they start with the questioning, "Have you ever heard of the Church of Latter Day Saints?" What do they think you are, an idiot? Of course you've heard of Mormons. How couldn't you? They stop by every other week, for Christ's sake!

The WTF Approach to Handling F*#!-ing Proselytizers

➤ **OPTION #1:** *Answer the Door in a Devil's Costume*

It's good to keep some Halloween Satan horns and a pitchfork lying around so that when unexpected and unwelcome missionaries come pounding on your door, you can scare the crap out of them. Just look through your peephole to make sure that you're dealing with proselytizers and not the little kid next door. It's not hard to spot them: Look for the pontific smiles, cheap suits, and the subtle gaze of wasted youth.

➤ OPTION #2: *Flip the Switch*

Two can play at the proselytizing game. Let them in and hear what they have to say. After listening intently as if you might be interested, break out some of your own literature on the religion of your choice—like satanic transsexual worshipping, for instance. After having listened so politely to their spiel, they'll feel compelled to hear you out. Try to waste as much of their time as possible, just like they had planned to do with you.

➤ OPTION #3: *Try to Seduce Them*

This will (most likely) *not* work out, but it will make sure that these proselytizers won't come back. And if they do, you know what they're back for. They want to get to know you . . . in the biblical sense.

PROGRESS IN PROSELYTIZING

Fanatical proselytizers are, in this country at least, at worst, just annoying. Not that long ago, saying "no" to a conversion didn't end with a polite, but admonishing, "God bless your soul"—it ended with them tying you up and setting you on fire.

Heaven Is a Restaurant

Think of your favorite television evangelist as the maître d' at a restaurant called Heaven's. How much you donate determines where you get to sit. Here's a breakdown:

$100	Sit at the bar
$1,000	Get a shitty table in the back
$10,000	Great table with good view of Jesus
$100,000	Seat at a table with Jesus
$1,000,000	Sit on Jesus' lap

82. Your Best Friend Is Still on Your Couch

When Vinnie told you he was moving to your town, you were ecstatic. It was like old times! But now it's getting old. When one month became two months, you shrugged your shoulders. When two months became five months, you clenched your teeth. You're now in one of the most awkward situations in life. Your best friend won't leave your couch, and he ain't paying to stay on it.

The WTF Approach to Getting That F*#!-ing Bum Off Your Couch

➤ STEP #1: *Question Him*

Ask him what his plans are, and how the job search is going. If you're uncomfortable being direct, be sure to pepper those questions with: How do you like it here so far? Have you made any new friends? What area do you like best?

➤ STEP #2: *Encourage Him*

Your friend seems to have motivation issues, so get involved. Help him fix his resume and look for apartments. Maybe he hasn't yet found a job where he can best apply his many God-given talents. Perhaps he can find a job eating cereal all day as some kind of product tester. Or since he likes the couch so much, maybe he has a future in the furniture business. Spend a little time mentoring him to help him get on his feet. He ain't gonna do it by himself.

➤STEP #3: *Give Him a Deadline*

You've tried being subtle, you've tried being helpful, but neither has worked. It's time to talk eviction dates.

➤STEP #4: *Find Him a Girlfriend*

The unfortunate truth is that some guys don't do shit unless a girl tells them to. Find him a lonely, desperate, generous woman with a mommy complex to take care of him. Now he's her problem, not yours. You can find these women *anywhere*.

➤STEP #5: *Learn to Live with It*

Let's face it. You're never going to kick him out. The deadline has come and gone—twice. He's your best friend. But if he ain't going to pay rent, he's going to have to pay in other ways. Make him clean up his shit—and yours. Make him do the laundry, the dishes, and scrub your bathroom until it's so clean you could eat off it. Then, make him eat off it.

Interpreting Couch Potato Speak

He says: "I applied to ten jobs on craigslist."
He means: *"I applied to one job, jerked off, took a nap, and jerked off again."*
He says: "I saw about five apartments."
He means: *"I drove by a few for-rent signs on the way to the pub."*
He says: "I met this really great chick and she was way into me."
He means: *"The barista smiled at me."*

83. You Got a Dog Trainer and Your Dog Still Pees on the Floor

Your heart was in the right place when you bought the little, cute four-legged pain in the ass. And you thought you were doing the right thing by forking out the cash for a trainer, but now you're still finding yourself knee-deep in dog shit in your own house. If you can't seem to housebreak the monster, try our tips.

The WTF Approach to Dealing with a F*#!-ing Piss-Happy Puppy

> **OPTION #1: *Call Cesar Milan***

You got screwed by an amateur—now it's time to call in the pro. Known as the "Dog Whisperer," Milan is a famous dog trainer who will turn the most untamable canine into Lassie. To sign up to be a guest on his hit show *The Dog Whisperer*, just look him up on Google. You can find your own link, bozo, you don't need us.

> **OPTION #2: *Buy a Doghouse***

Just keep the dog outside at all times or in a doghouse. Snoopy had to live that way, for Christ's sake, why can't Fido?

> **OPTION #3: *An Unfortunate "Accident"***

If you don't want to break your kid's heart (or at least not be held responsible for doing so), kill the puppy, but make it look like an accident. Here's how:

Kill all the dogs in the 'hood: This idea won't make it look like an accident, but it will take the suspicion off you. Plus, it would allow your kid to join other grieving kids on the block and draw strength from one another. And, it will make the neighborhood more peaceful—once the wails and moans of grieving children quiet down.

Poison the puppy: You can use just about anything in large amounts. Yes, rat poison works for dogs, too.

Let the dog out: Carefully take the puppy's leash off your child's sleeping arm and let the puppy out so you can later blame your confused, sobbing kid for not watching it. Chances are, it will die out there. This experience will also serve to teach little Billy about the importance of responsibility. Not to mention, you can look like a hero by keeping your cool in the face of his incredible lack of responsibility.

WTF: UP CLOSE AND PERSONAL

Any dog can live outside. Take my uncle's Alaskan Husky. When Uncle Bob bought a new house, he wanted to keep it nice and didn't want to get dog fur everywhere. So he built a beautiful, luxurious doghouse in the big backyard.

Bob happened to live in Phoenix, where temperatures can reach 130 degrees. The dog may not have been predisposed to that kind of heat, being from Alaska and all, but Bob's house sure was gorgeous.

—AWH

REMEMBERING RODNEY

"Some dog I got, too. We call him Egypt. Because in every room he leaves a pyramid."

—Rodney Dangerfield

84. The Cops Show Up at Your House Party

There's nothing that spoils the mood of a nice, quiet, debaucherous get-together more than the po'. When your neighbors finally get sick of all the noise, they won't hesitate to call the cops. But that doesn't mean the party's over, as long as you follow our step-by-step guide.

The WTF Approach to Survive a F*#!-ing Party-Crashing

➤ STEP #1: *Turn Down the Loud Music*

Nine times out of ten, the cops are there because of a noise complaint. Close your windows, use your inside voices, and keep the music down.

➤ STEP #2: *Hide the Evidence*

Get anything illegal out of sight. This includes: drugs, underage girls, buddies who skipped out on parole, and hookers. Send them down to the basement or into the bathroom, stat.

➤ STEP #3: *Don't Answer the Door*

Police need a warrant and they're not getting one in the middle of the night. If they do come in, you can meet them in court. A loud noise does not constitute grounds for probable cause. And the worst that can happen if you try to ignore them is they come in anyway.

Not Invited?

Never get invited to house parties? Then call the cops on the cool kids and shut down their fun. Say that you're their neighbor and that you've asked them to be quiet and they won't. Say that you have seen them doing narcotics, and you believe there are underage kids there. Also, say that you have reason to believe that the party is really the meeting place of a violent, antigovernment group that harbors a particular hatred of local police.

IN THE FUTURE . . .

Keep the cops away by keeping your dirtbag friends off your lawn. No one likes to see a bunch of creeps drinking cans of Pabst in their neighborhood. Bring them inside.

Also, don't let anyone in who's more than two degrees of separation from you. You're buddy's brother is fine. But his friend is not. This way you keep down fights, thefts, and vomiting. Although, if it's a really hot chick, f*#! the rules.

85. Your New House Is Infested with Termites

As you toured the house before the sale, you wondered what all those little particles were on the kitchen floor, but dismissed them for dust and crumbs. It wasn't until you moved in and saw one of the buggers did you realize, "Yep. That's termite shit." Well, here's what to do:

The WTF Approach to Getting Rid of F*#!-ing Termites

➤ OPTION #1: *Call the Exterminator*

If you're lucky, he'll put a bug circus tent over your house. Don't forget to take your pets—and your kids—to the hotel with you. If you really need the cash, you can hire a clown to stand out front to try to get kids to go in.

➤ OPTION #2: *Sell Them to Africa*

Fried termites are considered a tasty snack in Africa. Selling off your nasty pests will not only make a little kid over there happy when he gets a handful of yummy bugs, as an export it will help offset our massive trade deficit.

➤ OPTION #3: *Eat Them Yourself*

Termites are a good source of fat and protein, and have a nice nutty flavor when cooked. Yum!

➤ OPTION #4: *Learn to Live with Them*

Feed your termites scraps of wood and learn to communicate with them by wiggling your ears.

➤ OPTION #5: *Move*

Pretend you never saw the little bastards and sell your house to some other schmuck.

WTFACT: Termites cost Americans more than $1 billion each year. So, if you see one, step on it.

86. Someone's Growing Marijuana on Your Property

M any people have a soft spot in their heart for pot. But that doesn't mean you want to play Waco with the feds or get caught in a gang war. So when you come across a secret stash of dank being raised on your property, it's best to know all the potential hazards of your next move.

The WTF Approach to Dealing with a F*#!-ing Hidden Pot Garden

➤ **OPTION #1:** *Call the Cops*

This is the most logical option, unless you think whoever put the weed there might come after you for the money. So know your neighborhood and get a shotgun.

➤ **OPTION #2:** *Throw a Party*

If you're looking for a good time, a giant party might be just what you need to solve your pot-garden problem, your no-friend problem, and your need-to-get-laid problem all at once. If some free green can't help you, you'll have to trade it for massage parlor services.

➤ **OPTION #3:** *Enter the Record Books*

Fly in the bozos from *Guinness*, use all that weed to roll the biggest blunt ever, and become immortalized. You'll share space with athletes, politicians, humanitarians, and the guy with the longest fingernails. Good work!

➤ OPTION #4: *Start Dealing*

Though you never dreamed of getting into the drug trade, you don't miss an opportunity when it falls in your lap. It's a riskier but much more lucrative venture, and you'll want to make sure whoever planted it isn't coming back. Once your dealers hit the streets, your competition is going to start wondering where all that bud came from. You'll need a small posse of gun-toting cowboys to keep the banditos away.

WHERE TO SELL THE GANJA

- College campuses
- Medical-marijuana distribution sites
- ~~High schools~~
- Rock concerts

- Video game conventions
- ~~Elementary schools~~
- Local parks
- ~~Kindergartens~~

> **NOTE:** If you think your operation is going to be an easy street of laughs like *Weeds*, think again. You're going to be involving yourself in some *Wire*-type shit. Don't say we didn't warn you.

➤ OPTION #5: *Burn It*

F*#! the police. F*#! drugs. F*#! Jerry Garcia. Make it look like someone threw a cigarette out of their car window and torch the shit. This way, no one can blame you. You didn't know anything about it. You didn't tell the cops. And you'll get the whole damn town as high as a kite.

. . . But do you think you could grab an ounce for your two favorite authors before you do it? We have glaucoma, swear to Chong. Come on dude, WTF?

87. Your Parish Priest Is Accused of Child Molestation

Turns out, Father O'Brien was really Father O'BlowJob.

The WTF Approach to F*#!-ing Kiddy-Diddling Priests

➤ **STEP #1:** *Don't Feel Slighted*

You were a good-looking kid, with hair as pale as wheat, with eyes as blue as the sea, and with delicate features, chiseled to perfection by the hand of God. Any servant of the Lord would've been lucky to have you bowed on your knees before him.

➤ **STEP #2:** *Don't Move*

Stay where you are, because before you know it, he'll be transferred to another parish, with the full support of the Catholic Church, to tend to a new flock of kids.

➤ **STEP #3:** *Pray for Him*

If your faith in the Church hasn't been tarnished, pray for him. After all, he's simply a glorious servant of God who, seduced by the devil, has taken the wrong path.

➤ **STEP #4:** *Become a Real Catholic*

You know, the kind that only goes to church on Easter and shows her tits at Mardi Gras. The kind that skips church during football season, as well as baseball season, basketball season, hockey season, and NASCAR season. If you aren't in church, you're not going to have a problem with sicko priests.

Or . . .

➤ STEP #4: *Convert*

Maybe Luther was right, after all. And if you're worried about any funny business going on with Protestants, don't. They're only interested in one kind of coming: The Second Coming.

HOW TO STOP PRIESTS FROM SEXUAL ASSAULT

- Castrate them. They aren't supposed to use it for anything other than pissing, anyway.

- Require them to get married. Maybe the ability to get laid will keep the creeps out of the seminaries.

- Hold more nun/priest mixers.

- Stop moving them to another Parish when they get caught diddling kids!

It Happens in All Religions

Ask any Catholic about the ubiquity of child molestation in the Catholic Church and you get the same answer: "It happens in all religions. You just hear more about it in Catholicism." Really? You really believe that rabbis are playing hide the challah with young boys at synagogues across America? You know they aren't. That goes for Muslim and Protestant religions too, no matter how fanatical. And say what you want about how nuts Tom Cruise and his Scientologist cronies are, but at least they're not raping boys. Cruise gets to bed women like Nicole Kidman, Penelope Cruise, and his new plaything, that *Dawson's Creek* chick—who does kind of look like a boy, come to think of it . . .

WTFACT: In 1992, a nonprofit organization was founded in Australia to help victims of church-related sexual abuse. The organization has reported that approximately 90 percent of the victims who have contacted them have been Catholic. About 25 percent of the country is Catholic. Need we say more?

88. Your Dog Knocks Up Your Neighbor's Dog

Man's best friend can't be much smarter than his master. All those times he's watched you ride bareback has apparently rubbed off on him. Then, one day, your neighbor comes over with an ugly little pregnant bitch and claims that your Fido is the daddy. But don't fret, and don't throw Fido under the bus quite yet.

The WTF Approach to Handling Your F*#!-ing Fertile Pooch

➤ STEP #1: *Don't Admit Anything,* Ever

Just like when you crashed your car, drank too much and got into a fight, or fathered your first illegitimate child, don't admit guilt. It's not for you to decide. It's for lawyers, judges, insurance agents, and ultimately God to figure out.

➤ STEP #2: *Blame the Bitch*

"You know she wanted it, she's such a slut. Always sniffing Fido's ass." If you say it straight, your neighbor will never bother you again. Nor will he ever let his kids outside.

►STEP #3: *Offer to Help*

Without accepting any responsibility, tell your neighbor that you'll be more than happy to take care of the puppies once they're born, no matter who screwed his pooch. You'll take care of them, all right—by burying them alive in the backyard.

HOW TO TELL IF YOUR DOG IS SLEEPING AROUND:

- When you went to work, there was one dog food bowl; when you came home, there were two.

- He used to squirm when you took him to the groomer's; now he gets excited.

- The vet always gave him a clean bill of health. Now he tells you Fido has AIDS.

Neuter the Little Bastard

Do like Bob Barker always said and whack off his nuts. If you still believe that you might one day breed him, get your head examined and then whack off his nuts. People who breed dogs live on farms, not in condos. They have kennels, not duct tape and sticks. And, they know much more about dogs than how much weed it takes to get 'em stoned. If you're a weirdo and think that a dog without balls is embarrassing, you can pay an extra few bucks and get plastic gonads installed. It's worth it. Would you want to walk around with an empty sack?

***WTF*ACT:** Every year, animal shelters kill about 5 million dogs. Not only is that brutal, it's expensive and your taxes pay for all the cages, drugs, and vets. Don't be a bozo, chop off Fido's nuts.

89. You Accidentally Run Over Your Neighbor's Dog

Dogs are great. They're our loyal companions and our best friends—we even consider them members of our family. Despite that, they're stupid. They chase their own tails, eat their own shit, and enjoy nothing more than the smell of your crotch. So don't feel too bad when you turn your neighbor's golden retriever into a pile of bloody meat. You may have been speeding, on the phone, and only half watching the road, but it's not really your fault. He should have looked both ways.

The WTF Approach to Dealing with a Dead F*#!-ing Dog

► STEP #1: *Make Sure It's Dead*

If it's not dead already, it's going to be pissed and bite the shit out of you. Do the humane thing and throw your car in reverse.

NOTE: If there's a sensitive person in your car—like a woman, child, or vegetarian—she might try to persuade you to help the dog. Don't. Even if it doesn't bite you, you'll get blood on your clothes and your upholstery, the vet will charge you $500, your neighbor will hate you, and the dog will still die.

➤STEP #2: *Order Chinese Takeout*

Relax and treat yourself to a little sweet and sour pork and a nice cup of wonton soup. After all, you've had a hard day—you just killed a puppy. Eat your fortune cookie and then move its carcass over to your neighbor's porch in the cover of night.

➤STEP #3: *Make Up for It*

Donate a couple bucks to the local SPCA or adopt a puppy from impending eternal sleep.

➤STEP #4: *Compensate for Their Loss*

Your neighbors are no doubt torn up about the passing of their pooch—not to mention finding its bloodied remains on their porch.

Grab a DVD you don't watch anymore, hand it to your neighbor, and say, "Sorry for your loss."

➤STEP #5: *All Dogs Go to Heaven*

Don't beat yourself up over this. Most of these mutts don't even work for a living. Their jobs are to lie around and eat all day. Then they get sent off to heaven where they chase mailmen and sit on the couch. Overall, it's a far better life than yours.

WTFACT: Estimates put the number of dogs in the world at 400 million. There are more dogs in the world than there are people in the United States and each country of the world except for China and India.

90. You Think a Terrorist Just Moved into Your Neighborhood

In these troubled times, it's best to be extra careful. This is especially true when it comes to our families and our homes. When someone with an accent moves in next door, it's only natural to get a little anxious. Because of what's on the news, it may be tempting to only worry if the new neighbor is Middle Eastern, but that shouldn't be the case. According to the U.S. National Counterterrorism Center, only 21 percent of terrorism is perpetrated by Islamic extremists and more than half, a full 59 percent, is committed by unknown people with unknown motives. Be afraid—of everyone.

It's about time we add Nepalese Communists, Basque Separatists, and the Irish Republican Army—among many, many others—to our list of who to watch. Terrorists are white, black, and yellow. They're communist, anti-communist, and anti-anti-communist.

But there's one thing for sure. There's no way in hell they're moving in next to your family.

The WTF Approach to Your F*#!-ing Friendly Neighborhood Terrorist

> **STEP #1: *Organize***

Gather a group of concerned citizens and form a neighborhood terror watch. Post stickers on the windows of all participants' homes, allowing terrorists to know that their ideas, their way of life, and their bombs are not welcome in your community.

> **STEP #2: *Demonstrate***

Luckily, the first amendment allows for peaceable demonstrations of any point of view. A demonstration could make your would-be terrorists think twice about moving in next to such concerned, proactive citizens.

> **STEP #3: *Fight Fire with Fire***

While we can't condone illegal acts, nothing gets terrorists out of the neighborhood as quickly as

a house fire. Remember: Nothing fights terrorism better than counter-terrorism, which is always completely different and justifiable.

Is Your Son an Islamic Terrorist?

Forget about the boy next door—what about the boy upstairs? "The American Taliban" John Walker proved that anyone's kid might turn into an Islamic terrorist. Here are some signs that your son might be on the way toward dangerous fanaticism.

YOUR SON MIGHT BE AN ISLAMIC EXTREMIST IF . . .

- He used to eat hamburger. Now he eats lamburger.

- He used to watch *Girls Gone Wild*. Now he watches *Girls Gone Burqa*.

- He used to smoke a bong. Now he smokes a hookah.

- He used to ride a skateboard. Now he rides a camel.

- He used to dream of sluts. Now he dreams of virgins.

But again, you can't just look for telltale signs of Islamic terrorism—there are other terrorist groups your son might fall prey to.

YOUR SON MIGHT BE AN IRA MEMBER IF . . .

- He used to love apple pie. Now he loves shepherd's pie.

- He used to complain about his teachers. Now he complains about the British.

- He used to love soda. Now he loves soda bread.

- He used to bang cheerleaders. Now he bangs leprechauns.

- He used to read *SI*, *The Onion*, and *Rolling Stone*. Now he reads Joyce, Yeats, and Heaney.

YOUR SON MIGHT BE A NEPALESE COMMUNIST IF . . .

- He used to use a graphing calculator for his advanced algebra class. Now he uses an abacus.

- He used to drive around town in his convertible. Now he rides a yak.

- He used to go for walks in the park to get fresh air. Now he climbs on the roof.

YOUR SON MIGHT BE A BASQUE SEPARATIST IF . . .

- He used to eat anything. Now he refuses to eat tapas.

- He used to have a picture of President Bush on his dartboard. Now it's a picture of Franco.

- He used to watch *So You Think You Can Dance*. Now the flamenco makes him cringe.

91. Your Girlfriend Demands You Cut Back on the Internet Porn

Sometimes pornography seems infinitely more appealing than even the prospect of a woman. It's cheaper, there's less mess, and *you* always know exactly what you want. But that doesn't mean she's okay with you always opting for the e-porn. A healthy person should have a mix of porn and real women—but probably more porn. But still, you're going to have to learn how to cut back.

The WTF Approach to Beating Your F*#!-ing e-Beating

➤ **STEP #1:** *Block It Out*

Get a babysitter program for your computer and just smash keys like this—oeruwgfc3iuewacwqpoi—for your password. Or, call your Internet provider and have it block words like "interracial," "gang-bang," and "facial."

If, for some reason, you have to write an essay on the social impact of interracial marriage, the growing influence of gangs in the inner city, or new techniques in personal beauty, go to the library, where jerking off is frowned upon.

Nowadays, there's no social element to masturbation. Whatever happened to hanging out on 42nd Street, drinking a beer out of a bag, having a couple of smokes, talking to your buddies, and then excusing yourself to go into the booth and jerk off all over the floor. Peep shows, coin booths, and porno theaters weren't just places to get off, they were an indelible part of urban social life . . . a great place to meet interesting new friends—*and* jerk off.

> **STEP #2:** *Hang a Giant Crucifix Above Your Monitor*

Even if you're not particularly religious, this should turn you off from trying to access your porn—unless you're into bondage.

> **STEP #3:** *Go Old School*

Wean yourself off Internet porn by buying DVDs. Once the cravings subside, toss the DVDs, and buy a couple of dirty magazines.

THE SEVEN LEVELS OF PORN ADDICTION

I: You stay up late every night to look at porn.

II: You look at porn at work.

III: You turn down sex to look at porn. (But not if you're married—that's not addiction, that's marriage.)

IV: You keep asking your girlfriend if she's into gangbangs.

V: You've erased your favorite songs from your iPod to make room for all your favorite pornos—so you can watch them *wherever* you go.

VI: You bring a girl back from the bar and expect her to do double penetration with you and your parakeet.

VII: You stop banging your girlfriend altogether.

92. Your Bank Account Is Hacked Into

It's a disease of the information age. Cyberdorks do stupid shit online all day long. At some point, they come to the conclusion that they should stop coding dumb games and living in their momma's basement. So they start hacking into bank accounts, and today they just hit yours.

The WTF Approach to a F*#!-ing Internet Hijacking

➤ STEP #1: *Go into the Bank*

Waiting twenty minutes in line beats waiting five days on the phone.

➤ STEP #2: *Blame the Bank*

Remember, even if you're less than vigilant when it comes to account security, never admit it's your fault. Bankers are some of the cheapest, meanest, greediest people in the world, and you don't want to give them any reason not to give you back your cash.

➤ STEP #3: *Stop Banking Online*

The Internet is as perilous as it is convenient. You can satisfy most of your banking needs by using the ATM.

➤ STEP #4: *Stop Banking Altogether*

You don't trust bankers, so why do business with them? Those suits are just there to steal your hard-earned money. Put your cash in your cowboy hat and slip it under the bed.

93. Your Homemade Sex Tape Winds Up Online

While celebrities such as Pamela Anderson and Paris Hilton may have been sincerely disappointed by the release of their most private moments to the public, it significantly improved both of their careers.

That said, your career in corporate communications is probably not going to get a boost if this happens to you. That is, unless you performed much better than either one of those ladies did, which wouldn't be hard to do. (Sorry, ladies, we weren't that impressed—especially you, Paris. Now, the guys on the other hand, well, that's a different story.)

The WTF Approach to Seeing Yourself on F*#!-ing YouPorn

➤ **STEP #1: *Who Done It?***

If an ex uploaded the video, you have every right to kick his—or her—ass. It's one thing to masturbate to that digital trip down memory lane, but it's another to let the whole world get off on it. Now you'll never know if that attractive stranger across the bar is smiling at you because you're hot or if it's because she's seen a video of you begging for it like a dog in heat.

➤ STEP #2: *Wait It Out*

Luckily, however, there's so much porn online now that the chances of anyone you know running into your video is probably slim, unless you're both into some wacky fetish. And if that's the case, you probably don't mind.

WTFACT: About one out of every ten websites are porn and about 250 new sites are being added to the list of porn websites daily. So, the chances your mom will run across your video are not good. But when your pervert brother finds it, he'll be sure to let her know—after he whacks off, and, stricken with a sense of overwhelming guilt, cries uncontrollably.

➤ STEP #3: *Learn from It*

Just be happy you're not with her anymore. It's been a while, and you forgot what a hideous body she had. At least that will assure that the lifespan of this video will be much shorter than the herpes you gave her.

➤ STEP #4: *Milk It*

No, not *that*; you already did that. We're talking about the video. Ride your wave of porno success and start your own website. Start filming every time you get busy with a new friend—but be sure to check IDs. Monetize the site. Now you can say you're an entrepreneur with a technology company—even though you're really just a ho with a camera.

IN THE FUTURE . . .

Promise you'll never look like that again. Can you believe how you wore your hair back then? God, how embarrassing. Never go back to that style.

94. Your Computer Breaks Down and You're on a Deadline

When your computer breaks, the prospect of buying a new one can be daunting—and like most daunting tasks, you want to put it off. But you're on deadline, you lazy son of a bitch, so put your ass in gear and buy a new one. Yes, you'll have a lot of options to choose from, and yes, it's a lot of money, but it's essential. We know, all you want to do is get back to how it was before the meltdown, when you could merrily watch your favorite TV shows and porn at the same time—after you finished your report, of course.

The WTF Approach to Replacing Your F*#!-ing Computer

> **STEP #1:** *Don't Trust Anything a Salesperson Tells You*

Sorry, bud, you're going to have to do your own research. The salesperson is there to sell. He's not there to give you a good deal. Even if he isn't working off commission, his salary is tied to his sales.

> **STEP #2:** *Don't Just Buy Anything*

It saves you a lot of hassle to just walk in to the store and grab the first thing that will work, but these aren't socks. Be choosey.

➤ STEP #3: *Don't Believe Your Friends*

Unless your friend is a computer engineer, he's probably just as stupid as you are.

➤ STEP #4: *Don't Buy a Warranty*

They're just a way for the store to get another couple hundred bucks out of you because you're afraid. If you want to gamble, bet on yourself, not against yourself.

➤ STEP #5: *Get Your Old Files Recovered*

Take your old computer to a geek, and pay whatever it takes to get your data. You may have to sell your car or get a second mortgage, but at least you won't be canned.

How Much Should You Spend on a Computer?

A computer costs as much as you want to spend. Want one that's able to shoot a missile at another missile in the stratosphere? That'll be several billion bucks. Want one that'll let you look at porn and send e-mails to chicks around your town? Don't spend more than $500. Also, don't buy any software. You should be able to get everything you need from a friend or free on the Internet.

95. Your Connection Goes Down in the Middle of Warcraft

Oh my God! What's happening? I can't get online! I can't get online! My level 70 Blood Elf Paladin is going to die! My guild is going to be pissed! Someone help! I can't get online! *Aaaaaaahhhhhhhh*!!!

Relax. There is a world outside of cyberspace.

The WTF Approach to a F*#!-ing Broken Internet Connection

➤ **OPTION #1: *Fix It***

Unless you're a big-time techie, fixing it requires about two days. One day is spent on hold waiting for a "technician," and another is spent troubleshooting with this "technician."

➤ **OPTION #2: *Move to a Café***

Internet cafes are great because it's just like being at home, except the muffins are better and the coffee costs five bucks.

➤ **OPTION #3: *Don't Fix It***

Do something else for once. It may seem like living without one foot in cyberspace is equivalent to living like a caveman, but it isn't. Remember, you first got hooked up to the web in 1999—not 1979.

Alternatives to Being Online

Real life may seem more dull and trying than you remember. If you need ideas about what to do, try looking at the Yellow Pages, which is probably wrapped in cellophane under your sofa. Or try out some of these ideas:

Chat face to face: Instead of chatting with your buddy in Beijing, try chatting with your friend down the street—and I don't mean with a webcam. While he may not be into rare projectile weaponry of the Ming Dynasty like your pal who you met in a chat room of the same name, the "life-like" and animated quality of a face-to-face conversation might make up for it. It seems so real.

Go to a porno theater: Can't get your kicks online? Visit an old-fashioned theater that features pornographic films. If you have specific fetishes, such as goats in high heels ridden by nude midgets, you might be disappointed

with what these relics of the 1970s have to offer. After all, who can get off to two people just having sex anymore?

MAJOR CONTRIBUTIONS TO COMPUTING AND INTERNET TECHNOLOGY

IBM
Xerox
Microsoft
Apple
Al Gore

Go to an arcade: Remember the old days when you would go to an arcade with your friends to play Pac-Man and it was the most fun you could ever have? Relive that fun time. Beware, however, that for the good games, it's about $3.50 a pop. Oh, and do us a favor, beat the shit out of those kids making an ass out of themselves on Dance, Dance Revolution while you're there.

Pick up a newspaper: Get your news somewhere other than *Yahoo.com*. Marvel at the anachronistic black and white coloring and the feel of the paper between your fingertips. Relish that moment. They'll soon be gone.

96. You Keep Losing Your Cell Phone

These days, technology is making our lives more convenient. Cell phones are rapidly becoming smaller, faster, and more advanced. But there's one feature these gadgets seem to be missing: a feature that prevents you from losing the f*#!-ing thing.

The WTF Approach to Keeping Track of Your F*#!-ing Cell Phone

➤ **OPTION #1:** *Back It Up*

Keep all your important numbers and information not just on the hard drive of your computer or on a jump drive, but in a spiral notebook under your bed. Even if you're accident prone, losing your bed is difficult.

➤ **OPTION #2:** *Wear It as a Necklace*

You may think it looks stupid, but it's certainly practical. Not only that—if you're otherwise cool enough, you could rock it and make it work. God knows, there have been stupider fads, such as leaving the price tag on a baseball cap. If that can be popular, why can't wearing a Motorola around your neck?

➤ OPTION #3: *Get a Part-Time Job with Nokia*

Even successful professionals take part-time jobs at Starbucks for the health insurance. Work a few hours a week there. They could offer deep discounts on phones. Call them to find out. Make sure to put your phone back around your neck when you're done, bozo.

➤ OPTION #4: *Buy the Most Expensive Cell Phone There Is*

If you pay $50 for a phone, you might not pay too much attention to it. But if you pay $5,000 for a phone, you won't forget about it for a second.

➤ OPTION #5: *Go Old School*

Get a land line and an answering machine. These days they're dirt cheap. If you want to talk on the go, get the longest extension cord you can find. It may look stupid, but it's better than tying a phone around your neck, putz.

WTF: UP CLOSE AND PERSONAL

I speak from experience here. I've lost twelve phones in twelve months. Literally, a phone a month. FYI, insurance plans only cover two phones per year. Unfortunately, all the proceeds of this book will go to financing my expensive cell-phone-losing habit. FYI, I am a moron.

—GB

WHAT THE F*#! IS UP WITH . . . CONSTANT COMMUNICATION

It used to be easy to avoid people. Just let the message machine pick up and that was it. But with the advent of cell phones, all of a sudden, everyone became as reachable as a doctor on call. But even cell phones can be turned off, and you could always say that you couldn't get a signal. But not now. With text messaging and e-mail functions, avoiding people without arousing suspicion is virtually impossible. I guess you're going to have to just be honest and tell them you hate them once and for all. If you're a coward, text them.

97. Your Inbox Is Overloaded with Spam and Crashes

Spammers are the scum of the universe. With thousands and thousands of these pricks sending penis-enlargement plans, weight loss options, and hot stock tips every day, fighting them is going to be a losing battle. Here are some tips that just might put a dent in the amount of spam you get.

The WTF Approach to Avenging Your F*#!-ing Inbox

> **STEP #1: *Get a Spam-Blocking Program***

There are dozens of quality programs that will reduce the amount of spam that gets into your inbox. You've got enough penile enlargement pills to last you years, anyway.

> **STEP #2: *Never Reply to Spam***

That just tells the spammers that your e-mail address is a good one to send shit to.

> **STEP #3: *Never Make a Purchase Based on a Spam***

This makes spam campaigns effective. Punish anyone who uses spam to get them to stop.

➤ STEP #4: *Change Your E-mail Address*

If spam gets too overwhelming, change everything. Change your name, your apartment, and your sex. This *should* stop you from getting all that penile-enhancement spam, but we all know that it won't.

➤ STEP #5: *Tattle!*

Report the spam to the appropriate authorities. If you can't unsubscribe, it violates CAN-SPAM. If you get spam that you think is deceptive, forward it to spam@uce.gov. The Federal Trade Commission uses the spam stored in that database to pursue law enforcement actions against people who send deceptive e-mail. If it has a stock ticker, the Securities and Exchange Commission probably wants that address. Forward investment-related spam to enforcement@sec.gov. Since these are government agencies, they might take up to a decade to do anything, if they ever do anything.

Also tell Google, Yahoo, MSN, and anyone else you feel like. These are the real Internet cops (and robbers).

Our Favorite Spam

It's nice when spammers get a little creative instead of just being annoying. This one stood out and became a favorite.

"At last you've met a gal that's hot
You wanna hump her moistened twat.
She's full of passion, she's so nice!
But would your penile size suffice?
Not sure she will ask for more?
You need a wang she would adore!
But how to get it long and thick?
Your only hope is MegaDik!
You'll get so wanted super-size
And see great pleasure in her eyes!
Your shaft will pound her poon so deep,
Tonight you'll hardly fall asleep!
So try today this magic p'ill
And change your life at your own will!"
—Courtesy of an e-mail from jody@ms46.hinet.net

98. You Have to Open Another Flickr Account Because You Took So Many Damn Pictures

They say a picture is worth a thousand words. The reason they said that was because taking a picture used to be a pain in the ass. Between carrying and setting up the equipment and all the time in the darkroom, taking a picture wasn't easy. This long process meant that pictures weren't taken thoughtlessly. A "Kodak Moment" was something out of the ordinary—a moment worth capturing.

Now, in the digital age, you can take a picture effortlessly, post it online, and share it with friends at virtually no cost. People today take a picture of about every goddamn thing they do. "My new cool toothbrush," "Look, I'm wearing pants, dude," "OMG, I'm out having a drink with a friend I see five times a week." A thousand words, really?

It's okay. You can admit you're one of "those" people. You're among friends and we're here to help—even lame people like you.

The WTF Approach to Kicking Your F*#!-ing Photo Habit

➤ STEP #1: *Take a Class*

Photography is an art form, just like painting, sculpture, or writing humor books. Learn to appreciate the art form and pick your subjects—and your moments—more critically. With this new appreciation, you won't take a picture of your friend taking a piss outside a bar, unless you use a set of specific aesthetic guidelines and put it into a social perspective.

➤ STEP #2: *Leave It at Home*

If you're not traveling, seeing a friend you haven't seen in years, or witnessing a crime, you really need to ask yourself if this moment is worth capturing forever.

➤ STEP #3: *Just Have Fun*

Stop thinking that you have to document every smile. If you go out to some place with friends and want to take a picture, fine. Take *one.* Have everyone gather around and take a picture. That's all you need, so you can go back later and say "Oh, remember when . . . ." A hundred pictures aren't necessary.

➤ STEP #4: *Stop Sharing Photos*

If you *really* can't help yourself: Take all the pictures you want, but stop *sharing* them. If you really think everyone wants to see 400 pictures of you and your friends at the mall, you need to see a specialist. They don't. No one does.

for the ladies . . .

If you want to take a thousand pictures every time you leave the house, fine— just leave us men the f*#! out of it. We'll take our own. Like when Chris fell off his motorcycle and his feet were pointing the wrong way. Or our trip to Bangkok we never told you about. You would have been proud. We took *a lot* of pictures.

99. Some Creep Is Cyberstalking You

He's poked you on Facebook, messaged you on MySpace, and sent you an IM on AIM, all with creepy details about your personal likes and dislikes and daily life. But you haven't a damn idea who this person could be. Well now you do—he's your very own cyberstalker.

If your information is on the Internet, you're open to cyberstalking. Your cyberstalker could be an ex-girlfriend, an old classmate, or a sick murderer/pervert out to get you. No matter what, getting cyberstalked is f*#!-ing creepy. Here are some tips to avoid these creeps.

The WTF Approach to F*#!-ing Cyberstalkers

> **STEP #1: *Keep a Low Profile***

Don't publish your phone number, e-mail address, or physical address. Cyberstalkers can search for you in any city in the country. Keep your MySpace page private as well. You don't need potential cyberstalkers to see your photos, know your friends, and read your blog—unless they're about what you do to cyberstalkers when you catch them.

➤ STEP #2: *Spread Disinformation*

Only post phony information about yourself. If you're tall, say you're short. If you live in Nevada, say you live in Nebraska. And if you are into defecation during sex, keep it to yourself . . . always.

The downside of this method is, of course, your friends on the Net won't know the *real* you. But isn't that the point of this whole stupid social networking shit anyhow?

➤ STEP #3: *Give up Your Computer*

Not only will this keep you safe from cyberstalkers, it might open up a whole new world to you outside cyberspace. While living without a computer and the Internet can seem daunting, it isn't. Make sure to check out "Your Connection Goes Down in the Middle of Warcraft" (Entry 95).

Now, what to do with that guy in the e-bushes?

How to Cyberstalk Someone

Let's say—just as a matter of interest, not because you wanted to hunt down your ninth grade crush who never called you back after the prom—you want to cyberstalk someone. Let's call her Gregina Bergmina.

First, Google her. Since she has such an uncommon name, you'll probably be able to find any mention of her. Beyond the simple search, you might be able to find her address and phone number on *whitepages.com.* You'll be able to see her friends, videos, and photos on Flickr, Facebook, and YouTube. (If you're really lucky, you'll be able to find homemade porn films on *YouPorn.com.*)

Now that you know all about her, set up a fake Facebook account and start flirting, gaining trust, and laying the foundation for a meeting, in which you can try to rape and murder poor Gregina Bergmina.

100. You Broke Your iPhone and Can't Afford to Buy a New One

At first, breaking it didn't bother you; it was just another gadget. Surely, in a few months there would be another new product and there'd be no need to replace your old iPhone. But now, everyone has one—except you. You feel like a freak; the only iPhone-less person in the Western World.

The WTF Approach to Getting a New F*#!-ing iPhone

►**OPTION #1:** *Save Your Money*

Cut down on food, stop going out, and skip some credit card payments. Do you want to be cool or not? Grow up and buy everything that everyone tells you that you need.

►**OPTION #2:** *Do It Old School*

Go out with your giant cell phone, old laptop, and Discman. You have 1,300 CDs, so you might as well use them. And for those of you who still have a cassette Walkman, even better. Just make sure not to mess up your Flock of Seagulls 'do when you're bobbing your head to *Purple Rain*. And if you really want to play up the retro thing to compensate for not having an iPhone, get really nutty and walk around with a boombox on your shoulder. Make sure it's as loud as it can be, so even people browsing the web and listening to music on their iPhone will be able to hear your tunes.

➤ OPTION #3: *Steal One*

Go to a local junior high in a wealthy town. One out of every three kids will have an iPhone. Even though in a poor neighborhood, it's one out of every two, focus your thieving energy on the rich kids. They're easier to beat up. Seeing a ton of bratty kids with the coveted iPhone will induce the anger you need to pull it off.

WTF ABOUT TOWN

After scouring junior high schools and grammar schools and eventually preschools, we found the youngest PDA owner in the country. His name is William "Billy" Schmidt. He's from Sioux Falls, Idaho. He's four. We sat down with the lad to ask him about his life in the fast lane:

WTF: Do you like your BlackBerry?

Billy: Yeah, I like it. It's red. Red is my favorite color. I like blue too.

WTF: Me too. I really like blue. So who got it for you, Billy?

Billy: My dad. He works a lot. He got me this so we could talk sometimes.

WTF: Which features do you use most often, Billy?

Billy: I like to make my daddy videos from my baseball games. I play right field . . . sometimes. This way he can see me play and not have to miss his meetings.

WTF: Do you think that it makes your life easier?

Billy: Uh huh.

WTF: That's great. Just one more question for you, Billy. While handheld communications devices like cell phones and BlackBerrys are incredible tools that allow people to connect in ways that have hitherto only been imagined, many social commentators warn that these technological advances also have a dark side: They force us to be constantly available, thus limiting our private lives. What is your take on the matter?

Billy: Hold on. I have a call . . .

Bonus WTF: Your Eight Year Old Won't Stop Throwing Tantrums Because He Wants a Cell Phone

Since when did an eight-year-old need a BlackBerry? Our kids have all become little phony Donald Trumps—and one colossal prick is enough, if you ask us.

The WTF Approach to Handling Your F*#!-ing Tech-Savvy Brat

➤ **STEP #1:** *Shoot Him Straight*

Tell him, "When I was your age, my favorite toy was an empty soup can and a stick. I used to hit the soup can with the stick, naturally. Now go outside and play—like a f*#!-ing kid."

➤ **STEP #2:** *Trick Him*

Buy a couple of paper cups, tie them together with a string, and tell your kid it's the latest gadget.

When the tech-savvy little rascal complains, tell him he's adopted. Then direct him to "You Find Out That You're Adopted" (Entry 58).

➤ **STEP #3:** *Get Him the Phone*

Hey, it's your fault for having a child in this day and age. Just like you *had* to have a Cabbage Patch Kid (or if you're a real young parent, Pokémon) back in ancient times, he wants to fit in, too.

101. Your Teenager Only Communicates in Text Message Lingo

You get this text from your daughter: OMG D, IDK Y R U POD? SRSLY. BRB FRL. W BFF. G2G. TTYL. 143.

And all you can think is: WTF? What do all these acronyms mean? Whatever happened to picking up a phone and calling someone? That's what you're paying the bill for! Your kid's texting has gotten *way* out of control. Every time you look at her, she's typing some silly message. It's f*#!-ing annoying.

If you find your teen turning into a text-crazed lunatic like so many PPL out there, take a look at how to handle it.

The WTF Approach to Your F*#!-ing Texting Teen

➤STEP #1: *Make Her Call Someone*

Have her try talking to people for a change instead of typing messages. She might find out that they are not worth communicating with at all.

➤STEP #2: *Break Her Thumbs*

It would be better if you could break all of her friends' thumbs, but that's impractical. So break hers. No one will expect her to text back.

➤ STEP #3: *Force Her into Texters Anonymous*

Here, she'll be able to talk about her problem with her fellow texters. With luck she won't pick up their loathsome habit of actually saying "LOL" when they think something is funny or "G2G" when they have to go.

PHONES OF THE FUTURE

God phone: The only phone that can connect you straight to the Lord himself. The Pope will pay top dollar for it.

Straight-to-a-live-operator phone: Tired of talking to robots?

Talk-to-the-dead phone: Check in with loved ones who have passed on.

Find-my-real-parents phone: Calls them so you can ask why they didn't love you enough to keep you.

➤ STEP #4: *Have Her Write Out the Rules to Text Etiquette 100 Times*

1. You cannot text more than once every thirty minutes if you're out with someone. If you do, don't expect him to ask you out again.

2. You must turn off the beep when you get text messages. That beep is annoying and you will be associated with that annoyance.

3. Don't send important information via text. If you're too lazy to call someone to pick you up from the airport, and instead text, "C U @ LAX 10AM K?" don't expect to be picked up. You need to put in a little more effort.

MATCH GAME

In order to keep up with your kid's constant texting, we've devised this test for you. Match the acronym with the meaning.

Acronym	Meaning
A) OMG	1. Obese man gut
	2. Oh my God
	3. On my gash
B) LOL	1. Laugh out loud
	2. Lick on the lamb
	3. Lions on lionesses
C) BRB	1. Bring Reagan back
	2. Big round balls
	3. Be right back
D) IDK	1. In the Dakotas
	2. I don't know
	3. Igloo dog Canada
E) GTG	1. Gone to Georgia
	2. Got to go
	3. Going to a gangbang
F) ASL	1. Age, sex, location
	2. Ass-sucking lips
	3. After-sex feeling of existential loss
G) BF	1. Big and fat
	2. Boyfriend
	3. Buttf*#!

Acronym	Meaning
H) GF	1. Gay fruit
	2. Girlfriend
	3. Get f*#!-ed
I) IMO	1. In my opinion
	2. In my orifice
	3. Inuit make me orgasm
J) JK	1. Junk
	2. Just kidding
	3. Jew Kid
K) MMB	1. My mom's big
	2. Make my bidet
	3. Mail me back
L) NM	1. No more
	2. Never mind
	3. Arizona
M) WTF?	1. Want to f*#!?
	2. What the f*#!?
	3. I have a giant cock.

Answers: A2, B1, C3, D2, E2, F1, G2, H2, I1, J2, K3, L2, M3

Chapter 2

WTF?

COLLEGE

How to Survive 55 of Campus's
Worst F*#!-ing Situations

102. You Applied to Twenty Schools —and Were Only Accepted at One

Choosing a college can be a very difficult decision. Does it have a good reputation? Is it expensive? Do the chicks there put out? But for you it's even harder. Truth is your grades aren't perfect, so you apply to twenty schools just in case. Surely you'll get accepted to at least ten or so. But soon the thin envelopes start to arrive. *Rejected. Rejected. Rejected.* And yet another goddamn *rejected!* You have been turned down from every school you applied to except one. One! You are now the newest student at Loser University. WTF?

The WTF Approach to Handling F*#!-ing Rejections

➤ **OPTION #1:** *Make the Most of It*

So what if the school's motto is "We're a bunch of rejects, but we are really nice . . . and stuff." And who cares if the campus is old and dirty and the computer room looks like something out of a 1950s sci-fi film. Look on the bright side: Your professors probably grade on one hell of a curve.

➤ **OPTION #2:** *Transfer*

Get good grades the first semester and then get the fuck out of Dodge. Some slightly less shitty school might accept you now.

➤ OPTION #3: *Stay Home with Mom and Dad*

Fuck it. Get a job at Dairy Queen instead. Maybe you can work your way up to assistant manager or even manager one day. That's when the *big* bucks start rolling in.

EXCERPTS FROM RECENTLY DISCOVERED COLLEGE ESSAYS:

"I am a hard worker and true team player. I enjoy football, golf, and just about any type of physical activity that is hands-on. Above all, I consider family to be the most important thing."

> OJ Simpson
> Intended Major: *Forensic Science*

"I have a lot of leadership skills. People tend to trust that I know the final solution to even the most tedious of problems."

> Adolf Hitler
> Intended Major: *Jewish Studies, with a minor in Art*

"I believe in turning the other cheek, not coveting thy neighbor's wife, and that the meek shall inherit the earth. I think one day people all over the world will cherish these principles—to such an extent that they will kill, maim, and torture those who do not."

> Jesus H. Christ
> Intended Major: *Religious Studies*

"I like to grill hamburgers and hit people."

> George Foreman
> Intended Major: *Sports Medicine, with a minor in Culinary Arts*

"I am a true visionary, the kind you'll one day read about in history books. I enjoy writing, playing 'conspiracy against the King' with my pals, and having sexual relations with our many slaves."

> Thomas Jefferson
> Intended Major: *Government*

"My neighbor's dog told me I should apply to your school. You should really consider accepting me. Seriously."

> David Berkowitz
> a.k.a. Son of Sam
> Intended Major: *Abnormal Psychology*

"My last name is Bush, as in, the son of George Herbert Walker Bush. See you at school! The End."

> George W. Bush
> Intended Major: *Undecided, and honestly not really planning to try that hard. Did I mention my last name?*

"I will get into your school—by any means necessary."

> Malcom X
> Intended Major: *African-American Studies*

"I have always believed that it is important both in school and in life to 'back that ass up' when appropriate."

> Terius Gray a.k.a. Juvenile
> Intended Major: *Undecided, but mostly just going to chill and smoke weed*

"My grades aren't so good, but I have an enormous cock."

> John Holmes
> Intended Major: *Sexual Education*

IN THE FUTURE

Apply to fifty schools instead of twenty. Or, don't be a loser in the first place.

103. You Only Got In Because of Your Dad's Donations

Poor little rich boy. You didn't mind that Daddy threw some money around so you could wind up in the Ivy League rather than community college—and forgot all about the cash he sent you to pimp out your dorm room—but now you're pissed. Everyone's making fun of you because they know the only reason you're here is that your dad donated a ton of cash to the school.

The WTF Approach to Handling Your F*#!-ing Legacy Issues

➤ OPTION #1: *Change Your Name*

Chances are, if your dad's a campus big shot, there's some building or fund named after him. If you change your name, no one will know that you're related. Pick a cool, single-word name like Prince, Cher, or Madonna—realizing that you're obviously gay if you listen to any of them.

NOTE: This is more important if you have a unique last name such as O'Gubersteinsmith or something. If the Stern School of Business at NYU is named after your dad, it's not likely anyone will make the connection just because your last name is Stern. There are probably a few more Sterns there—and Steinbergs and Goldbergs and, well, you get the picture.

➤OPTION #2: *Beat Your Dad*

It may not be easy growing up in the shadow of a great man, but it is possible to outdo even your legendary pop. Many sons in history have outclassed and out-succeeded their big-shot fathers. For example, George H.W. Bush was a shitty president for only four years, while his son was twice as shitty a president for twice as long.

➤OPTION #3: *Use It to Get Laid*

So what if you're a dumb ass and your daddy paid your way into school? When you're getting your rocks off with a hot chick in your dorm room because of your last name, you might not care so much that the building you're screwing in is named after Dad.

➤OPTION #4: *Kill Daddy*

Time to put that Freud stuff you learned in psychology class to good use. Kill your father and end his evil reign over your soul just like Sigmund's theory of the Oedipus complex says every son wants to do.

> **PROFESSOR TIP:** Banging your mother, however, is ill advised. But it is always an option if you're experiencing a dry spell.

YOUR DAD MAY BE BETTER THAN YOU IF . . .

- ❏ His penis is *still* bigger than yours.
- ❏ He knows more about fly-fishing than you.
- ❏ He's more proficient with a carving knife on Thanksgiving.
- ❏ He can still beat your ass.
- ❏ Your girlfriend chooses to have sex with him over you.

Quit Your Bitching

There are worse last names and worse legacies than yours. How'd you like to show up to school with a last name like . . .

- Dahmer
- Manson
- Hitler
- Bush

104. Your Mom's Calling Everyday Because She Misses You

The beeping, the vibrating, the flashing light on your phone—to the average eye it looks like you're really popular. You're always blowing up with calls and texts. But what no else knows, and you pray they never find out, is that nine out of the last ten missed calls were from Mom. Yep, her little boy has gone off to college and she misses you. Aren't you glad you suggested that unlimited calling plan?

The WTF Approach to Dealing with a F*#!-ing Helicopter Parent

➤ OPTION #1: *Lay Down the Law*

Explain to her that this is part of life and she knew this day would come. Tell her you love her and you miss her, too (even if it's not true), but that you cannot grow as a person if your mommy keeps calling. Then set a calling schedule so you can set aside time between partying and eating pizza to catch up.

> **OPTION #2:** *Change Your Number*

If she's not paying for your cell phone bill, then you have every right to go off the grid. If the only benefit you get from Mom is an overcooked turkey on Thanksgiving or a bad Christmas sweater, cut the cord and don't look back.

> **OPTION #3:** *Use It to Your Advantage*

People like a popular guy. Change the name in your phone from Mom to something like Candy or Daisy, then whenever a call or text comes in, your friends will just think you've got a stalker.

NOTE: If your mom's name is really Candy or Daisy, be thankful you made it to college.

> **OPTION #4:** *Get Her Laid*

If your mom has been single for a while, it's no wonder she's holding on to you so tightly. Find her a man to take the edge off. If the sex is really good, you might never hear from her again.

Is Your Mom a MILF?

This might not be a bad thing. Have her come up and party with you instead of chat on the phone. It could make you very popular.

YOUR MOM IS A MILF IF . . .

❏ When she takes off her bra, her tits don't touch her belly button.

❏ Everyone thinks she's your older sister.

❏ When she leaves the house in a mini-skirt she stops traffic—in a good way.

105. You Call Your Mom Everyday Because You Miss Her

You couldn't wait to leave home and be on your own. You can eat what you want, wear what you want, stay out as late as you want. You can get drunk in the afternoon and dance naked until you vomit all over your room if you want. You were *so* ready for all of that. But what you weren't ready for was this strange aching in your belly whenever you think about home. Turns out you are really homesick and missing your mommy. Pussy!

The WTF Approach to Stop Being Such a F*#!-ing Mama's Boy

➤ OPTION #1: *Find a Replacement*

Date a girl who reminds you of Mom. Not looks-wise, sicko. Find yourself a girl who likes to take care of you the way Mom does, like make you soup when you're sick, do your laundry, and pay for your shit. When you get over that homesick feeling, dump her ass and find yourself a raging bitch . . . they're more fun.

➤ OPTION #2: *Numb Yourself*

Get drunk and stay drunk. Yeah you'll probably become an alcoholic, but at least you won't be a mama's boy.

➤ OPTION #3: *Spend the Weekend with Mom*

Chances are, by Sunday you'll remember all the reasons why you wanted to go away to school in the first place.

➤ OPTION #4: *Drop Out and Move Home*

If you really can't take the separation any longer, transfer to a school that is closer to home and commute—like the pathetic loser that you are.

Yo Mama So . . .

Everyone remembers this classic schoolyard slam. Here are some favorites:

- Yo mama so fat she goes to a restaurant, looks at the menu, and says, "Okay!"
- Yo mama so stupid it took her two hours to watch *60 Minutes*.
- Yo mama so greasy she sweats Crisco!
- Yo mama so poor her face is on the front of a food stamp.
- Yo mama so nasty that she pours salt water down her pants to keep her crabs fresh.

Are You Too Close to Your Mom?

You could be too close to your mom. Here are the top three signs that your relationship is a little too intimate.

1. She breastfed you until the end of the seventh grade.
2. The thought of her homemade apple pie makes you cream.
3. When she asks if you "want seconds," she's referring to intercourse.

106. You Run Up Your Credit Card on Non-Emergency Things

When your parents gave you a credit card to take to college they told you it was to be used explicitly for school supplies and emergencies. But when your dad gets the latest statement, he has a hard time believing that case of beer, a leather jacket, and the Wii console were *real* emergencies. In fact, you somehow managed to rack up over $2,000 in debt. WTF are you going to say?

The WTF Approach to Beating F*#!-ing Charges

➤ OPTION #1: *Report It Stolen*

It happens all the time. People steal credit cards and charge the shit out of them. Tell your parents that you lost your wallet at a frat party a while ago and when you got it back, you didn't even think to look for the card because you rarely use it. Remember, you're the victim here.

➤ OPTION #2: *Flip the Switch*

Explain to your parents that you don't agree with their definition of "emergency." It must be a generational thing. You were only trying to fit in at school by buying cool stuff like everyone else. Peer pressure is a nasty thing. Tell them they should be thankful that you didn't turn to drugs.

➤OPTION #3: *Fess Up*

Apologize and tell them the temptation was too great. Then promise to pay them back once you graduate and get a real job. By the time that happens, they'll be dead. Win-win. Well, not for them . . . so more of just a win, really.

WTFACT: When using your parents' credit card, buy beer and food at gas stations. The bill will only state the name of the gas station and not the items you purchase. This way you can claim that you were only buying gas. You're welcome, scumbag.

PROFESSOR TIP: Word to the wise: It's kind of suspicious to claim that you spent $100 on gas unless you're filling up a semi.

107. There's a Blackout on Campus During Your Study Session

You're in the middle of "studying"—playing video games and occasionally glancing at your closed book—when everything goes black. No lights, no television, nothing. At first you think you blew a fuse, but when you look out into the hall you realize it's the whole dorm. Then you look out your window and it's the whole campus. Damn.

The WTF Approach to Dealing with No F*#!-ing Electricity

➤ **STEP #1:** *Loot the School*

If you need some extra cash, get a couple friends together and start looting. Dress in black and hit the computer labs, video departments, and anywhere else with expensive equipment.

➤ **STEP #2:** *Engage in* **Frotteurism**

A *frotteur*—for those of you who have yet to take Psych 101—gets off by rubbing himself against others in public places. Use the cover of night to surreptitiously rub against whomever you fancy. Good times.

➤STEP #3: *Black Out!*

The lights are off and the power's out. Finish up your night of mayhem by throwing a party and getting so wasted that you black out. Get it, black out and *blackout*? In other words, do the same as you would any other night, just with the lights off.

What **Not** *to Do*

Cry like a bitch. If you are still afraid of the dark, then you're probably crying like the pathetic little piece of crap that you are. Call your mommy on your cell and then read Entry #105: You Call Your Mom Everyday Because *You* Miss *Her*—you'll need the help, baby.

WTFACT: One of the worst blackouts in U.S. history was the New York City blackout of 1977. The blackout lasted over twenty-four hours and resulted in massive looting and arson. In all, 1,616 stores were damaged, 1,037 fires were called in, and 3,776 people were arrested. Estimated cost of damages amounted to a little over $300 million— which, incidentally, is the current median price for a one-bedroom condo in Manhattan.

108. Your Ride Home for the Holidays Ditches You

The air is getting cold, holiday lights and decorations are everywhere, and the spirit of the season has slowly begun to warm even your cold, black heart. You have been looking forward to this time off to spend with your family for a while. But a few days before you are about to leave for the holidays, your ride leaves without you.

The WTF Approach to Getting F*#!-ing Home

➤ **OPTION #1: *Go Greyhound***

Unlike the airlines, some bus companies offer special deals around the holidays for losers, so it shouldn't cost you too much. While it might take longer and smell worse than a plane, you'll get there eventually.

➤ **OPTION #2: *Hitchhike***

Hitching a ride is a great way to see the country and possibly learn something about yourself. Bring a copy of Kerouac's *On the Road* and pretend that what you are doing is romantic. Make sure to jot your experiences down too. While your collection of stories might not end up as well-written or insightful as Kerouac's, in today's more dangerous world it might be more exciting—especially the part about you escaping from being held as a sex slave in the belly of a semitrailer driven by a bisexual born-again Christian ex-con named Billy Bob.

➤ OPTION #3: *Steal a Car*

Wait until about 1 A.M. then take off. By the time the owner realizes his car's gone you could be home. Tell your parents it's a friend's car. Then when you return to campus, leave it in a ditch. The cops will find it and return it to the owner. He'll be happy the car is in the same shape it was before—minus those few hundred extra miles.

COLLEGE KID QUOTE

"My mommy and daddy don't love me enough to pay my way home. I hate my life and I hate the holidays and I want to die."

—Jacob Stein, law student at University of Chicago

IN THE FUTURE

Be born to better parents who love you and won't strand you at school.

➤ OPTION #4: *Stay at School*

While the school will be pretty empty, the students who stay behind are just as depressed as you and want to forget their holiday gloom. So throw a party and get wasted. Remember, the only girls who are still at school during Christmas are filthy whores who were disowned by their parents a long time ago.

109. You Can't Lose the Freshman Fifteen

Welcome to real life, prick! You think you can just eat like a pig and drink beer all day and not gain weight for the rest of your life? Well, you can't. Those days are over, pal. Time to cut down on Dominos and do some friggin' exercise. *Capiche?* You'd know what that meant if you weren't failing Italian, fat boy.

The WTF Approach to Shedding the F*#!-ing Pounds

➤ STEP #1: *Stop Drinking Beer*

I know it sounds insane, but you can do it. Switch to drinking pure vodka or, if you're a pussy, Bacardi and Diet Coke. You'll get just as wasted but you'll stay slim.

➤ STEP #2: *Vomit Yourself Thin*

You'll be the only bulimic guy in your frat. Won't that be cool? You will be so trendy, like a model.

➤ STEP # 3: *Shit Yourself Thin*

Go one step further than becoming bulimic to really see the pounds shed. If you shit more, then you'll have less food inside you, which will make you skinnier. Take lots of laxatives every morning before class. Make sure to wear dark jeans in case you crap yourself. Yummy.

➤ STEP #4: *Screw Yourself Thin*

Hopefully after Steps #1–3, you're a little less chubby than before, and you can actually find a chick who *wants* to bang your fat ass. Now you just need to get laid more. Think of it this way: If you have more sex, then you will lose more weight, and therefore you will become more appealing, which in turn allows you to have even more sex. That's Logic 101, biatch.

NOTE: The skinnier you get, the bigger your dick looks!

for the ladies . . .

Just go with it and become a fat slut. If you have already gained fifteen pounds it's probably due to drinking beer, which means that you're getting wasted a lot, which means that you are probably already getting your fair share of dick. That's Logic 101, biatch.

NOTE: The fatter you get, the bigger your tits get!

WHAT THE F*#! IS UP WITH . . . BLAMING A "BAD METABOLISM"

Listen up, fat America: bad metabolism, *shmad* metabolism. If you eat a lot and don't move, you get fat. Simple. So don't give us that metabolism nonsense—just get the Krispy Kreme out of your mouth and hit the gym, fat ass.

Diets to Beat the Fifteen

Following are some new diets that you might want to try:

Rock diet: Eat rocks. They're cheap, plentiful, and very low-calorie.

Rock cocaine diet: Smoke crack and you'll never be hungry again.

French diet: Nobody knows how they stay so skinny with all of their fatty foods, but somehow they pull it off. Warning: Side effects include spontaneous cowardice, rapid armpit hair growth, and overall ennui.

Sushi diet: Avoid the tempura and just stick to raw fish and you'll be slim in no time. Warning: Side effects include spontaneously breaking out into karaoke, dressing like an anime character, and radiation poisoning.

Endangered species diet: Because they're illegal to kill and hard to find, dinner is going to be difficult. That said, until you've had a bald eagle sandwich you just haven't lived.

IN THE FUTURE . . .

Be that overconfident, beer-belly college guy. You know, the guy at the party that's the loudest and most obnoxious and is convinced that every girl wants him? Be him. He gets laid despite his belly—and doesn't have to deal with any of that exercise bullshit.

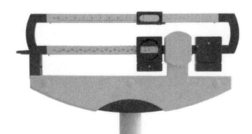

110. You Don't Receive as Much Financial Aid as You Expected

You somehow managed to survive your first year of school despite spending the majority of your school loan money on party expenses like plastic red cups, paper plates, and phat bags of weed. So why should this year be any different? Anticipating your loan for this year, you decided to skip saving for school costs and pay for the good stuff first—like that new video game console you wanted, the cruise to Mexico with your boys for Spring Break, and a whole lot of beer and expensive booze. Then you get this year's financial aid package and realize you're not getting as much as last time. You're all out of cash and you haven't even paid tuition yet . . . WTF?

The WTF Approach to Paying Out of F*#!-ing Pocket

➤ OPTION #1: *Get a Job Fast*

Believe it or not, it's relatively easy to get a job in a college town. Unless, of course, you are going to school in California, Arizona, New Mexico, or Texas, where illegal aliens will work far harder and for far less than you.

➤ OPTION #2: *Sell Yourself*

That's right, head over to your local sperm bank and make a deposit. You can make several deposits in a week and get paid in cash. You might as well get paid to do something you do for free four to five times a day!

➤ OPTION #3: *Sell Your Blood*

You won't be able to make as many deposits as with the sperm, but it still pays. Don't mix this with Option #2 though. That can give you AIDS.

➤ OPTION #4: *Hock Your Roommate's Shit*

He probably has something of value. Take it, sell it, and then stage a break in. You can report it to the police and file a claim.

for the ladies . . .
Become a prostitute, duh!

IN THE FUTURE

Be born to rich parents and/or don't be a moron.

111. An Epidemic of Crabs Breaks Out in Your Dorm

Lately you've been dancing around like a jerk. At first you thought it was the new laundry detergent you were using, then you thought it was some kind of food allergy, but now you're not the only one doing the shuffle. Other students in the dorms seem a little extra fidgety as of late. The good news: It's not epilepsy. The bad news: You've got crabs—and so does half your dorm! Here's what to do when your genitals have been turned into a twenty-four-hour seafood buffet . . .

The WTF Approach to Recovering from F*#!-ing Crabs

➤ STEP #1: *Get Treatment*

Remember those lice outbreaks in grade school? Same treatment, different patch of hair. You can pick up a lice kit in any drug store. After application of the pesticide, you must then comb out your uninvited guests. It is important to treat the infected area thoroughly, which will include anal hairs and those on the thigh area. It is also a good idea to treat anyone whom you're in a sexual relationship with to reduce the chance of reinfestation. You might want to make a night of it: little bottle of wine, little crab removal . . . hot!

➤ STEP #2: *Damage Control*

Now that you're clean—of crabs anyway—it's time to clean house. Although the primary way to contract crabs is from sexual contact, it's also possible to get them from infected bedding, towels, and clothes. Wash everything thoroughly in hot water to kill the creepy crawlies.

➤ STEP # 3: *Shave It Baby!*

That's right, shave it all off. It may sound extreme, but this way you won't have to use the ointments or a comb. Start from scratch. Strippers and porn stars do it. Why can't you? And for you crabby guys out there, shaving your pubes might make your dick look bigger. Bonus!

WTFACT: Studies show that crabs reproduce faster than Mormons—though they are far less annoying.

To Blame or Not to Blame?

There's plenty of sexual revelry in your dorm, and not everyone is as clean as you. However, don't waste your time trying to figure out who to blame for this outbreak. Crabs spread fast on bodies and clothing. You can even get crabs from a toilet seat (don't bother squatting—crabs can jump). So unless you plan on never taking a dump in public again, you need to accept that crabs are an occupational hazard of college life.

WTF: UP CLOSE AND PERSONAL

The Great Crab Outbreak of 1993

Hurricanes are bad, earthquakes are worse, and tornadoes are just plain scary, but until you live through a crab outbreak you don't know the true nature of terror.

It was a chilly night in 1993 when the crabs took control of my dorm at East Strousburg University. I'll never forget the sight of hundreds of girls running down the halls scratching themselves wildly, as if they were possessed by demons. Horrible. Just horrible.

The outbreak was so bad that we all had to leave the dorm for the weekend so that it could be decontaminated before we returned. Rumor has it that regular decontamination efforts didn't work, and the school had to hire a priest to finally oust the little bastards. Luckily, with God on his side, he was successful, and we could return that Monday to a crab-free environment for the rest of the semester.

But it wasn't over for me. I still can't bring myself to eat shellfish to this day. At least, not intentionally.

—JM

IN THE FUTURE . . .

Examine your partner's genitals closely before engaging in sexual conduct. Before doing the deed, head down south and look carefully at the pubes, if you see something move, abort! If not, just pump and pray.

112. You Clog the Only Stall on Your Floor

You're not actually sure what the hell you ate last night, but whatever it was, it didn't agree with you. You just spent a good forty-five minutes in the dorm bathroom clearing the pipes, so to speak. Done, you take a moment to look at your accomplishment. Damn, how the hell did that even fit inside you? Not your problem anymore, it's out and all you need to do is flush and get on with your day . . . but not so fast. You push down on the toilet's lever only to find the waste isn't going down but coming up, and up, and up. *Shit!* Literally.

The WTF Approach to Dealing with a Clogged F*#!-ing Toilet

> ➤ OPTION #1: *Take Off*

Get the hell out of there and let someone else take the blame. You're feeling light on your feet now anyhow, so you should be able to get away quickly.

> ➤ OPTION #2: *Close the Lid and Pray*

Shut the bowl tight and hope the mountain of feces doesn't escape. Put a sign on the door that says out of order—or full of shit—either will work.

➤ OPTION #3: *Trash the Bathroom*

Make it look like some drunken students ransacked the can in the middle of the night. Then report it. You will look like the good guy in this scenario.

➤ OPTION #4: *Mark Your Territory*

Take the shit out and smear it on the wall and claim that stall is yours. No one else will go near it—or you—ever again.

***WTF*FACT:** The human small intestine can reach up to eight meters in length. Why do you want to know that? Because all knowledge is important, fuck-face.

WHATEVER THE F*#! YOU DO— DON'T FLUSH THESE:

- Cotton balls
- Unused herpes ointment
- Condoms
- Chopped up body parts
- Newborns

for the ladies . . .

This doesn't really apply to you. Everyone knows girls don't poop. At least, not the hot ones.

IN THE FUTURE . . .

Get a monthly enema—if you can't afford one, have one of your buddies shove a hose up your ass and turn the water pressure on high.

113. You Go to Do Laundry, but All the Machines Are Taken

You've put it off as long as you could. You've gone through every shirt and pair of pants in your wardrobe, and now your clothes are so dirty they are practically walking around by themselves. And to top that off, you have a hot date tonight. You really, *really* need to do laundry, but as usual, all the machines are taken.

The WTF Approach to Cleaning Your F*#!-ing Clothes

➤ **OPTION #1:** *Double Up*

Toss your stuff in with someone else's. Make sure to stand guard. You will need to retrieve all of your things before that person comes back.

➤ **OPTION #2:** *Use an Occupied Machine*

Desperate times call for desperate measures. This is tricky, though, and must be carefully executed:

1. Remove the clothes out of one machine and place on the counter.
2. Take the clothes from another machine that's just been started and place them in the machine you initially emptied.
3. Put your stuff in the machine you emptied last.

This way when the guy with the clothes in the first machine comes back and sees his stuff wet on the counter, he will find someone else's in his machine—and blame him. You will still need to stand guard though in case the guy from the second machine comes back first.

➤ OPTION #3: *Use the Sink*

Only wash what you will be wearing that night. And make sure you have a couple hours to let the clothes air-dry. Be certain the clothes are clean before hanging them out to dry.

> **NOTE:** Toothpaste does *not* make a good laundry detergent.

➤ OPTION #4: *Wear Your Room-mate's Clothes*

Just make sure not to ruin them. If you do, just burn them. Dirty clothes shouldn't ruin the rooommate relationship. That's a girl's job.

➤ OPTION #5: *Head to Another Dorm*

Suck it up and take your dirty shit to another dorm. Don't go to the girls' dorm—those machines are *always* taken.

➤ OPTION #6: *Fuck It*

Just wear the least dirty thing you have, then take your date to a crowded, sweaty, smoke-filled frat party. All the repugnant odors, including yours, will blend in.

IN THE FUTURE . . .

Always save a clean outfit for such an occasion. You don't have to do much in college to get laid, but at the very least make sure you're not a smelly piece of shit.

114. You're Trying to Sleep and Your Roommate Is Having Sex

Now, screwing in front of roommates is par for the course in college, but sometimes a person's got to get some sleep. Lately, it seems like every night you wake up to what you think is a sex dream—a very vivid and loud sex dream—only to realize it ain't no dream—it's a nightmare! A real, live nightmare. You open your eyes yet again to find your roommate's skinny white ass high in the sky pounding away at a very vocal, boozed-up floozy.

The WTF Approach to Battling Your Roommate's F*#!-ing Booty Call

➤ OPTION #1: *Leave*

Just quietly slip out and go crash on the couch in the common area. Its sucks, but one day you will be able to repay the favor to your roommate.

➤ OPTION #2: *Go Off*

That's right, turn on the lights and start screaming. This will surely stop the lovebirds in their tracks and send her out the door. Your roommate will probably kick your ass, but at least when he's done you can get some shut-eye.

➤ OPTION #3: *Get It on Tape*

Since you're not sleeping, you might as well do something to pass the time. After they're done, post it on YouTube. Chances are your roommate will never see that girl again and he'll probably have a hard time getting any other chick to go home with him.

➤ OPTION #4: *Drown It Out*

Put on your iPod and turn up the volume. Listen to the sounds of spring and pretend you are in a peaceful green meadow far, far away from your roommate's gyrating.

➤ OPTION #5: *Join In*

Shit, the girl might be into it. Just walk up and see if you can stick yourself in her mouth. If your roommate objects, stick yourself in his mouth to shut him up.

IN THE FUTURE . . .

If you and your roommate plan on getting some ass on a regular basis, you should institute a code system using different color clothes. Place an item of clothing that's the necessary color on the doorknob outside the door. See the chart below.

COLOR	MEANING
White	Come back in an hour.
Blue	Come back in two hours.
Red	Come back tomorrow.
Black	Go get help.
Yellow	Join in.

115. You Get Caught with Beer in Your Room

You and your friends are right in the middle of some serious gaming while downing a couple of beers. What a great day, until your RA pops in unexpectedly and finds the beer. There is a no-alcohol policy on campus and, guess what, you just got nabbed.

The WTF Approach to Avoiding a F*#!-ing Write-Up

➤ OPTION 1#: *Drink Up*

Down it, bitch! Your RA can't prove you're drinking if there isn't any alcohol. If he smells the alcohol, tell him it's not beer, but that you are drinking your own piss according to this new cleansing diet you heard about.

➤ OPTION #2: *Make It a Party*

Get your RA wasted and let him join in. Most RAs are a bunch of nerds that are in desperate need of fun. Show them what you're actually supposed to do in school.

➤ OPTION #3: *Beg for Mercy*

Get down on your knees and beg the prick to overlook it. RAs are like cops and other assholes—they just like the power.

PROFESSOR TIP: Most campuses have a no-alcohol policy. But that doesn't mean you shouldn't keep alcohol in your room, you just need to be clever about it. Hide vodka in a water bottle or keep beer in the ceiling panels.

COLLEGE IS NO LAUGHING MATTER

"A telephone survey says that 51 percent of college students drink until they pass out at least once a month. The other 49 percent didn't answer the phone."—Craig Kilborn

IN THE FUTURE . . .

Do drugs that you can hide easily. Pills are a good bet. Enjoy!

116. Your Roommate Eats All Your Food

College is a great learning experience. You not only improve your academic skills, you also learn to live with people—and that some people are not worth living with.

The WTF Approach to Stopping Your F*#!-ing All-Consuming Roomie

➤ STEP #1: *Label It*

The time for sharing is over. Put labels on everything you buy and tell your thieving roommate to do the same. That'll put an end to that "was that yours?" game.

➤ STEP # 2: *Poison Your Food*

If the labels don't stop him, this'll show him. Buy something you know he likes and lace it with something that will *at least* make him sick, if not kill him. Be careful,

if you do murder him, not to get caught—you don't get to pick your roommates in jail either.

WTF: UP CLOSE AND PERSONAL

Back before I was the internationally renowned author of the *WTF?* series, I rented a room the size of a latrine (and almost as smelly) in Staten Island, New York, for $400 a month.

My landlord and roommate was Manuel—a five-foot-tall,

handicapped Mexican who, rumor had it, was dying of AIDS. Manuel dressed in a kimono and sported a half-mustache. (Yes, he would only shave half of his mustache.) And despite his dark skin, jet-black hair, and the fact he was born and raised in Mexico City, Manuel claimed he was Scandinavian. As a tribute to his heritage, Manuel decorated his room with posters, paintings, and statues of famous Nordic gods and heroes.

A nineteen-year-old community college student at the time, I was always broke and chose to spend what I had on beer rather than food. So what did I do? I ate Manuel's, mostly his mozzarella cheese. You see, if you take a little slice at a time, there's a good chance the person won't notice. However, Manuel did. He would yell at me in his thick Mexican accent: "Stop eating my cheese! You are making my Viking blood boil!" (I am not making this up.)

Luckily, however, Manuel had a crush on me (what, the kimono didn't tip you off?), so he let me get away with my cheese-eating activities. Oh, college.

—GB

IN THE FUTURE . . .

Find a roommate with an eating disorder—specifically anorexia. You don't want a bulimic vomiting all over the joint. You can also ask to be roomed with a vegan. They don't eat anything. Plus, they always have weed.

117. Your Loser Roommate Is Getting More Action Than You

You don't like to be a spoilsport, but this is getting ridiculous. Every time you come home with your head down after striking out yet again, you open the door to see your roommate with his head between another chick's legs.

The WTF Approach to Getting More F*#!-ing Ass

➤ **OPTION #1:** *Watch and Learn*

If you have a good view of your friend while he's banging away, pay attention and take some notes. Maybe he's getting laid more than you for a reason—he's better at it.

➤ **OPTION #2:** *Get Sloppy Seconds*

If he is such a hot shot, maybe he can help you out by convincing the chicks he brings over to screw you after he is done with them. Better to have sloppy seconds than to cry every night with your hand down your pants wishing that you were dead.

➤ **OPTION #3:** *Get Plastic Surgery*

Maybe you can't get laid as much as your roommate because you're a fat ugly pig. If you're chubby, get liposuction. If you're ugly, get a face-lift and a nose job. And if you have a little pecker, get a penile implant—or just go after Asian chicks.

➤ OPTION #4: *Sabotage Him*

Ruin his relationships by leaving other girls' numbers in his pants, or put bras and panties and other dumb shit like that in his bed. If you aren't getting laid, might as well spoil it for him. You can also play the good guy and tell his girlfriends that he's a prick and cheats on them. Maybe they'll do you just to get back at him.

➤ OPTION #5: *Cut His Dick Off*

Pull a Lorena Bobbit and chop his pecker clean off. Then take a good look at it and see what a real man's dick is supposed to look like.

***WTF*ACT:** Your roommate is better than you. Loser!

IN THE FUTURE . . .

Make sure your roommate is lamer than you. If your roommate looks too cool when you meet him, request another roommate right away. Don't overestimate yourself and think you'll turn as cool as him.

118. You Accidentally Burn Down Your Dorm

Every student heads off to college with the basic necessities. Clothes, school supplies, and a hot plate. Can't live without that hot plate. From making soup to making meth, it's a must-have. The only problem is sometimes you forget to turn that shit off when you're done. One day on your way back to the dorms, you notice several fire trucks and hundreds of students outside. Looks like some asshole left his hot plate on and burned down the dorm. Oh wait, that asshole was you. Bummer.

The WTF Approach to Handling F*#!-ing Accidental Arson

➤ OPTION #1: *Take Off*

Just split and never return. Fuck it.

➤ OPTION #2: *Break Out the Marshmallows*

Shit, you can't do anything about it now, so might as well make the most of it. Material things don't matter anyhow. Make s'mores for everyone and maybe they'll forgive you.

➤ OPTION #3: *Sue*

That's right: sue. Sue the company that makes the hot plate. Even if this model wasn't defective, their hot plates should have an automatic turn-off switch. They should know only drunk, stupid, and high college students use these. Settle out of court and drop out of school. You'll be rich; you don't need a degree now.

➤ OPTION #4: *Become an Arsonist*

Fire is pretty. Get some more hot plates or, better yet, some matches and gasoline and burn down all kinds of shit. Come up with a cool arsonist name like "Franky the Fire Starter" and become infamous.

> **NOTE:** Congratulations on your new career choice. Way to prove to your parents that you don't need a college degree for *everything*. Just don't come crying to us when you can't beat your arson rap, or give yourself third-degree burns over 90 percent of your body.

THINGS THAT WILL SET ON FIRE:

- Alcohol
- Aerosol hairspray
- Bedding
- Gasoline
- Dirty underwear

THINGS THAT ARE FUN TO SET ON FIRE:

- Fireworks
- Homework
- Ex-girlfriends
- Feces
- Malibu

WTF: UP CLOSE AND PERSONAL

I once burned down a hotel room in a small town in northern Laos. Let me explain . . .

After college, I backpacked throughout Southeast Asia for a few months. One night, during a binge, I apparently left a candle burning in my room when I went out. The candle somehow started my backpack on fire, which contained my toiletries—including an aerosol deodorant can. The bag blew like a stick of dynamite, scattering scorched pieces throughout the room and ceiling.

One of my travel companions came to find me at a bar to tell of the inferno. In his thick Norwegian accent, he said, "Your voom Greig is on fire!" I laughed and shrugged, thinking he was bullshitting. However, I returned to the hotel to find the owner and his family cleaning up my disaster of a room. Luckily, my money and passport were hidden behind the mirror in the bathroom, which the fire did not reach.

When the hotel owner told me that we would "work this out in the morning," I tried to escape into the night, but the town was so small there was no late-night transportation. I was stuck. So I went with Plan B: Tell them that my money was in my bag and that because it was destroyed, I was left with nothing. Yes, that would be my story.

In the end, they took me to jail as a negotiation ploy when I refused to pay the full $400 damage cost. On the way to the station, I worked out a deal to pay about $130. Overall, I am very proud of my negotiating skills that day— though it might have been better not to have burned down the room in the first place.

—GB

119. Your Parents Are Up Your Ass Because Your Major Is Undeclared

What's your major? It's perhaps the most commonly asked question in college behind the omnipresent: *What dorm do you live in? Where is the keg?* and *Do you have a condom?* And yet, despite mounting pressure from your peers and parents to choose a major, you just can't seem to make up your mind.

The WTF Approach to Choosing a F*#!-ing Major

> **STEP #1:** *Examine Your Interests*

Besides *Family Guy* and porn, what do you like to do? If you can't come up with an answer in a few minutes, you should probably watch a little *Family Guy* and then whack off to some porn. It might help clear your head so you can think straight.

> **STEP #2:** *Examine Your Abilities*

If you can't do basic arithmetic then you should probably steer clear of accounting. Then again, if you can't do basic arithmetic, you should probably steer clear of life and commit suicide for being a moron.

➤ STEP #3: *Examine Your Dick*

No reason in particular, we just figured since you were examining things and had nothing else to do right now it might pass the time.

➤ STEP #4: *Take Classes*

Don't worry about your major right now, and just take classes that engage you. Think of this time as a kind of courtship period between you and your intellect before you commit her to a specific discipline. In other words, bang the shit out of every subject that interests you before you choose one to marry.

➤ STEP #5: *Major in Communications*

Trust us; it's a total fucking joke.

WTFACT: According to recent studies, one in four people have claimed psychology as their major at one time during their college tenure. But just because you majored in psychology for a half a semester doesn't give you the right to psychoanalyze that hot girl who won't hook up with you. Yeah we get it—she has daddy issues. Who doesn't?

How to Choose a Major

Before you pick a major, you need to be able to recognize which majors pertain to which professions.

POP QUIZ

Match the following majors with their corresponding professions.

1. Math	A. Crook
2. English Literature	B. Dry Cleaning or Acupuncture
3. Accounting	C. Blockbuster Video clerk
4. Political Science	D. Accountant
5. Film	E. Alcoholic high school teacher with a beard, working on unpublishable novel, prone to fits of depression and suicidal rage

Answers: 1B, 2E, 3D, 4A, 5C

Or, pick your major by what you actually *like* doing:

- Working with kids? Become a teacher
- Taking care of sick friends? Become a nurse
- Smoking a lot of pot? Become an environmentalist
- Getting your dick sucked? Become an adult film performer

Or, pick one of these majors if you want to score a hot chick:

- Design studies
- Psychology
- Elementary education
- Nursing
- Art history

120. It's Too Late to Change Your Major from Philosophy to Business

You didn't want to major in philosophy, but after taking six philosophy classes and with your parents on your case, you figured you'd just major in it for now while getting your generals out of the way before picking something more useful. But when you go to change majors you're told it's too late. Now you will be graduating with a degree in existentialism. Useless!

The WTF Approach to Graduating with a F*#!-ing Bullshit B.A.

➤ OPTION #1: *Get an MBA*

A bachelors in business is useless anyhow if you don't get a masters. So, don't worry about what's on your certificate, you can always go back to school for business later.

➤ OPTION #2: *Lie*

Just put down that you majored in business. Who is really going to doubt you? In fact, say you have an MBA while you're at it. Just make sure to read enough *Business for Dummies*-type books to pull it off.

➤ OPTION #3: *Go to Law School*

Studies show that students who studied history and philosophy end up making more money in the long run. Why? Because they have no choice except to go to law school. Become a lawyer; Lord knows we need more of them.

➤ OPTION #4: *Be a Philosopher*

There are still real philosophers out there, but they are few and far between. If you're not smart enough to be a great academic, then just wear a toga and philosophize on the corner.

NOTE: Do yourself a favor and buy *The Little Bathroom Book of Philosophy.*

➤ OPTION #5: *Become a Nihilistic Businessperson*

If you want to be a cold-hearted corporate suit, study your nihilism and Nietzsche. Remember: *might makes right*, biatch!

WTF ABOUT TOWN

We had the privilege of talking to one of the most promising philosophers in the country. The following conversation ensued:

WTF: We heard that you are a philosopher.

Philosopher: Indeed, I am.

WTF: Is that your cardboard box? Do you live there?

Philosopher: That is a good question. Well, it certainly seems that way doesn't it? But how can we be sure that our senses are perceiving reality as it truly is? How, for instance, do you know that you are not dreaming this experience entirely? How, for instance, can you prove that these words "cardboard" and "box" are actual representations of real objects or just terms we used to differentiate certain visual "forms" that comprise our reality?

WTF: Interesting. We never thought if it that way.

Philosopher: Thank you. Now can I interest either of you in some crack?

COLLEGE IS NO LAUGHING MATTER

"I took a test in existentialism. I left all the answers blank and got 100."
—Woody Allen

121. Your Girlfriend Has a Crush on Her Professor

She talks about him constantly—about how "smart" and "funny" he is, how he "knows everything," and how he has "really opened her eyes." Recently, you notice she's stopped referring to him as Professor Richard Long, PhD, and started calling him by his nickname, Dr. Dick. Not only that, she's also texted him several times about some "assignments" late into the night. Seems as if your girlfriend's professor has ignited her intellectual curiosity, and sparked a burning flame in her pants.

The WTF Approach to Squashing Your Girl's F*#!-ing Crush

➤ **OPTION #1: *Spread Rumors About Him***

If your girl is getting too close, spread rumors that he has herpes or some other unfortunate sexually transmitted malady. When the grapevine gets to your girl, she'll be more than happy to keep her crush to the classroom and leave the bedroom just for you.

➤ **OPTION #2: *Become Smart and Interesting—Quickly***

If you can become smarter and more interesting, maybe your girl won't have to chase her teachers to satisfy her intellectual needs. Stop working on your cardio and exercise your brain.

➤ OPTION #3: *Get Him Fired*

If things are really getting out of hand and you're sure it's only a matter of time before your girl ends up playing the skin flute with her music teacher, use any means necessary—fair and unfair—to get him the boot. Plant drugs in his office, pay one of his female students to accuse him of sexual harassment, or just beat him up so bad that he'll end up looking like Stephen Hawking. Because even with those kinds of smarts, when you look *that* bad, you don't get laid.

YOUR GIRL MIGHT HAVE A CRUSH ON HER PROFESSOR IF . . .

❑ She gets all dolled up before class—just his.
❑ She quotes him on a daily basis.
❑ She sits in on his other classes.
❑ She laughs at all his jokes.
❑ She's a little dirty whore and you *know* it.

IN THE FUTURE . . .

Research the professors that teach the classes your girlfriend is considering. Find out what they look like, if they are married, what their reputation and accomplishments are, and so on. If the course book says that the professor is TBA, whoever ends up teaching the class probably won't be an academic big shot and therefore shouldn't be a threat.

122. You Get an Erection During Your Physics Presentation

There you are in front of a large classroom explaining how the force of one object can affect the space of another. Now you're not sure if it's the fact that you're really nervous or if it's the girl with the big tits that you've been eyeing all semester, but suddenly you can't focus. In fact, the force of something is definitely affecting the space of something else. You are getting a raging hard-on in your jeans and there is no way to stop it.

The WTF Approach to Welcoming F*#!-ing Unexpected Wood

➤ OPTION #1: *Get Creative*

When an actress on television is pregnant in real life but her character isn't pregnant on the show, the writers find a way to conceal the baby bump. Your bump should be much easier to hide. No offense. Stand in front of the desk. Turn your back to the class, or hold a book over your crotch. Then think of Rosie O'Donnell bent over covered in margarine and pray it goes away.

➤ OPTION #2: *Use It*

Point it out. Explain that this is part of your presentation: to show how something *so* large can expand

and contract in such a confined space. Maybe McTitty in the front row will want to conduct her own experiment after seeing it.

➤ OPTION #3: *Jerk Off in Class*

Hey, this is the most surefire way to get rid of it. It probably won't take you long. Aim at McTitty. That will teach her to wear tight T-shirts without a bra—and teach the class about projectiles.

for the ladies . . .

This may not seem like it's something to worry about, but having hard nipples can also be very embarrassing and distracting. Wear band aides over the areola.

Erection Equation

$$\frac{\text{Mass of tits} \times \text{Mass of dick}}{\text{Speed of blood flow}} = \text{Erection}$$

THOUGHTS THAT KILL AN ERECTION:

- Dead kittens
- Your grandmother (unless she's a cougar)
- Michael Moore
- Michael Jackson
- Colonoscopies
- Nipple hair
- Nipple hair on Holocaust victims
- Cankles
- That birth video from health class
- Photos of STDs
- AIDS
- A dead baby sandwich on rye, with that mustard that you *hate*

IN THE FUTURE . . .

The next time you have to stand in front of a large group of people, wear a cup.

123. You're the Only Guy in Your Women's Studies Class

When you signed up for women's studies you thought it would be a class about how chicks think. You figured you would learn how to get into their heads so you can score. But on the first day of class you realize what kind of hell you've just stepped into. You're surrounded by a mob of angry, embittered women looking for a face to blame.

The WTF Approach to Surviving a Class Filled with Angry F*#!-ing Chicks

➤ **OPTION #1: *Use It***

Just because these girls hate men, doesn't mean that they don't need dick. Being the only dude in class might have its advantages.

➤ **OPTION #2: *Come Clean***

Tell everyone you're considering a sex change and since you will one day be the proud owner of a vagina you really wanted to learn everything you can about your future gender's history.

➤ **OPTION #3: *Divide and Conquer***

Get the women to hate one another despite their feigned solidarity in class by starting vicious rumors. Turn these so called feminists into the real yentas that they are. Sit back and laugh as the claws come out.

124. Someone Cheats Off You During the Final Exam

You've been studying hard the last couple of weeks for finals. So hard, in fact, that you have cut down to ten beers a day. True, they were 40-ounce beers, but still. The point is that you were making an effort and it paid off: You totally aced it. And so did the kid next to you—though not because he studied. You thought you saw him looking at your test, but you were too busy concentrating to be sure. It was only when that freckle-faced prick got his exam back with the same grade you did that it was undeniably clear: He cheated.

The WTF Approach to Dealing with a F*#!-ing Cheat

> ➤ **OPTION #1: *Tattle***

Why should this lazy prick get the same grade you did when you were studying all night while he sat on his ass? Don't let him get away with it. Tell the professor that you absolutely saw your neighbor cheating off you. Make sure to add that you feel bad doing this but that it isn't "fair" since you worked so hard. The professor will still probably think that you're a little tattle-tale pussy, but so be it.

➤ OPTION #2: *Let It Go*

Don't be such a hard ass. It's not like his cheating affects your grade—unless, of course, your professor grades on a curve. In that case, go with Option #3.

➤ OPTION #3: *Beat the Shit Out of Him*

Grab him by the collar after class and slam him into the wall. Make him confess to his sins and then, when he does, beat him up some more. This will not change anything, but it will make you feel good (assuming that you are a sick fuck).

➤ OPTION #4: *Blackmail Him*

What good is it to tattle like a baby or to beat him up? Maybe it's best that, instead, you make him give you something for cheating off you. Quid pro quo.

Things to Consider Before Telling on the Cheater

Before you go and tattle on or blackmail your cheating classmate, you might want to factor in a few things. Sometimes it's good to keep your mouth shut, not out of principle, but to save your ass. Consider:

- Height, weight, and muscle density of the cheater
- Ethnic background of the cheater; don't mess with the Irish—they'll beat your ass.
- The cheater's shoes: you can tell how rich or poor a man is by his shoes. If he's wearing sneakers from Target, don't bother blackmailing because he doesn't have any loot. And don't tell on him either. Let the poor schmuck off the hook.

NOTE: Converse sneakers are neutral. They don't tell anything about your cheater's financial status, since everyone and their mother now wears them. In this event, look at his watch.

125. You Get Caught Cheating and Are Thrown Out of Class

You were caught cheating. And you can't deny it by saying that you have some sort of crossed-eyed problem that makes it seem like you are staring at your neighbor's paper. No, the professor caught you with the notes written on your desk—and this is the first exam he's given out. No excuses. No bull. You've been caught red-handed . . . now what?

The WTF Approach to Beating the F*#!-ing Cheating Rap

> **OPTION #1:** *Give a Sob Story*

Go to his office and beg him to let you retake the exam. Tell him you couldn't study because your mom died or that you just found out over the weekend that you had AIDS—not HIV but full-blown AIDS . . . you have six months to live.

Make sure that if you are going to conjure up a sob story to explain your being a cheater, that it is as devastatingly sad as the aforementioned stories. Everyone has a dead grandma and has gotten the flu—don't go there. Go the dead mom or the AIDS route and cry like a baby. Even the coldest, by-the-book professors will crack and give you a break.

➤ OPTION #2: *Bribe Him*

Offer him money to forget about the whole thing. If he accepts, offer him more to just go ahead and give you an A.

➤ OPTION #3: *Change Your Major*

What were you doing studying biology anyway? Now that you know you're a sneaky, cheating liar with no integrity whatsoever, change your major from pre-med to pre-law. You'll do wonderfully.

➤ OPTION #4: *Compromise*

If your professor is too square for a bribe and doesn't give a shit about your sad life, then try and convince him to just fail you and not bring it to the dean's attention.

BEST WAYS TO CHEAT—AND GET AWAY WITH IT:

Get a cast: Break your arm if you must, but just make sure you get a cast. Get people to sign it and then write the information for the test in between the signatures.

Get a doctor's note: Have your doctor say that you have a bladder issue and need to urinate frequently. Make sure to inform your teachers at the beginning of the semester that you *must* go to the bathroom every ten minutes. This will make it easy for you to check your notes during test time while you're in the john.

Write the answers on your baseball cap: Jot the information on the inside of a baseball cap's bill. During the exam, take the cap off and place it in front of you upside down for easy viewing.

IN THE FUTURE . . .

Study, dick wad.

126. Your Professor Is Out to Fail You

Your friends think you're paranoid, your parents think you're lying, but you know it's the truth. Your professor hates you and is out to fail you for no good reason. Maybe you remind him of someone—a bully from high school, a mean uncle, or that jerk in the blue pickup truck who knocked up his daughter—whatever the reason, you're on his naughty list and you just can't seem to get off.

The WTF Approach to Getting Around a F*#!-ing Professor Out to Get You

➤ **STEP #1:** *Drop the Class*

Even if it's past the date to drop, you can still drop it for an incomplete. While an incomplete sucks, it beats failing. Retake the class at another time with another professor who isn't a prick.

➤ **STEP #2:** *Pucker Up*

If an incomplete means you won't graduate—or worse, get tossed from the school—you're going to have to kiss some ass, big shot. Bring a new shiny red apple to class every day, and if that doesn't work offer to suck him off.

➤ STEP #3: *Poison the Apple*

Put a little arsenic in the apple every day until he chokes on his own spit and leaves this world forever—double the dosage come finals just to make sure.

NOTE: While we here at *WTF* want to see you succeed, we don't want to see you go to prison. (Eh, maybe we do.) Keep in mind that believe it or not, homicide does look worse on a resume than a failing grade in biology.

for the ladies . . .

Based on what you have read of this book so far, what do you think our advice is to you? We'll give you three options:

A. Spread your legs.

B. Spread them wider.

C. Attach your ankles to your ears.

Yes. The answer is C. Wow, you're getting so smart!

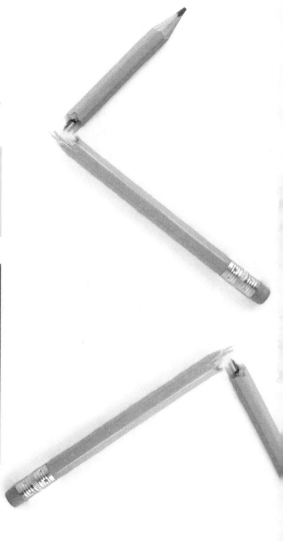

127. You Can't Stop Falling Asleep in Class

You thought that you could party all night and still be alert enough to take copious notes during psych class. But these all-nighters are starting to wear you down. You know that you should stay in and study instead of chug beer and take body shots off a freshman coed's tanned abs, but you just can't seem to stay away from the fun. Luckily, we at *WTF* can help. Here's a crash-course on how to stop turning your desk into a puddle of drool and your professor against you.

The WTF Approach to Handling the F*#!-ing Classroom Zzzs

➤ **OPTION #1:** *Party in Class*

Rather than stay up all night partying, take the party to the lecture hall. Top off half a bottle of Pepsi with some rum. This way you can have all the fun you would at a party, while still being an enthusiastic participant in class (perhaps a little too enthusiastic). The pro-

fessor will love you and so will your classmates . . . if you share!

➤ **OPTION #2:** *Break Down and Start Crying*

If your grade is in jeopardy, force a tear and tell your professor that you haven't slept well because you've been spending all your nights at the hospital, where your poor girlfriend hovers between life and death. Make sure to know a hospital offhand so you can be specific, which will make your lie more believable.

PROFESSOR TIP: To perfect the crying game, make sure to take an acting class early in your college career—you're going to need those lying skills to make it through the next four years.

➤ **OPTION #3:** *Think Fast*

If you're called out for dozing off, explain to your professor that you have been practicing the art of meditation . . . very Eckhart Tolle. This *is* the way you absorb your material.

➤ **OPTION #4:** *Say You're a Narcoleptic*

Tell the professor you have a slight case of narcolepsy. If he believes you, now you have an open invitation to fall asleep in class whenever you want.

for the ladies . . .

If you sleepy ladies are reprimanded by a male professor for constantly dozing off, you might want to tell him (again, with tears) that financial troubles have forced you to take a night job as a stripper, which has ruined your sleeping patterns. As you tell this sad story, be sure to gently sway back and forth in a progressively seductive manner. Your professor will be so turned on and saddened at the same time he won't know what to do—except cut you a break.

128. You Have a Paper Due Tomorrow That You Haven't Started

You have always been a procrastinator, but usually it all turns out okay. You can study the night before an exam and still ace the test. No problem. But this time you really screwed up, and there's no way to wing it. You know that big paper that's worth half your grade? Well, it's due tomorrow and you haven't even begun.

The WTF Approach to Finishing a F*#!-ing Paper by Deadline

➤ **OPTION #1:** *Sit Down and Write It*

If you sit down with a few hundred Red Bulls and double-shot lattes you should be able to bang it out. Writing papers is easy. Just make sure your thesis is clear and then prove your point. If you don't have time to write real transitions between ideas, just keep using words like "furthermore," "in addition," "also," and such. Furthermore, use a lot of quotes to take up lines. In addition, make sure to draw attention to the subjective nature of paper grading by using phrases like "in my opinion," "it is my contention," and so on. Also, make the font as big as you can without being too conspicuous.

➤OPTION #2: *Buy One*

If you've ever been on the Internet, you probably already know this type of service is available. There are several sites that offer term papers for sale on just about every subject. We suggest finding one that charges a monthly membership fee and then splitting the cost with your roommate or a friend. Of course, if you go with this option, you will never really learn anything, but when have you ever learned anything from writing a paper that you didn't forget by next semester?

➤OPTION #3: *Steal One*

Hack into a classmate's computer and take his paper. Destroy his hard drive so he has no record of it. While you may not learn anything, you will be teaching your classmate a valuable lesson about trusting others.

➤OPTION #4: *Get Your Girlfriend to Write It for You*

Tell your girlfriend that you had a wildly romantic night planned for her but you have to cancel because of this damn paper. She knows how slow you type. Odds are she will offer to help, and by help, we mean she'll do all the work. Grab a bottle of wine and get loaded while she types away. Then bang her as her reward. If you don't have a girlfriend, find one fast. That's what they're for, anyway.

COLLEGE KID QUOTE

"I once had this paper due and I was like, oh shit, it's like the night before. And then I like totally didn't have time and failed the class."

—Wayne Smith, *still* a freshman at University of Arizona online (he's 28)

The WTF Sample Paper

Most term papers follow the same structure and format, which means you can get a jump on the one you didn't start by using this template. By inserting a few pieces of key information and making a few choices between the supplied choices, you'll have one hell of paper.

While researching _____ it is clear that
[insert: subject, book title, or article title]

the main _____ is intended as a metaphor for
[choose: idea, theme, or bullshit]

_____. This is symbolic because it represents a
[choose: life, death, or existential woe]

classic case of man versus _____. The questions
[choose: man, nature, or society]

raised by the author are _____. In my
[choose: controversial, profound, or who-gives-a-shit?]

opinion, this _____ novel focuses on the struggle
[choose: classic, brilliant, or lame-ass]

of the individual to maintain his _____
[choose: identity, humanity, need to feel like a big shot]

in the modern world. In conclusion, I found _____
[insert: subject, book title, or article title]

to be one of the most moving examples of the natural human desire to

give life _____. The End.
[choose: meaning, purpose, or . . . God this is fucking boring!]

129. You're the Dumbest Kid in All Your Classes

They say it is better to be a big fish in a little pond than a little fish in a big pond. Perhaps you should have thought over that expression a little more before deciding to go to a school that you knew should not have accepted you. It looks good on your resume to graduate from a fancy school, but it doesn't look that great if you barely get by. You just weren't Yale material. Don't feel bad, there have been others in the same boat—a recent U.S. president comes to mind . . .

The WTF Approach to Surviving as the F*#!-ing Stupid Kid

➤ **OPTION #1:** *Switch to an Easier Major*

If you are in the Ivy League when you should be in community college, you're going to have to get off that pre-med track. It's the only way to shine academically and stop embarrassing yourself. To stay at the top, pick from the left field of academic majors. Choose a major like drama, art, or sociology.

➤ **OPTION #2:** *Downgrade Schools*

In a less prestigious school, you'll not only perform better, you'll have more fun too. When you're getting As on tests and blowjobs between classes, you'll forget all about your former school.

➤ OPTION #3: *Ignorance Is Bliss*

Okay, you're the dumbest kid in class. Who cares? Keep a low profile and your mouth shut so you don't make a jackass out of yourself. Study hard and you'll graduate, not with honors or the respect of your peers, but graduate nonetheless. Remember, you'll never have to see these pricks again—unless you're fixing their office's elevator.

How to Pass—When You're a Moron

Here's how to handle questions when you don't know the answer, as well as how *not* to handle them.

WHAT TO SAY . . .

Question: What is your take on the situation in Kashmir?
Answer: That is such a complicated issue. I don't even know where to start. But *something* has to be done.

Question: What do you think should be done about Darfur?
Answer: I think I'm in the majority here. What's *your* take?

Question: How should the government handle the current economic crisis?
Answer: Well, it certainly is a crisis. And therefore should be dealt with as such.

WHAT *NOT* TO SAY . . .

Question: What is your take on the situation in Kashmir?
Answer: I don't even wear cashmere. It sheds.

Question: What do you think should be done about Darfur?
Answer: I don't believe in cruelty to animals. I don't care what kind of fur it is.

Question: How should the government handle the current economic crisis?
Answer: What crisis?

130. You Choose to Plagiarize So You Can Party . . . and Then Get Caught

It's the night before your mid-term essay is due. You put it off forever and now you have no choice but to buckle down. But then you hear about this amazing party . . . shit! You go online to look up some resources—wow, these people really know what they're talking about—and so you decide to just copy their thoughts. A week later, your professor calls you in to talk about plagiarism. Thief! Maybe it wasn't such a good idea . . .

The WTF Approach to Talking Your Way Out of F*#!-ing Plagiarism Charges

➤ OPTION #1: *State Your Case*

Explain that these are also your ideas and that great minds think—and sometimes write—*exactly* alike. If he doesn't buy it, offer to write the paper again. Then pay a really smart kid to write if for you. In fact, that's what you should have done in the first place. You deserve to be caught, dumbass!

➤ OPTION #2: *Lie*

Admit that you used other people's work but forgot to attach your sources. If you copied word for word, you'll have to say that you accidentally turned in a rough draft of your paper. Go home and quickly pull up the material you ripped off, change the words around, and list them on your works cited page.

➤ OPTION #3: *Flip the Switch*

That's right; tell this professor he is insulting you as an academic and that you will not be accused of something so outrageous. Then drop the class and file a complaint. Don't go too far, however, or they might call your bluff and actually read your paper.

IN THE FUTURE . . .

Buy a paper online.

The WTF Guide to Good Plagiarizing

Learn how to copy, dipshit!

Text to Copy

> **COLLEGE KID QUOTE**
>
> "I'm glad I'm not bisexual. I couldn't stand being rejected by men as well as women."
>
> —Bernard Manning

The Wrong Way to Copy

I'm glad I'm not bisexual. Because, I couldn't stand being rejected by men as well as women.

The Right Way

You see I could never be bisexual. I couldn't stand getting rejections from both sexes.

HOW TO WRITE A PAPER:

1. Sit at your desk.
2. Read over the assignment carefully to make certain you understand it.
3. Walk down to the vending machines and buy some Red Bull.
4. Stop at your friend's room.
5. Talk about banging chicks and *Family Guy*.
6. Go back to your room and sit back at your desk.
7. Read over the assignment again to make absolutely certain you understand it.
8. Check your e-mail; reply to everyone who sent you a message.
9. Check your cell phone; return any missed calls and texts.
10. Go take a shit.
11. Check your e-mail again.
12. Watch porn on your computer.
13. Whack off to that hot girl from Bio class.
14. Nap.
15. Eat.
16. Read over the assignment again.
17. Check your e-mail to make sure no one sent you any urgent messages since the last time you checked your e-mail.
18. Watch *Family Guy*.
19. Look through your roommate's personal stuff.
20. Sit down and do some serious thinking about your plans for the future.
21. Decide what kind of super powers you would want if you were on *Heroes*.
22. Read over the assignment one more time, just for the hell of it.
23. Whack off to the *other* hot girl from Bio class.
24. Lie face down on the floor and moan.
25. Type the paper.

131. You Pull an All-Nighter and Still Aren't Prepared for the Final Exam

Every semester it's the same story. "I've got time," you say. "Finals aren't until the end of the semester. I'll just have to really hit the books a couple weeks before." Then a couple weeks become a couple days and now it's only a couple hours. It's the night before and you're freaking out in the middle of an all-nighter. You're just not ready.

The WTF Approach to Making It Through the F*#!-ing Exam

➤ OPTION #1: *Sit Next to a Smart Kid and Cheat*

That's what they're there for, right? If you were smart you would have picked a seat next to this kid early on so it wouldn't look weird the day of the exam, but then again if you were that smart you would be the smart kid and not the loser sitting next to him.

➤ OPTION #2: *Pull the Fire Alarm*

Right before you head in to the class, pull the alarm. Everyone will have to exit. When they do, grab a test and start looking up the answers. It will take a while before everyone is allowed back in. Class might even get canceled and now you have the test. Score. You can sell it to your classmates and cash in.

➤ **OPTION #3: *Drink Ipecac***

Ipecac's a liquid designed to make you instantly puke, usually reserved for mothers to give their little kids if they swallow poison. Right before you walk in, take a swig and then puke all over the desk. The professor will have to excuse you, giving you some more time to study.

WTF: UP CLOSE AND PERSONAL

As I've confessed already, I wasn't exactly the greatest high school student. In fact, I sucked. I sucked so bad that in order to graduate, I needed an A on my senior project, which included a paper and a speech about the paper. I aced the paper. Whew. Next was the speech. But on the day in question I wasn't ready. What the fuck would I do? I decided to do what any student serious about graduating would do: I went to the drugstore and bought ipecac.

When it was time for my speech, I went around the corner, took a big swig, and came back in class. Within thirty seconds I vomited all over the bag of the redhead girl next to me. Heading for the door and covering my mouth, I continued to vomit violently through my fingers. And I mean *violently*. By the time I was finished, the school bathroom looked like it had hosted a food fight.

As I waited for a friend's mom to pick me up, lying in a pool of my own barf, my teacher had the audacity to ask if I would be okay enough to do my speech. I just glared at him through the globs of puke hanging from my eyelids. He got the message. He told me that he would make a rare exception and go against school policy by letting me make it up. A couple days later—and just twenty-four hours before graduation—I did just that. And yes, I got an A!

—GB

132. You Overslept and Missed Your Mid-Term

The alarm goes off and you hit Snooze and think, just ten more minutes. When it goes off again, you turn it off and think, I'll count to sixty and get up. 1, 2, 3, 4 . . . The next thing you know you wake up an hour later. Shit, you missed class, and what's worse, you had your mid-term today. WTF?

The WTF Approach to Recovering from F*#!-ing Oversleeping

➤ OPTION #1: *Just Make Something Up*

Go see your professor and tell her the electricity went out in your room and your alarm never went off. Then beg her to let you take a makeup exam. Not quite the truth, but there will be no way for your professor to prove you wrong. Just be prepared if she asks you to take the exam right then and there.

➤ OPTION #2: *Fess Up*

Go see your professor and confess. Honesty is the best policy. Explain that you were up all night studying and that you just couldn't get yourself out of bed. While she probably won't let you make up the exam, at least you'll know you did the right thing. Lame ass.

➤ OPTION #3: *Call in a Bomb Threat*

You will have to do it from a land-line so no one can trace it back to you. The classroom and building will be evacuated and class will be canceled. You're not only saving yourself, you're also helping out those who didn't study for the exam. You're a hero. Whoo-hoo!

➤ OPTION #4: ~~Blow Up the Building~~

While it would get the job done, it's a bit drastic. And you'd probably get thrown in jail. If you think college exams are horrible, try giving an oral presentation to Bubba every night before bed.

IN THE FUTURE . . .

Take Adderall. That shit will keep you up for days. You'll be so wired you'll have to study. Substitutes for Adderall include crack cocaine, crystal meth, and intravenous Red Bull.

133. You Partied Too Much and Failed Out of School

Maybe it was the booze, maybe it was the drugs, or maybe you're just a fucking idiot who was destined for failure; whatever the reason, you are now in the middle of a collegiate catastrophe. You just received a letter asking you not to come back next semester due to your academic performance. As in, you've failed, flunked, get no college degree at all (sorry, figured we'd spell it out for a moron like you).

The WTF Approach to Life after F*#!-ing Flunking

➤ **OPTION #1: *Welcome to Wal-Mart***

Without a college degree in this country your fate is sealed. Get a job working at Wal-Mart and just wait to pass away.

➤ **OPTION #2: *Work on a Fishing Boat in Alaska***

Because it sucks really, really bad, just about anyone can get a job on a fishing boat off the coast of Alaska for a surprisingly good pay—around $1,500 per week.

➤ **OPTION #3: *Steal a Smart Kid's Identity***

Make sure this kid is a total loser so that no one misses him after you off him. Take over his life, get a great job, marry a hot chick, and call it a day.

> **OPTION #4:** *Jerk Off*

Why not? You've obviously masturbated your academic career away anyhow. Might as well go back to doing what you do best.

HISTORY'S FAMOUS FAILURES:

Abraham Lincoln went to war a captain and returned a private. Afterward, he was a failure as a businessman. After that he was shot in the head.

Albert Einstein's childhood grades were so poor that his parents thought he was mentally handicapped. Turns out they were just typical overly critical Jewish parents.

Winston Churchill failed sixth grade. He was subsequently defeated in every election for public office until he became Prime Minister at the age of sixty-two. He later wrote, "Never give in, never give in, never, never, never, give up." Churchill finally did give

up on January 24, 1965 when he forever left this world. Hypocrite.

Sigmund Freud was booed from the podium when he first presented his ideas to the scientific community of Europe. A strict Freudian, he still charged the attendees for the full hour.

Charles Darwin once said, "I was considered by all my masters and my father, a very ordinary boy, rather below the common standard of intellect." Ironically, the same thing can be said of anyone today who still doesn't believe his theories.

Thomas Edison's teachers said he was "too stupid to learn anything." He tried 9,000 experiments before he invented the light bulb, inspiring the famous joke opener: "How many experiments does it take to develop a light bulb . . ."

Adolf Hitler tried to kill every Jew. He failed too.

134. Your Parents Make a Surprise Visit and You're Drunk

"Surprise! We were just driving through and thought we would drop in!" And boy did they. Unfortunately you're wasted and what's worse, your parents are very religious and do not believe in the consumption of alcohol. You try to think fast but the four beers and three shots of tequila you slammed down in the last ten minutes are making it very difficult.

The WTF Approach to Enduring a F*#!-ing Unexpected Drop-In

➤ **OPTION #1: *Play Sick***

Quickly run to the bathroom and pretend you are getting sick, and if you really drank a lot, you might not even have to pretend. Then crawl in bed and explain that you really need to get some sleep. Hopefully your parents will leave so you can get back to the party.

➤ **OPTION #2: *Lie***

Tell them you were participating in a class project for a science class that monitors the effects of alcohol in your blood stream over a certain period of time. You know drinking is wrong, but this was for school and you want to excel.

➤ OPTION #3: *Blame It on Your Roommate*

Tell them he must have slipped some vodka into your Red Bull and you had no idea. This was not your fault, and you feel violated.

➤ OPTION #4: *Admit It*

Tell them you're drunk and proud of it. This is college, and you want to have fun while getting an education. What are they going to do, ground you?

➤ OPTION #5: *Make It a Party*

Break out a case of beer and get your parents wasted too. Explain to them that while you appreciate their views on the consumption of alcohol, even Jesus drank wine now and again.

135. You Get Caught Using Your Fake ID

Your heart is pounding, your palms are sweating, you feel dizzy, and you haven't even had a drink yet. This bouncer is just not buying that the skinny white kid in front of him is Ahmed Karim. He has your fake ID and he's calling your bluff.

The WTF Approach to Using a F*#!-ing Fake

➤ **STEP #1:** *Stand Your Ground*

Even if you're shitting your pants, keep up the front that you're Ahmed. Don't back down. Start rattling off the license info. If you're smart, you memorized every detail of that fake ID, Ahmed.

➤ **STEP #2:** *Make a Scene*

That's right. Scream out, "This is ridiculous!" Then say that you have been here plenty of times and insist to see the manager. Tell the bouncer that you're going to

get his ass fired. This is a risky move, but we have seen it work several times.

> **PROFESSOR TIP:** The more of an obnoxious prick you are, the more willing people are to believe you.

➤ **STEP #3:** *Play It Cool*

If making a scene didn't work in your favor, there is a chance that this bouncer will now call the cops. So calm down and start making a graceful exit.

➤ STEP #4: *Lie*

Tell him you know that it's not you. You found it on the ground and you were only kidding when you tried to use it. You wanted to be a good citizen and return it. Then spilt.

WTF: UP CLOSE AND PERSONAL

I was not only the owner of several fake IDs while I was at college, I also made them. I was very popular. They worked in every bar except one, Rudy's. This was one of those bars where the doormen have special bullshit-detecting powers, and if they caught you using a fake ID, they would sound a loud fog horn, turn off the music in the bar, and announce to everyone that you were just caught using a fake. Then they would take a Polaroid of you looking mortified and hang it up with the other underage losers. Not a risk I was ever willing to take. Some bars are worth the wait.

—JM

136. You Throw a Party and No One Comes

You have been planning it for over a week. Facebook invites have gone out. Texts and e-mails have been sent. You got the keg and are ready to go. At first you just think everyone is fashionably late. They'll be here, you say; they're just at another party first. But when it's gets to be 1 A.M., it's quite clear that no one is coming to your party.

The WTF Approach to Dealing with a Failed F*#!-ing Party

➤ **STEP #1:** *Cry*

Yes, a good cry is always helpful. Now continue to Step #2.

➤ **STEP #2:** *Get Drunk and Pass Out*

Drink everything you have until your body shuts down. There's a good chance you'll black out and forget everything, so when you wake up you'll think that you must have thrown a real rager. Or you'll overdose and die, and therefore you won't care, and everyone will immortalize you.

➤ **STEP #3:** *Lie*

Tell everyone they missed the party of a lifetime. Download some pictures of other parties from another school and post them on your Facebook page.

When someone asks you who came, just tell them there were too many people to keep track. In fact, you think there were people from another college there, then tell them you blacked out and don't remember the rest of the night.

PROFESSOR TIP: Next time, throw a theme party. People love that cheesy shit. Any excuse to dress like an ass and get wasted.

GREAT THEME PARTY IDEAS:

- '80s party
- Toga party
- Cross-dressing party
- Famous dead celebrities
- Virgins and hos

NOT SO GREAT THEME PARTY IDEAS:

- AA meeting
- Famous serial killers
- 9/11

IN THE FUTURE . . .

Get some friends, asshole!

137. You Run Out of Booze at a Party

The party is going great. Everyone is having a blast. The girl you have been hitting on all night is almost drunk enough for you to bang; all she needs is that last drink to get her wasted enough to find you attractive. You rush over to the keg . . . empty. You run over to the table with the hard stuff . . . gone. People are starting to leave when they realize there is no more booze, and your slutty conquest is about to bail.

The WTF Approach to Fixing a F*#!-ing Dry Party

➤ **OPTION #1:** *Go Buy More*

Do you really need a handbook to figure this out, dipshit?

➤ **OPTION #2:** *Party Like a Rock Star*

If all the stores are closed, then you're going to have to get creative. When Mötley Crüe ran out of heroin one night, these rock and rollers famously mainlined Jack Daniels instead. Collect all the booze and beer bottles you can and pour whatever is left in them into a big jug. Then, get some needles (if you don't have any, then you don't know how to party anyway—there's got to be one junkie among you), and take turns shooting the alcoholic mixture into your veins. If you don't get drunk, at least you can say that you did it. If you survive, that is.

NOTE: Before attempting, look at Mötley Crüe now.

➤ OPTION #3: *Drink Listerine*

Listerine has 35 percent alcohol—that's 70 proof! (Most whiskeys are about 80 proof.) Vanilla extract and cough syrup also make for delicious cocktail mixers.

NOTE: Before attempting, watch an episode of *Intervention.*

WHAT THE F*#! IS UP WITH . . . ROBO-TRIPPIN'

The undisputed "king" of household, over-the-counter drugs that can really spice your party up is Robitussin. Robitussin contains a high concentration of dextromethorphan, a chemical that gets you really fucked up. Robitussin is such a popular choice for teenagers looking to get high that the slang term *robo-trippin'* has entered into the vernacular of morons around the country.

WOMAN GETS DUI FOR CLEAN BREATH

After a wild night of three glasses of Listerine, Carol Ries, 50, of Adrian, Michigan, rear-ended a vehicle. She pleaded guilty to drunk driving and will serve two years' probation. She blew a .30. on her BAC test; Michigan's legal limit is .08.

On a related charge, she plead not guilty to gingivitis.

➤ OPTION #4: *Get High—Somehow*

Not only is your house a veritable cocktail bar once you know how to find that hidden alcohol, but it's also a veritable pharmacy as well. You'd be surprised how many common household items can be party savers. You can do "whip-its" with whip cream, or sniff things like glue or magic markers.

NOTE: Before attempting, . . . *really?*

➤ OPTION #5: *Rock Out with Your Cocks Out*

Who needs liquor and drugs? Have everyone strip down and rock out with their cocks out. Do it, bro!

138. Your Trip Goes Bad During the Homecoming Parade

Mushrooms are completely natural, and they last for hours. So when your friend offered you some you thought it would be a good idea. But what wasn't a good idea was to take more than you could handle during the homecoming parade. Now you are tripping balls in a crowd of thousands!

The WTF Approach to Surviving a F*#!-ing Bad Trip

➤ **OPTION #1: *Join the Parade***

Get in back of the marching band and move to your own groove. Everyone will think you are part of the interpretive dance group.

➤ **OPTION #2: *Hide Out***

The last thing you want is to be in a large mass of people, especially when your magical ride takes a turn for the worse. Head back to your dorm or apartment ASAP, but don't go alone. You should have at least one other person around you, preferably someone who also took the mushrooms and is a veteran.

IN THE FUTURE . . .

Plan your drug use to coincide with trip-appropriate events.

➤OPTION #3: *Man Up*

Conquer your fears, and deal with your haunted past. Tell the 'shrooms who's boss and turn your bad trip into a good one.

WTFACT: Psilocybin mushrooms (also called psilocybian mushrooms or teónanácatl) are fungi mainly of the *Psilocybe* genus that contain the psychedelic substances psilocybin and psilocin, and occasionally other psychoactive tryptamines. They also grow on cow, horse, pig, sheep, or even goat shit. Happy eating!

THINGS TO AVOID WHILE TRIPPING:

- Ex-girlfriend that you cheated on
- Thanksgiving dinner with the family
- Finals
- A root canal
- Hunting
- Gym class
- Walking a tightrope
- Car crash

THINGS TO DO WHILE TRIPPING:

- Finger paint
- Compose music
- Walk on the beach
- Hike up a mountain on a star-sprinkled night
- Group sex after hiking up a mountain on a star-sprinkled night
- Drive through a car wash
- Go to the planetarium
- Watch Pink Floyd's *The Wall*, or an actual wall—equally entertaining

POP QUIZ

Match the drug to the event.

1.	Ecstasy	A.	Pink Floyd Concert
2.	Weed	B.	Cleaning the Garage
3.	Meth	C.	Rave
4.	Cocaine	D.	Anytime
5.	'Shrooms	E.	Strip Club

Answers: 1C, 2D, 3B, 4E, 5A

139. You Need to Build Your Resume but You Hate People

You have never really liked others—and they never really liked you. With the exception of a few close buddies, you're a loner and you prefer it that way. But unfortunately, employers and graduate schools have this crazy idea that it is important to be able to work well with others. So it's time to bite the bullet and sign up for some social activities—even though inside you hate everyone.

The WTF Approach to Picking a F*#!-ing Activity

➤ **OPTION #1:** *Join the Suicide Prevention Hotline*

Misery loves company. You'll get to volunteer to talk to miserable fucks all day. And since you hate people anyway, you'll probably get a kick out of it.

➤ **OPTION #2:** *Join the Chess Club*

These nerds are also socially challenged loners. They sit in silence for hours devising strategies to destroy their opponents, but the minute anyone fucks with them in real life they bow down like the cowardly dogs that they are. This club would be perfect for you. Not only is there very little social interaction, but you can also bully anyone who does try to talk to you. Watch out for the one Russian kid who might be tougher than you think.

➤ OPTION #3: *Work with Animals*

Join a group that rescues animals or finds stray puppies loving homes. Hopefully you can spend most of your time with the animals rather than other human beings.

➤ OPTION #4: *Lie*

Put whatever you want on your resume. Employers don't even call to check on your last job, let alone what friggin' clubs you belonged to. This is your first lesson about real life. Just don't go overboard and say you were the president of the Spanish club when all you know in Spanish is *hola* and *Taco Bell*.

CLUBS *NOT* ACCEPTED BY THE
STUDENT GOVERNMENT BOARD:

- Waterboarding club
- 2 + 2 = 5 club
- Inquisition Reenactment club
- My Girlfriend Is a Whore club
- Professors We Want to Fuck club
- Kill Whitey club
- 9/11 Was NOT a Conspiracy club
- AIDS is Hip club

140. Your Knee Gives Out and You Lose Your Wrestling Scholarship

You were born to wrestle. Gifted with speed and strength, you were a natural from the start. And you loved it. After all, who doesn't get off on grabbing another sweaty man tightly from behind and violently pinning him down on a mat? Your hard work and genetic predisposition for whipping ass paid off big time when it earned you a scholarship to an Ivy League school—it certainly wasn't your essay in which you painfully attempted to use wrestling as a metaphor for life. But just when things are going great, your knee gives out and with it your scholarship, your future, and your reason for living. Now what?

The WTF Approach to Getting Back on Your F*#!-ing Feet

➤ **OPTION #1: *Make a Miraculous Recovery***

Prove your teammates, your coach, and all the doctors wrong and make a recovery no one could have predicted. Make sure to write about your experiences so you can sell it as some shitty television movie of the week. Think *Lifetime*.

➤ OPTION #2: *Get a Lawyer*

The terms of your scholarship might need scrutiny from a legal eye. If it does say that you are screwed in the event of an injury, sue anyway. You can sue for anything in this country, and now that you're a crippled jackass with no way to finance your education you don't have many other options.

➤ OPTION #3: *Do Gay Porn*

Come on, you know you like dudes or you wouldn't have picked this sport. You think it's a coincidence that wrestling was passed down from the ancient Greeks, who spent all their free time philosophizing, sucking dick, and philosophizing about sucking dick? Seriously, and you're used to being on all fours anyhow. Just think of it as wrestling without the tights—and with a cock in your ass.

WHAT THE F*#! IS UP WITH . . . OLYMPIC SPORTS

Every four years Americans go gaga over athletes who are good at crap that no one cares about—like wrestling or swimming. Consider the hype over Michael Phelps. When was the last time you watched a swimming contest at your local sports bar? Four years ago when some shaved freak was squirming his way toward another gold medal, that's when.

The time has come for us to be honest about these so called "sports." Who gives a shit about fencing except for the French? And what about the shotput? When was the last time a kid in grade school wanted to be the world's best archer?

So, new rules for the Olympics: The more competitive, the more weight the award carries. Events can be broken down into gold, silver, and bronze events—just like the winning positions are now. But there will only be one winner for each event—no more three winners. After all, the only thing less impressive than being the world's best discus thrower is to be the second- or third-best discus thrower.

So let's stick to real sports that we like and are good at. Sports like baseball, basketball, volleyball, and tennis (as long as one of those hot sisters is playing or John McEnroe comes out of retirement). Game over.

---

141. You Try Out for the Basketball Team and They Make You the Mascot

Jocks get all the hot chicks. This has been true for centuries, and probably won't ever change. You can bet that the gymnastics majors in ancient Greek schools were probably getting a lot more ass than philosophy students. True, it was probably little-boy ass, but that's not the point.

So you figured you'd try out for the basketball team in college, even though you sat on the bench for most of your high school basketball career. And surprise, you didn't make it. However, you were so awesomely bad that they asked you to become the mascot.

The WTF Approach to Getting Over Getting F*#!-ing Cut

➤ **OPTION #1:** *Go with It*

While you may look like a complete jerk-off dancing around in a big bird outfit, you'll be invited to all the team events and parties. If you play your cards right and act like the fuzzy little friendly creature you pretend to be, you might just be able to bag a hot pom-pom girl who recently broke up with the quarterback.

➤ **OPTION #2:** *Hit the Gym*

Maybe you didn't make the cut because you just aren't pumped up enough. Start lifting heavy weights and bulk up for tryouts next year. Even if you don't make it on the team, at least you'll be so ripped that you can get laid anyway.

➤ **OPTION #3:** *Kill the Team*

Think of the 1972 Olympic Games in Munich when Arab terrorists killed all those Israeli athletes. If you get away with it, you might just make second or third string.

WTFACT: "Knickerbocker" refers to the style of pants New York City's Dutch settlers wore, known as "knickerbockers," or "knickers."

Give Geronimo a Break

Look, if Native Americans object to the way in which they're portrayed in sports—like in the case of the Washington Redskins or the Cleveland Indians—then pick another name for your team. We stole their land, killed their buffalo, and gave them small pox. Let them bitch; they've earned it.

WTFACT: "Dodger" as in the Los Angeles Dodgers (formerly the Brooklyn Dodgers) refers to the many trolley cars that crisscrossed Brooklyn in the early twentieth century—so many in fact that Brooklynites literally had to "dodge" them.

142. You Can't Afford to Go on Spring Break

You have been looking forward to Spring Break ever since you got into college. Every time you watch a *Girls Gone Wild* video you imagine yourself right in the middle of a naughty coed's massive breasts. But you have only five bucks in your bank account and your parents refuse to give you any money for something that is not a learning experience (little do they know).

The WTF Approach to Being a F*#!-ing Broke Spring Breaker

➤ OPTION #1: *Sell Drugs*

This is the quickest way to make some good cash, as well as some good connections. Don't smoke your own stash—or the only place you'll be going to for Spring Break is rehab.

➤ OPTION #2: *Stay Home*

Tell your friends that you and a buddy from home are going to Amsterdam for Spring Break, then go home to Mom and Dad and catch up on your sleep. Photoshop some drunken pics of you in the red light district and brag about how awesome your trip was.

" My girlfriend went on Spring Break without me, so I decided to have sex with as many girls as I could. That's what I call a break. "

—Elliot Jameson, junior at the University of Massachusetts

► **OPTION #3:** *Mooch*

Borrow some cash from your friends for airfare and just wing the rest. Go to the bars and drink other people's drinks. Buy a loaf of bread for food, then crash on the floor in your friend's room. If you're resourceful, you can really get by on almost nothing and still have an awesome time.

for the ladies . . .

Please, when was the last time you paid for a fucking thing?

WTF ABOUT TOWN

We went to Cabo to check out the Spring Break scene:

WTF: Hey there.

Anna: Whoo-hoo party!

WTF: You're beautiful.

Anna: Thanks! Whoo-hoo party!

WTF: I thought you might want to be in the next *Girls Gone Wild* video.

Anna: OMG, are you like a producer?!

WTF: Sure, okay.

Anna: I totally want to be in that video! Whoo-hoo party!

WTF: Okay, do you have a problem taking off your top on camera?

Anna: Oh no, I hate my dad! Whoo-hoo party!

WTF: Action!

IN THE FUTURE . . .

Date rich girls. Girls love to take care of their guys. Let her pay for your trip. Then suggest Amsterdam.

143. You Get Kicked Out of Your Hotel Room

Turns out that hotel managers frown on running through the hotel halls singing "Happy Birthday" while wearing nothing but your birthday suit at 5 A.M. Go figure.

The WTF Approach to Finding Another F*#!-ing Place to Stay

➤ OPTION #1: *Hit the Motels*

Most places sell out quickly for Spring Break, but there just might be one or two rooms left. If not, you might have to offer Javier the hotel manager an extra fifty or a hand job to free up a room.

➤ OPTION #2: *Sleep on the Beach*

Hopefully you went somewhere warm with a beach. If not, you're a moron. Lay a blanket down and crash on the sand. You'll be so smashed anyway, you probably won't even know where you are. Just make sure you shower each morning, sand has a way of getting caught in your ass pipe.

➤ OPTION #3: *Get a Chick*

If you aren't bagging a chick every night on Spring Break then you're doing something wrong. If you can't seem to get the hot ones to take you home, go after a desperate-looking girl who's as horny and unlucky in love as you. Sure she might be a beast, but at least she's a beast with a bed. So get really wasted, then hit on her. When she takes you home, bang her good and you'll have a place to stay for the rest of the trip.

➤ OPTION #4: *Get Arrested*

Okay, it's not exactly how you wanted to spend your little vacation, but at least you'll have a place to stay and hopefully three squares a day. That's better than most of the natives in Cabo, so consider yourself lucky.

THE MOST OUTRAGEOUS PLACES TO CRASH:

- On a giant peach
- In the wardrobe to Narnia
- In a shoe with an old biatch
- Graceland
- Never, Neverland
- The Statue of Liberty
- In a whale

144. You're Sleeping on the Beach and Your Friends Use Sunblock to Draw Phallic Shapes on You

Everyone knows when you drink in the sun you get drunk faster. You'll also get burned, and if you pass out around your drunk, immature friends, don't be surprised if you wake up with the tan lines of a giant dick on your face.

The WTF Approach to Dealing with F*#!-ing Dick Friends

➤ OPTION #1: *Self-Tanner*

Apply the lotion on the outline of the dick and blend it in with your current tan.

➤ OPTION #2: *Embrace It*

Make it your thing and have everyone call you Dick. Then act like one so people think you're cool.

for the ladies . . .

If this happens to you, just be thankful that it's just the tan lines of a dick and not a real dick on your face. Odds are if you pass out drunk in the sun on Spring Break that might actually happen!

➤ OPTION #3: *Play It Off*

Tell everyone it's a birthmark and play the sympathy card. Some chick with a good heart (and a love of cock) might take pity on you.

➤ OPTION #4: *Get Even*

They fucked with the wrong freshman. Drug them and carve "I love dick" into their chest and back using an ice pick. Not enough to kill them, but enough so that when they wake up they'll wish they were dead.

COLLEGE KID QUOTES

❝I woke up with a big schlong on my face. I mean, not a real one, like a drawing of one. No seriously, it wasn't like a real one.❞

—Anthony Depala, grad student at Princeton University

IN THE FUTURE . . .

Get tattoos all over, including your face. This way your friends won't be able to create inappropriate tan lines. Of course, you will look like a freaky piece of shit but at least you won't have a dick on your face.

145. You Get Arrested for No Good Reason

Spring Break has begun. The drinking, the girls, the sun. This is going to be a twenty-four-hour party, until you try to inconspicuously pull down your pants to take a piss and get arrested for indecent exposure and drunken misconduct. Now the only "happy hour" you know is the one hour a day you're not getting ass raped.

The WTF Approach to Beating Those F*#!-ing Foreign Charges

> **OPTION #1: *Wait It Out***

Unless you have committed some serious crime, most college kids who are arrested during Spring Break get released within twenty-four to forty-eight hours.

> **OPTION #2: *Flip the Switch***

Call a lawyer and tell the police that you plan on suing the shit out of them for sexual harassment, slander, and emotional damages. Then call *Jerry Springer* and tell them what "happy hour" means in Mexican prison.

> **OPTION #3: *Break Out***

Take off all your clothes; tie them together to make a long rope. Then attach your belt to the end. Throw the homemade rope out and knock down the keys. Drag them to you and break out. Wait . . .

that was an episode of *The Brady Bunch*. Forget it, you're fucked!

➤ OPTION #4: *Pay Off the Cops*

The good thing about corrupt countries that arrest you for nothing half the time is that you can get out for pennies. Throw them a few bucks and go home. Here's a rough estimate as to what it takes to get pardoned by *policía corrupta*:

- Drunk in public: $1
- Vandalism: $2
- Theft: $3
- Murder: $4—plus a $2 international processing fee if you kill an American

---

COLLEGE KID QUOTE

"The only day out of my Spring Break I remembered, was Spring Break court, because I was semi-sober there."

—Jonathon Freeman, senior at University of Nevada

HOW YOU SPEND YOUR TIME ON SPRING BREAK

50%	drinking
10%	screwing
20%	bragging about all the chicks you scored
10%	vomiting and swearing never to drink again
10%	unaccounted time due to blackout

SPRING BREAK COURT

Did you know that many places have set up Spring Break courts? Yep, Spring Break court is where you have a quick trial and you carry out the sentence (usually community service) with a group of other Spring Breakers who committed a similar crime. This translates to cleaning the streets or the outside of the bars that kids partied in the night before. It sucks, but you are done quickly and usually don't have to pay a fine.

146. You Lose Your Passport and Can't Get Back in the Country

Well, Spring Break is over and after a week of nonstop boozing, smoking, and the occasional blackout, you're looking forward to getting home to rest. But just as you get to the airport, you realize that somewhere in your drunken travels you lost your passport. WTF?

The WTF Approach to Breaking Back into the F*#!-ing Country

➤ STEP #1: *Call Your Parents*

Have them come and get you. They should have your birth certificate and other proof of your citizenship. If they don't have your birth certificate, then they don't love you or you were adopted, in which case you don't want to go home anyway.

➤ STEP #2: *Live in the Airport*

If it's good enough for Tom Hanks, it's good enough for you. You have everything you need in an airport. Plus, you can bang hot chicks and you'll never have to see them again. That beats college.

➤ **STEP #3: *Learn the Language***

It looks like this is your new home for now, so you better learn to communicate with the locals. Get a job and a place to stay. Maybe one day you'll see your family and friends again.

➤ **STEP #4: *Cross Illegally***

When you've finally tired of tequila and dysentery, do what thousands of Mexicans do all the time. Hire a coyote—a guide that will take you over the river and through the desert—and head to the Promised Land. Then get a job bussing tables or picking strawberries until you save up enough money to get the rest of the way home.

Nontraditional Spring Break Destinations

For those of you who are sick of Daytona Beach and Cancun, there are other more exotic places to go for Spring Break.

Here are the top five worldwide destinations:

1. **Thailand.** Want to have more sex in the sun than you could possibly imagine? Bangkok makes Cancun look like New Hampshire—in the winter. Why do you think they call it Bangkok? Because that's all they know how to do.
2. **Rio.** Ever seen that *City of God* movie? Doesn't that look fun?
3. **Australia.** Sun, surf, blondes. It's like California but with fucked-up English-type accents.
4. **Tokyo.** These little people like to party big. Enjoy some sake and some sucky at the same time!
5. **Amsterdam.** Legal prostitution. Legal marijuana. Little cute Jewish girls who like to keep diaries while hiding from Nazis. What more could you want?

147. Your Dad Wants You to Pledge His Frat but It's Full of Losers

You have been wearing Kappa Phi T-shirts and sweatshirts ever since you were a little kid. Your father has recounted his glory days as a Kappa Phi countless times, and ever since you can remember you were expected to be a Kappa Phi too. One problem, the Kappa Phi chapter at your school is a bunch of nerds. Dungeons & Dragons-playing, Trekkie-loving, computer-center nerds, and if you ever want to get a date in college you can't pledge this fraternity.

The WTF Approach to Pledging a F*#!-ing Nerd Frat

➤ **OPTION #1: *Tell Dad the Truth***

Just explain that you love him and you're sure his Kappa Phi was amazing and there is no way your experience could ever live up to his if you pledge this chapter. If he still doesn't get it, invite him up for the weekend to introduce him to the fraternity at your school.

When he sees that the all-night toga parties are now late-night discussions of Aristotle, he'll understand.

➤ **OPTION #2: *Pimp Your Frat***

Do an Extreme Makeover: Fraternity Edition. Once you're a brother, start changing the image of this fraternity for the better. They can still have their Dungeons & Dragons nights, just add a couple kegs, a stripper, and you got a party.

> **PROFESSOR TIP:** Rent *Revenge of the Nerds*.

➤ **OPTION #3: *Transfer to Another School***

If your father is dead set on you becoming a Kappa Phi, this might be your only option.

Most Exclusive Fraternities

These are great fraternities but very difficult to get into:

Kappa Big Cocks: must be nine inches or more to pledge . . . very popular at Howard University

Theta Eskimos: have to be able to field dress a polar bear

Delta Pulitzer Prize Winners: if you can't write, forget it!

Phi Gamma Giants: under seven foot need not apply

PROS AND CONS OF GOING GREEK

Pros	Cons
Meet lots of people	Hazing
Parties	Being part of a herd
Working with others for a common goal	Pledging is a huge time commitment
Parties	Living with a bunch of dudes

148. Your Frat Strands You in the Middle of Nowhere

It's common knowledge that fraternities haze their pledges. One little prank they like to pull is to leave the pledges in the middle of nowhere without any money or a phone. Hysterical, right?

The WTF Approach to Finding Your F*#!-ing Way

> **OPTION #1:** *Man Up*

Start walking. Forrest Gump ran across the whole country, and he was an idiot. So you can make it a few miles. Use this time by yourself to think about all the fun you'll have when you get to torture the next batch of pledges.

> **OPTION #2:** *Hitch a Ride*

You have two thumbs—use them. People used to hitchhike across the country all the time. But be careful about accepting rides from long-haul truckers. They just love dem fresh young boys.

> **OPTION #3:** *Fake Your Own Death*

Turn your back on school, your friends, your family and start over with a new identity—and no student loans.

149. You Finally Move In to the Frat House and It's a Dump

After weeks of torture and hazing you have made it into the brotherhood. You can now sit back and enjoy all the perks of belonging to a fraternity, including living in the frat house. One problem though—the house is a total shit can! There is garbage everywhere, holes in the walls, mold on the ceiling, and fuzzy food in every corner of the house as well as what appears to be a human fetus on the couch. What's worse is that nobody seems to care. Sure you survived Hell Week, but will you survive living in this hellhole?

The WTF Approach to Living in F*#!-ing Filth

➤ **OPTION #1:** *Call in the Pros*

Hire a cleaning crew of hot, half-naked girls. Believe it or not, there is such a thing. Imagine: Hot girls in little French maid outfits, waxing your candlesticks. If every brother chips in a little cash, you'll be able to afford it—no guy is going to fight this one unless he's gay, in which case you'll probably find a way to throw him out of the frat. Once you see these girls on their hands and knees sucking up the dirt, it will all be worth it. Of course there'll probably be another mess to clean up after.

➤ OPTION #2: *Make the Pledges Do It*

Shit, that's what they're there for. They should be cleaning night and day. How else will they learn about brotherhood?

➤ OPTION #3: *Move*

If it's not required to live in the fraternity house, get your own place. Maybe you can room with another not-so-disgusting brother. Odds are you'll probably get laid more. No girl wants to screw you in a room with vomit in it.

➤ OPTION #4: *Deal with It*

You're in college for Christ's sake. Join the fun and stop being a whiny pussy. Men are programmed to be slobs. And you want to be a man, don't you?

➤ OPTION #5: *Screw It*

Become an addict. If you're high 24/7 you won't give a shit about anything else. Careful not to overdose and die though—if the place really is a shit hole, they might never find your body.

➤ OPTION #6: *Get on* Extreme Makeover

Call ABC. Of course, they usually only help families who have suffered some traumatic event, or have gone out of their way to do good for others. So you might have to sponsor some poor, starving Ethiopian child. Or maybe tell them one of the brothers is dying and that his last wish is to see his fraternity house transformed. ABC loves that crap. However, if they do pick your house to makeover, you will have to deal with that annoying dipshit Ty Pennington.

WTF: UP CLOSE AND PERSONAL

My sister's room was always disgusting, but one month the stench was so bad that even she knew something was up. Every day it became more and more unbearable. Finally, she asked me to check her room out and see if that smell was "normal." It wasn't. In fact, I almost passed out instantly.

So she cleaned. And cleaned. And cleaned. Finally, she found the culprit of the unbearable smell under the bed: a badly decomposed bird.

Apparently, the cat dragged in a dead bird and put it under her bed. If you can imagine how gross a room has to be for someone not to notice an animal decomposing under their bed, then you have a clue to just how filthy my sister is. Sorry sis, 'tis the truth.

—GB

YOUR FRAT HOUSE MIGHT BE WORSE THAN A THIRD WORLD COUNTRY IF . . .

❏ There are more cigarette butts around the ashtray than in the ashtray.

❏ There are more maggots and roaches living there than brothers.

❏ You're starting to like the smell of urine.

❏ You or someone you know had a tapeworm in the last six months.

❏ You have an unexplainable rash spreading all over your body.

❏ The kitchen sink is sometimes used as a second toilet.

❏ You have fallen into a pool of semen.

150. Your Fraternity Is Caught Hazing Pledges

We all know the Greeks are known for their hazing of new pledges. But most of what happens is kept on the DL. However, every once and a while you get the one crybaby pledge who runs to the dean and tattles on a fraternity. Now your frat is on probation while an investigation ensues.

The WTF Approach to Handling a F*#!-ing Hazing Charge

➤ OPTION #1: *Deny It*

Unless there's a videotape, it's just his word against you and your bros. Assure the dean that your frat just partakes in harmless fun. Then kidnap the rat, tie him down, and force him to drink a mixture of lukewarm beer and hot piss.

➤ OPTION #2: *Call in the Big Guns*

Most fraternities are national. Call in the national representatives to deal with the situation. You have better things to do, like beating the shit out of more pledges.

➤ OPTION #3: *Change Your Ways*

Take the lead in publicly apologizing for the hazing that goes on at your frat. Become the John Kerry of fraternity pledging (we all know how well his outspokenness against the Vietnam War worked out for him!). Go around the country and preach about the dangers of hazing. Write a book, get on *Oprah*, and eventually get a show of your own. Then haze all of your guests.

> **NOTE:** *WTF* does not support or encourage hazing of any kind . . . unless, of course, it's really funny.

Cool Hazing Ideas

Make your pledge . . .

- Eat a bowl of cereal laced with thirty hits of LSD.
- Pull his own eyelashes out one at a time
- Listen to *Phantom of the Opera* or anything by Andrew Lloyd Webber over and over again
- Cut off his balls and eat them while humming "God Bless America"

Hazing in the Ivy League

Sometimes the spoiled rich kids haze their pledges in different ways from regular common folk.

Rich brothers in frats often make pledges:

- Drink white wine with meat in red sauce, and red wine with chicken in white sauce
- Register as a Democrat
- Suspend fencing lessons for up to a month
- Publicly reject the notion that Ronald Reagan won the Cold War
- Cancel their lifetime subscription to the J. Peterman catalog

for the ladies . . .

If by hazing you mean you circle the fat on your pledges, then please by all means continue. A lot of horny college guys depend on taking advantage of these emotionally damaged girls. Mess them up psychologically as much as you can so we can benefit!

Asian Student Hazing

Predominately Asian frats haze their pledges in slightly different ways than their Caucasian counterparts. Asian frats often coerce pledges to:

- Work on excruciatingly elementary and unchallenging math problems.
- Call their parents and tell them they don't want to study medicine anymore.
- Tell their ancient ancestors to go fuck themselves.

Hazing No-Nos

Hazing is an indelible part of the fraternity experience. But it can go too far. Avoid these techniques:

Water boarding: Now that a new administration is in office in Washington, you might actually get in trouble for this practice.

Crucifixions: While it would be a blast to make a pledge—crowned with a ring of thorns and carrying the crucifix on his back—walk to a desolate place as you lash him with a whip, it might make the pledge out to be a martyr if some of his close friends bear witness.

The rack: A trusty hazing tool since the Inquisition, the rack might not be as accepted by the campus police or local authorities as it was by the Catholic Church.

Burning at the stake: This could get your fraternity a shitload of heat so don't even think about it.

MOST INTENSE HAZINGS IN HISTORY:

- Spanish Inquisition
- Salem Witch Hunts
- The Pogroms
- Armenian Genocide
- The Holocaust

COLLEGE KID QUOTE

"Me and the brothers once forced this kid to eat shit and then stab himself in the eye with an ice pick. That was so awesome!"

—Danny Whackostein, junior at the University of Massachusetts

151. You Find Out That You Knocked Up Your Professor

You have been sleeping with your hot professor for a few months now and things are going great. It's a fantasy and a dream come true. Except that lately you've noticed something is different about her. She's been looking a little pale and fatigued, and seems to be getting sick to her stomach every morning. Is it a passing flu or something? No. Your professor is knocked up, and you're the goddamn baby-daddy!

The WTF Approach to Coping with a Big F*#!-ing Surprise

➤ **OPTION #1:** *Man Up*

You know what you have to do, so do it. Get a job, start a savings account, and offer your unconditional support. If that sounds like no fun, go to Option #2.

➤ **OPTION #2:** *Deny It*

If you really don't want anything to do with this whole situation, deny everything. If she wants to keep her reputation, she won't do much about it, except maybe fail you. It's not like she's going bring you on *Maury* and make you take a paternity test—unless she happens to teach a class called White Trash Studies.

➤**OPTION #3: *Abort!***

It's sad. It's difficult. But it's legal. Offer to pay for it if you feel that bad. Better to pay a couple hundred bucks than a couple hundred thousand raising a kid.

for the ladies . . .

That would make absolutely no sense. Why the fuck did you even look here, dipshit?

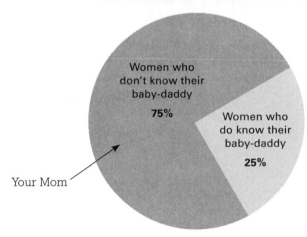

DO YOU KNOW YOUR BABY-DADDY?

Women who don't know their baby-daddy
75%

Women who do know their baby-daddy
25%

Your Mom

152. You Run into Last Night's Hookup and Forget Her Name

You had an all-night sex-a-thon with some girl you met at a party. It was great, except you can't remember her name. No biggie, it's a big school; chances are you'll never see her again . . . until you run into her on campus the next day and can't remember her name. Shit!

The WTF Approach to Filling in the F*#!-ing Blanks

➤ STEP #1: *Deflect and Distract*

Use common phrases such as "Hey you" and then pray someone calls out her name while you're talking to her.

➤ STEP #2: *Go with a Nickname*

If the conversation goes any deeper, use a cute nickname like Bunny, Cutie pie, or Cuntie. She'll be so flattered that you like her enough to come up with a pet name just for her.

➤ STEP #3: *Be Slick*

To get to the bottom of it, make her put her name and number in your phone. This is a classic way to deal with not knowing a chick's name. Tell her how happy you are to run into her again then give her your phone and tell her to put in her digits. She'll include her name no doubt as well.

➤ STEP #4: *Be Direct*

When that doesn't work, knock her purse or backpack onto the floor.

Clumsily kick it around a little and pray that student ID or license falls out, then grab it, get her name, and give it back to her.

> **NOTE:** You and your friends should come up with a code word to use when you don't remember someone's name. Upon hearing it, your buddy will introduce himself and ask her name.

Slutty Girls' Names

You can tell if a girl will be easy by her name. Use this guide so you don't waste any time:

Heather: Big time ho name. Heathers are usually blonde and either really skinny or a little chunky with huge tits.

Christy: She's been with more guys than you want to know about. Wear two rubbers.

Veronica: Brown hair, big butt and tits, massive areolas. She likes to please and loves giving head.

Jennifer: This tall California blonde runs five a day, does yoga, and keeps in impeccable shape. She has a small, upturned nose, big blue eyes, and a rack to die for. She's a hottie, but she's also a fucking dumb bitch.

Melissa: Spoiled rotten and always gets her way, this chick will do you good, but it may cost you financially and emotionally more than it's worth.

Ellen: This is the kind of girl who lies in bed and does the *New York Times* crossword puzzle while you fuck her in the ass.

Sally: Lame, brown-haired Midwestern chick who might not put out right away but when she feels comfortable she'll turn the kink way up.

Anastasia: She's an unbelievably hot Russian chick with a body that could melt a cheese sandwich in Siberia. She'll be good to you, but if you cross her she'll stab you in the back . . . literally. Don't let her scowl throw you; Russians always look pissed.

Sharanda: This ebony princess is sexy beyond anything you could ever imagine and better in bed than every other chick you've been with combined. If you didn't vote for Obama, lie and say you did.

Emily: This sweet hometown girl loves her family and the church, but she also likes pleasing her man. Get in good with her and God and she'll do whatever you say.

Rebecca: Red hair, freckles (but not too many), big green eyes and legs that go up to her neck, this hottie smells like Irish Spring . . . everywhere. She'll do you after a couple pints of Guinness if you play your cards right. Refrain from asking if the "curtains match the drapes" if you want to score.

Tasha: White trash hood rat that probably got around as a teen. She is so sexualized that having sex is the only way she can express herself. Keeper!

Crystal, Daisy, Star, Candy, Bambi, Barbi, Lexxxi, Destiny, Savannah: Strippers. All of them.

Bobbi Jo: She loves riding four-wheelers almost as much as being on all fours. Bobbi could suck the chrome off of a trailer hitch. In fact, one time when she was so bored in her trailer, she did just that.

Buffy: Buffy loves playing tennis, wearing tennis skirts even when she isn't playing tennis, and taking frequent vacations to Jamaica where she "gets away from it all" ("all" meaning her stressful life as heiress) by getting ferociously gang-banged by hordes of angry natives.

Jodi: You wish. You could never get a chick this classy and hot!

for the ladies . . .

Who cares if you forget his name? Guys couldn't give a shit if you remember their names. Now, forgetting their cock? Well, that's just plain rude.

153. Your Roommate's Girl Wants to Screw You

You both met her at a party at the same time, and you always had a sneaking suspicion that she liked you. She laughs at everything you say, she holds on a little too long when you hug her goodbye, and once in a while she'll shoot you a look that sends a shiver down your spine and puts your cock in overdrive. These little flirtations were harmless, just good college fun. That is, until one night when she whispers in your ear, "I want to toss your fucking salad!" WTF?

The WTF Approach to Handling Your Roommate's Horny F*#!-ing Girl

➤ OPTION #1: *Do It*

This is college, okay? Turning down pussy is a big no-no. In fact, you could even say it is immoral.

➤ OPTION #2: *Just Say No*

If you happen to be governed by a different set of ethical principles (you are free to do as you please, though we strenuously object), then you might want to reconsider butt-fucking your roommate's girlfriend behind his back. Either keep your mouth shut or tell your roommate that his chick is after you. Then, take the first in a series of cold showers and cry like a baby for what you have given up.

HOW HOT IS SHE?

Since you can justify and rationalize whatever you decide to do (this is the beauty of being the shithead that you are), you might as well determine whether or not to face-fuck your roomie's girl according to how hot she is. Here's a hot scale to help you decide whether she's worth the trouble, with 1 being "maybe" and 10 being "fuck yes":

1. Hot enough to have sex with drunk

2. Hot enough to have sex with sober

3. Hot enough to masturbate to

4. Hot enough to masturbate to every night

5. So hot that you can't stop thinking about her

6. So hot that you get a hard-on just thinking about her

7. So hot that you'd give her a rim job if she wanted one

8. So hot that you'd beg her to let you give her a rim job

9. So hot that you'd let her pee on you

10. So hot that if you found out she had a dick you'd overlook it

COLLEGE TEN COLLEGE COMMANDMENTS:

I. Thou shalt NOT turn down good pussy . . . *ever.*

II. Thou shalt NOT study until the very last night before an exam.

III. Thou shalt eat shitty food and become a fat ass.

IV. Thou shalt remember thy pledge night and keep it holy.

V. Thou shalt NOT kill thy neighbor's beer.

VI. Thou shalt NOT date rape a chick that's passed out.

VII. Thou shalt NOT steal thy roommate's socks just because you can't find yours.

VIII. Thou shalt do as many mind-altering substances as humanly possible.

IX. Thou shalt NOT rat out thy neighbor unless he date raped that passed-out chick.

X. Thou shalt NOT covet thy neighbor's weed.

154. You're One of Ten Competing for Your Dream Internship

It's your senior year and it's time to prepare for life after college. You just found out that one of the best companies in your field is accepting applications for an internship position. This is just what you need, but when you go to drop off your resume, you find out there are at least ten other students from your school applying for the coveted position, many of whom are more qualified than you. Shit!

The WTF Approach to Securing the F*#!-ing Spot

➤ OPTION #1: *Flood the HR Department with Resumes*

Have you and your friends send in a ton of very impressive resumes under different names and then schedule a bunch of interviews, only to flake. This might convince them that a great resume isn't the most important thing in a candidate, giving you and your shitty one a shot if you can score the interview.

PROFESSOR TIP: If you get the interview, wear a suit with a power tie and look the guy or girl who is doing the hiring in the eye. Nobody knows how to interview people, and usually getting the position or not depends on bullshit like that. Also, read Dale Carnegie's *How to Make Friends and Influence People.* Maybe this will help you ace the interview. If nothing else, you can at least say that you read one book this semester.

➤ OPTION #2: *Lie*

We've told you this several times, and we cannot be more serious: nobody checks a resume! All they do at most is call your references. Get your friends Vinny and Joey to pretend to be whoever you want from whatever company you want. All they need to do is change their cell phone message for a couple days. This is not rocket science. Never let a bad resume stop you from applying to whatever job or internship you want.

➤ OPTION #3: *Come Clean*

Simply state your case. If you're an honest putz and there is nothing we can do to corrupt you, come clean in your cover letter that, while there may be more qualified candidates than you, it has been your dream since childhood to intern for a paper distribution company and you will do anything for this opportunity.

➤ OPTION #4: *Bribe Them*

Send gifts to secretaries and the HR people at the company—baked goods, bottles of wine, or a stripper if the internship is for a stockbroker trainee. Everyone knows stockbrokers love strip clubs.

DREAM INTERNSHIPS FOR COLLEGE STUDENTS:

- Medical marijuana tester
- Towel boy for girls' locker room
- Adult film reviewer
- Assistant to campus gynecologist
- *Girls Gone Wild* cameraman

WHAT THE F*#! IS UP WITH . . . FIRST JOBS

What is up with the fact that every job requires experience, even for an entry-level position? How the hell are you supposed to get experience if you need it to get a job in the first place? Even some internships say they prefer the candidate to have experience. It's a fucking internship! This is the Catch 22 of getting your first job—you need to have experience to get one, but you can't get experience without having a job. WTF?

---

155. You're Graduating with a Degree in Art History

It's a week till graduation and you're ready to get out there and make your way in the world. One problem: You have a degree in art history. So unless you are planning on becoming a professor or work in an art gallery, you're screwed.

The WTF Approach to Graduating with a F*#!-ing BS Degree

➤ **OPTION #1:** *Become a Famous Artist*

Even if you can only draw stick figures this can be accomplished. Art is subjective. Making it big has more to do with how you dress, where you hang out, and your personal mystique than it does the quality of your art. Remember, art history effectively ended with Andy Warhol and Pop Art, so there is nothing you can do that is new and interesting. Toss your cat in some paint, let him walk around on a canvas, sign your name, and hang it up somewhere in Manhattan with a $50,000 price tag. Rest assured, some jackass will buy it.

➤ **OPTION #2:** *Go Back to School*

Go back and get your masters. Then your PhD, then your postdoctoral. You'll be the most educated person you know. Sure, you'll still be a curator at the local museum, but at least you'll know your Monet from your Manet.

➤ **OPTION #3:** *Backpack through Europe*

Go to France, study art, bang some French girls, and eat croissants. The art degree will be very impressive over there. Europeans love useless shit.

CAREERS YOU CAN GET WITH A USELESS DEGREE:

- Pharmaceutical rep
- Bank teller
- Nurse
- Police officer
- Truck driver
- Legal assistant
- Bookkeeper
- Advertising salesperson
- Drug dealer

NOTE: If you have to resort to any of the above careers why did you go to college in the first place?

COLLEGE IS NO LAUGHING MATTER

"I have a friend who owns a Picasso painting. I'm ashamed to tell him it's been hanging upside down for nine years."
—Jackie Mason

156. After Four Years of Partying—It's Time for the Real World

It's been a long, fun ride and one that you might have taken for granted. You learned a little, and partied a lot. Now it's time to graduate and get a job. Congratulations, welcome to the real world. It blows.

The WTF Approach to Life After F*#!-ing Graduating

➤ OPTION #1: *Go Back to School*

That's right, stay a student as long as you can. People tend to expect less from you when you're a student. Don't disappoint them.

➤ OPTION #2: *Deal with It*

We've all been there—that "what the fuck am I supposed to do now" feeling. Well, now you have a degree, so go get a job. (We mean when there actually *are* jobs out there, that is.) You can always be the guy who's in his thirties but still goes to college parties. You'll probably get more action—or at least have money for better weed.

➤ OPTION #3: *Join the Military*

Sure, the military is not like it used to be. You can't join the Reserves and putz around with guns every fourth weekend of the month. You'll end up in Iraq or Afghanistan. But at least you'll get to drive a tank to work instead of taking the subway. Commuting is such a drag.

for the ladies . . .

Do what you are expected to do. Get a job, marry some guy, and quit to take care of the baby. When he inevitably leaves you for a younger woman and splits town to avoid child support payments, go back to work and live a shitty life as a single mom. Better yet, sue your superior for sexual harassment and live off the settlement.

➤ OPTION #4: *Write a Book*

It served us well. We'll never do *real* work again.

➤ OPTION #5: *Kill Yourself*

We've suggested you off other people to get your point across, now it's time to turn on yourself. Take the hint. Hopefully if this book sells we can afford the lawsuit. Seriously, bro—do it!

➤ OPTION #6: *Take a Trip*

Search your soul and backpack through Europe, or better yet, somewhere cheaper and shittier. Make sure to write down what you mistakenly believe are interesting insights about the cultural differences in a little journal like every other backpacking piece of shit.

WORK IS NO LAUGHING MATTER

"My father taught me to work; he did not teach me to love it."—Abraham Lincoln

"I only go to work on days that don't end in a 'y.'"—Robert Paul

"A good rule of thumb is if you've made it to thirty-five and your job still requires you to wear a name tag, you've made a serious vocational error."—Dennis Miller

"The reason why worry kills more people than work is that more people worry than work."—Robert Frost

"Hard work never killed anybody, but why take a chance?"—Edgar Bergen

Chapter 3

WTF?
Work

How to Survive 48 of the
Office's Worst F*#!-ing Situations

157. You Have No Qualifications

People always say that if you do something you love, the money will follow. But what if you only love to jerk off and play video games? After years of school and thousands of dollars in student loans, you still have no useful, marketable skills. How the hell are you ever going to land a job?

The WTF Approach to Having No F*#!-ing Qualifications

> ➤ **OPTION #1:** *Lie*

Everyone does. It's the American way. And if you're not an American, then shame on you for trying to take our jobs. Get out and stay out!

> ➤ **OPTION #2:** *Go Back to School*

When people ask what you do you can always say that you are "in school." Now you have an excuse to be a loser, albeit an extremely educated one.

> ➤ **OPTION #3:** *Offer a Bribe*

Find out who is in charge of hiring and start sending gifts like pots of jam, fruit baskets, and whores— standard stuff. They'll probably admire your determination and hire you on the spot.

> ➤ **OPTION #4:** *Marry the Boss's Daughter*

Find the richest son-of-a-bitch you can and start nailing his little girl.

Make sure to knock her up to seal the deal. He'll get you a job at his business in no time so you can take care of her. Then, once you are bored with her, dump her, and collect half in the divorce settlement. If he fires you out of rage, sue him for even more cash.

How to Creatively Doctor Your Resume

There are ways to make even the most innocuous work experience sound more significant. Take a look at these examples to see how you can get creative with your past experience:

BEFORE	AFTER
Raked leaves	Landscape architect
Babysitter	Early education administrator
Worked at a fast-food drive-through	Food service manager
Planned friend's bachelor party in Vegas	Event coordinator
Chronic masturbator	Massage therapist

HEADHUNTER'S TIP

Positive action verbs make your resume achievements sound even more impressive. Use these on your resume:

- Accomplished
- Analyzed
- Anticipated
- Applied
- Appointed
- Appraised
- Approved
- Awarded

NOTE: You can also look up some *B* words, but we both know you are too damn lazy.

158. You're Over-Qualified but You Need the Job

You're having a hard time trying to find a gig that is commensurate with your experience. But the job market's tough. You need the work so bad that you're willing to put aside your pride and take a pay cut. The only problem is your stellar resume keeps getting rejected even for these bullshit jobs. WTF? Don't they know that this is way beneath you and they should be lucky to have you? Don't they know that they will never find someone as qualified as you for this position? Don't they know that they should actually get down on their goddamn knees and thank God that you would even consider applying for a job at their company? Well, apparently not, hot shot.

The WTF Approach to Getting a Job That Is F*#!-ing Beneath You

➤ **OPTION #1: *Dumb Down Your Resume***

We've all lied to beef up our resume to make it more impressive (if you haven't then perhaps you should start), so why do the opposite and lie to make your resume *less* impressive? For example, if the position you are applying for is as an assistant, take out the shit about your managerial experience. Get creative. If you put your mind to it you can be working a really shitty, depressing job in no time.

➤ **OPTION #2:** *Get a Lobotomy*

If you are such an egghead that you can't hide your innate genius and über-developed skill-set no matter how hard you try, then you might have to get part of your brain cut out. Sure, you might not be the wittiest guy at the water cooler, but it's better than being the smartest guy at the homeless shelter.

HEADHUNTER'S TIP

If you do become a complete vegetable incapable of even the most basic thought, we suggest you apply immediately for a position as CEO of a major financial institution. You'll do superbly by comparison—just by doing absolutely fucking nothing.

How to Dumb Down Your Resume

You don't have to start from scratch. Change the wording of your responsibilities to make them seem less impressive.

Original Version: Spearheaded marketing initiatives designed to maximize company sales
Dumbed Down Version: Hired moronic telemarketers off craigslist to peddle inane product

Original Version: Able to multitask in high-paced environment with tight turnaround
Dumbed Down Version: Somehow managed to turn in work even though I spent most of my time making personal calls while I checked my Facebook account and planned my next jerk-off session in the restroom

Original Version: Forged key synergistic partnerships based on comprehensive market analysis
Dumbed Down Version: I don't really remember what I actually did there, but I have references who say that I was good if you want to call them

159. Your Resume Sucks Balls

There you are hitting the pavement day in and day out. You are looking high and low for a job, any job. You have sent out your resume to over 1,000 listings. Not one phone call. So you decide to take control and call one of the companies to find out what is going on. When you get the head of HR on the phone, she starts laughing. "Oh," she says, "we thought this was a joke." Turns out your resume blows and even McDonald's won't consider you.

The WTF Approach to Sprucing Up Your F*#!-ing Resume

➤ OPTION #1: *Steal Someone Else's Resume*

Shit, you probably cheated off the smart kids in school anyway—this is the same thing. Ask to look at one of your friend's resumes then copy it. Or better yet, pose as a company and place a fake ad looking for the position you want. Collect all the resumes that come in then pick the most impressive and copy that.

➤ OPTION #2: *Buy One*

Go one online and pay a professional to write it. Or better yet just pay another kind of professional to rid you of all your anxiety—and we don't mean a therapist.

➤ OPTION #3: *Protest*

March in front of the companies
that won't grant you an interview. You might end up on cable
news and become a celebrity—
the voice of a disenfranchised
generation.

Things You Shouldn't Include on Your Resume

- Violent felonies
- Weird hobbies like necrophilia
  or stamp collecting
- A nude photograph (unless
  you're really hung)
- A list of your favorite Polish
  jokes

HEADHUNTER'S TIP

If you still can't come up with some qualifications, try beefing up your resume by
adding *anything* positive about yourself.
Examples:

- Non-smoker
- Good at pinball
- Tall

Sample Cover Letter—Mad Libs Style

_____

[Your Name]

_____

[Your Address]

_____ • _____

[Your Phone Number]   [Your E-mail Address]

_____

[Person in Charge]

_____

[Name of Company]

_____

[Their Address]

Dear _____ ,

[Person in Charge]

I am interested in learning more about and establishing my qualifications for

your available position, which I found through _____ .

[Stupid Internet Website]

I believe I am aptly suited to work within your organization. As a

_____ at _____ I managed to _____

[Former Shitty Position]   [Former Shitty Company]   [First Lie]

significantly. As an employee, I am _____ .

[List of Fictitious Attributes]

Finally, I am a _____ worker and believe that my qualifications

[Huge Lie]

and personal attributes will enable me to excel in this position.

Sincerely,

_____

[Your Name Followed by PhD]

Resumes from Hell

It could be worse. Your resume could look like one of these people's . . .

Adolf Hitler

112 Escaped Nazi Road, Buenos Aires, Argentina
Adolf@JewFreeWorld.net

OBJECTIVE

To attain a position in the genocide industry in which I can demonstrate my knowledge and experience in the extermination of whole populations from the face of the earth.

WORK HISTORY

STRUGGLING ARTIST (1905 TO PRESENT)
Self-Employed
Austria, Germany, and now Argentina
Painted amateurish watercolor landscapes of Jew-free meadows and brooks.

COAUTHOR, MEIN KAMPF (1923 TO JAN. 1924)
Eher-Verlag (Eher-Publishing)
Prison cell somewhere in Germany
Wrote poignant treatise calling for enslavement and/or removal of Jews and other sub-humans, as well as the development of a revitalized German Empire.

I am currently working on *Mein Kampf . . . for Kids!* scheduled for release this fall. In addition, I am working on Spanish language version for distribution in my adopted country of Argentina titled *Mi Kampf Es Su Kampf* (also set for an autumn release).

DER FUHRER (JAN. 1933 TO APRIL 1945)
Third Reich
Berlin, Germany

Accomplishments included:
* Killed a lot of Jews
* Killed a lot of Russians
* Killed a lot of Poles
* Killed a lot of Homosexuals
* Killed a lot of Gypsies

EDUCATION
High School Dropout
Austria, 1933

MEMBERSHIPS
* Future Fuhrers of Austria and Greater Germany
* Nazi War Criminal Glee Club
* Big Brothers for wayward (but racially pure) German youths

LANGUAGE SKILLS
German (and un poco Español)

REFERENCES
* Eva Braun
* Heinrich Himmler

Lucifer
666 Eternal Damnation Road, Hell
Devil@EnjoyYourStayinHellLOL.com

OBJECTIVE
To attain a position back in heaven; I miss it there.

WORK HISTORY

ANGEL (DAWN OF MANKIND TO FALL FROM HEAVEN)
Heaven
Performed various services for God, including acting as a messenger for His word. I admittedly lost my way and was therefore cast down from heaven. In my defense, I was drinking a lot at the time. I have been clean and sober now for over five millennia.

SATAN, THE DEVIL, SUPREME LEADER OF HELL (AFTER FALL FROM HEAVEN TO PRESENT)
Hell
Responsibilities included corrupting the virtuous, destroying goodness wherever it lurked, and generally fucking up the world and turning man against man to the best of my ability. If you want to know the truth (not that I'm big on honesty LOL), it wasn't that difficult.

Accomplishments included:
Jesus, where do I start? I have done so much over the last 10,000 years it's almost impossible to sum up. From famines to genocides to making that little bitch's head spin around in *The Exorcist*, I have had an indelible impact in human history. (I'm not boasting here—though vanity is one of the seven deadly sins and you know how I feel about those!)

Here are some highlights of my work:
- The slave trade
- The Holocaust
- Wars (All of them!)
- AIDS
- Investment banking

EDUCATION
Angel Trade School Diploma
Heaven, Dawn of Mankind

MEMBERSHIPS
- Satanists of America (duh!)
- Hell Health & Racquet Club

SPECIAL TALENTS
- Ability to shape shift
- Flying
- Can touch nose with the tip of my tongue

REFERENCES
- Adolf Hitler
- Idi Amin
- Bernie Madoff

160. You Don't Have the Proper Attire for the Interview

Dress for success. It's a phrase you've probably heard before, and if you haven't, then you're probably a poorly dressed loser. The first impression is a lasting impression, so put your best foot forward—preferably covered in some decent dress shoes.

The WTF Approach to Looking like a F*#!-ing Human Being

➤ OPTION #1: *Goodwill*

There's a place for schmucks like you, it's called Goodwill. True, you'll probably only find a plaid suit from the 1970s, but it's better than wearing your favorite T-shirt that reads: I Like Pussy.

➤ OPTION #2: *Beg, Borrow, Steal*

Not necessarily in that order. You should probably try to borrow first. If that fails, get on your hands and knees and beg in the street for change. If you can't get enough—even for a Goodwill leisure suit—find a way to steal one. Don't worry about the morality of it, you'll pay for it when you get the job.

➤ OPTION #3: *Get Creative*

Design and sew a suit out of your old pairs of pants. Wait. If you actually had a marketable skill like that, you'd probably own at least one decent suit already.

➤ OPTION #4: *Wing It*

Just buy a clip-on tie and smile, dumbass. Though it's best to be overdressed for an interview, if you present yourself with a certain confidence being underdressed can actually work in your favor. It says, "I'm too good for this and I don't give a shit; you're lucky to even have me interview at this shit hole." Often times really, really, rich and successful people play it down. Just wear a polo shirt and khakis like some spoiled, "old" money, East Coast WASP and talk about how much you like sailing and voting Republican.

HEADHUNTER'S TIP

Just because it's better to be over-dressed than underdressed for an inter-view doesn't mean you should wear a tux with tails and a top hat. It just means that you should try not to look like a fucking scumbag for once in your life.

Dress for Success: Matching Game

Each profession has a different dress code. See if you can match the proper attire to its corresponding profession.

1.	Double-breasted Italian suit	A.	English professor and/or child rapist
2.	White short-sleeve shirt and tie with cartoon characters on it	B.	Conservative prick
3.	Corduroy jacket with elbow patches	C.	Mafia boss
4.	Suit and red tie	D.	Wal-Mart manager
5.	Astronaut uniform	E.	Astronaut

ANSWER KEY

1. C, **2.** D, **3.** A, **4.** B, **5.** E

161. You Show Up Hung Over to the Interview

It was only supposed to be a quick beer then off to bed early. And you did just have one beer—followed by twelve shots of tequila, a bottle of wine, and two bong hits to wash everything down. After that, the party really got started. Now you are headed to your interview with a pounding headache and the taste of tequila and toothpaste in your mouth.

The WTF Approach to Dealing with a F*#!-ing Hangover

➤ STEP #1: *Boot and Rally*

You know you always feel better after you vomit. (Plus, you drop a few pounds.) Before you head to the receptionist's desk, head to the bushes and let last night's partying fertilize the company's garden.

➤ STEP #2: *Start Drinking, Again*

If your puke session didn't make you feel better, it's time for the hair of the dog, baby. Excuse yourself to the restroom, then run out of the building and find the nearest liquor store. Buy a bottle of whatever you drank last night and take a few power swigs. That should get you through the interview. Buy some gum while you're at it too, shit breath!

➤ **STEP #3:** *Keep the Party Going*

Once you start to tank the interview (you do smell like vomit and tequila), break out the bottle you bought at the store and do some shots with your interviewer. Chances are they'll decline and probably either tell you to leave or have you arrested. But fuck it, at least you'll go out in style.

Signs You're Hung Over from a Crazy Night

- Dehydration
- Dry mouth
- Fatigue
- Headache
- Sore in strange places

HEADHUNTER'S TIP

Make sure you get a lot of sleep before an important interview. If you are a heavy drinker, drink during the day and go to bed early. After all, if you're going to an interview chances are you have no job anyway and are a loser, providing ample time during business hours to get shit faced.

IN THE FUTURE . . .

Avoid hangovers; stay drunk—always.

162. You Realize You Had Sex with the Interviewer and Never Called Her Back

You recognized the chick interviewing you immediately. Where have you seen her before? Hmm. You rack your brain. Those eyes, those lips, those perky breasts, that camel toe; they all ring a bell but you just don't know why. Then it hits you like a ton of bricks: You banged her after meeting in a bar and then never called her back. Now she's got you by the balls . . . again.

The WTF Approach to Lying to Your F*#!-ing Interviewer

➤ STEP #1: *Play Dumb*

If she doesn't recognize you, then you're golden. Of course, this means that sleeping with you is not memorable, which is a bit of a downer. But at least you can avoid any confrontation. If she does recognize you, move on to Step #2.

➤ STEP #2: *Make Up a Story*

Time to put those lying skills into action. However, we know how good you are at thinking on your feet, so here are a few stories to memorize for such situations.

OPTION A: IT HURT *SO* BAD

Tell her that you were scared because you liked her so much and you were afraid to get hurt. Then really lay it on thick by saying she reminds you of your ex fiancé who was killed in a tragic accident and that the one night of drunken sex—great as it was—brought up too much pain.

OPTION B: OFF-THE-WAGON ACCIDENT

Say that you were blackout drunk. Sell her on a sob story about how you had been sober for ten years, but fell off the wagon that night. Remember to reassure her that you are clean again and plan on staying that way so she doesn't hold it against you.

OPTION C: FLIP THE SWITCH

Tell her you did call, but the number was disconnected and you were so pissed and hurt that she gave you a fake number. Tell her that she really hurt your feelings.

When she begins to deny it tell her that you would like to be interviewed by someone else because looking at her is too painful. She will be so moved she'll hire you on the spot. Then bang her again out of gratitude.

for the ladies . . .

Here are the top five reasons why that guy never called you back:

1. He has a girlfriend.
2. He has a boyfriend.
3. Your vagina is stinky.
4. You don't know how to give head.
5. He is a guy.

163. You Can't Stop Staring at Your Interviewer's Massive Deformity

They liked your resume. The preliminary phone interview went well. And now you're in the door. Yes, you are just a smile and a handshake away from getting the job. But before you can charm your new boss into hiring you, you'll have to get through the first level of interviews with the HR person. But there's one problem. This "person" might not even be a person at all. She is a monster with a face so deformed she looks like the singer Seal had a baby with an actual seal—and then that baby's neck threw up. Whatever you do, don't stare or she'll catch you. Shit, you already did! Did she notice? She *must* have; you stared right at it. Shit, you looked again! What the fuck is that thing?!

The WTF Approach to Dealing with a F*#!-ing Repulsive Deformity

➤ STEP #1: *Keep Eye Contact*

Look your interviewer directly in the eyes. You should be doing this anyway in order to appear confident and build a rapport with the grossly disfigured pig-person.

➤ STEP #2: *Blur Your Vision*

If you make a slight adjustment to your vision to make the beast appear out of focus and fuzzy, it might help you stop staring at her monstrous deformity. Make sure you don't cross your eyes, however, or you will be the one that appears the most freakish.

➤ STEP #3: *Think of* **Schindler's List**

If you are on the verge of laughter and you can't seem to control it, think of the most depressing scene from the most depressing movie ever. Liam Neeson's departure from the factory at the end of *Schindler's List* is a good one, when he breaks down and realizes that he could have saved more lives. (If you actually *were* in the Holocaust, then you probably have an even more depressing scene of your own to recall.)

➤ STEP #4: *Compliment It*

If it is too late and you are certain that she saw you staring, compliment the interviewer on whatever disgusting disfigurement she has. If it's a big fat hairy mole, tell her she has a beauty mark that reminds you of Cindy Crawford. If it's a scar, tell her it makes her look exotic and dangerous. If she's a severely scarred burn victim, tell her that you used to want to be a fireman when you were a kid.

164. You Realize You Have No Idea What You're Doing

Well, you bullshitted your way through the interview process, got the salary you asked for, and have now started your new job. There's only one problem: You have no fucking clue what you are doing.

The WTF Approach to Getting a F*#!-ing Clue

➤ **OPTION #1: *Stare at the Screen***

That's it, just like that. Eventually it'll come to you.

➤ **OPTION #2: *Fake It 'til You Make It***

Just look around and start spying on what your coworkers are doing, and then follow suit. Ask questions like, "Hey I notice you finish your projects so quickly, what's your secret?" Someone might be willing to share.

➤ **OPTION #3: *Start Screwing a Smart Female Coworker***

Find a girl who appears to have no life outside of work. She's probably so desperate she'll bang anyone. As you two get closer, bring up the fact that you're slightly overwhelmed at work. If you are decent in bed she'll be more than willing to help, mostly because she doesn't want you to get fired—even she doesn't like to bang the unemployed. You might not only keep your job, but you may even get a promotion.

165. The Person in the Cubicle Next to You Smells like Ass

Every day it's the same thing. You're stuck in a 4' × 4' cubicle for eight hours. That's bad enough. Now add the fact that the person in the next cell smells like a steaming pile of shit and you have all the makings of a murder/suicide situation. But before you do that, follow these Steps . . .

The WTF Approach to Being a F*#!-ing Team Player

➤ **STEP #1:** *Go to HR*

Explain that the smell of ass, halitosis, and ball sweat is impairing the quality of your work. If they refuse to do anything, then send your smelly coworker down for a visit. Once they get a whiff of Mr. Shit Muppet they should reconsider.

➤ **STEP #2:** *Organize an Intervention*

If the pricks in HR refuse to help, it's time to take matters into your own hands. Get a couple of like-minded coworkers together and take Mr. Poop Bucket out for a drink (if you can stand it) and explain to him that no one will ever love him if he smells like road kill.

➤ **STEP #3:** *Out Stink Him*

When he rebuffs your intervention, it's time to fight fire with fire or in this case, shit with shit. Stop showering and using deodorant. If it's really bad, piss yourself every chance you get and wipe your ass with your hand. Show Mr. Stank Ass that two can play at this game.

> **STEP #4:** *Hose Him Down*

If he still won't clean himself, do it for him. Bring in a hose and start spraying him like a dog or a child from the Third World. Treat this like a nuclear waste emergency. Careful, don't touch him.

for the ladies . . .

If you stink, you should be shot. Women are supposed to smell like flowers, not fertilizer. If you just can't stop the stink, move to India. Compared to those people you'll smell like Coco Chanel.

WTF: UP CLOSE AND PERSONAL

In high school, a foreign exchange student from Russia named Artoom (most certainly the wrong spelling, but who gives a shit?) lived with us for a few months. On the first day, my mother bought him deodorant due to his repulsive stench. When I walked into my room and met him for the first time, he was putting the deodorant all over his neck and back. Yummy. I walked up to him, took it out of his hand and pointed to my armpits. "Just here," I told him, and walked out. Fucking animal.
—GB

Worst Smelling Places

- Slaughter house
- Porta-potty
- Chinatown

Best Smelling Places

- Florist
- KFC
- Medical marijuana dispensary

166. Your Boss Catches You Falling Asleep at Your Desk

Maybe you were out partying, maybe you were just stressing out over life, or maybe you were "experimenting" with massive amounts of crack cocaine—whatever the reason, you're dead tired and you just can't stop dozing off at your desk. The next thing you know your boss is standing over you with that "you're about to get fired" look on his face. Think fast!

The WTF Approach to Getting Out of F*#!-ing Trouble

➤ OPTION #1: *Play Dumb*

Claim that this has never happened to you before and it might be a sudden case of narcolepsy. Tell him you should really leave work early and go to the doctor. Then go home and take a nice nap. When your boss asks what the doctor said, tell him it was just a case of low blood sugar.

➤ OPTION #2: *Start Crying*

Beg for his forgiveness and make up some bullshit story about a death in the family or your wife leaving you. Just keep crying, odds are he'll tell you to take the rest of the day off. Everyone will make fun of you behind your back, but fuck 'em. While they're busting your ass you'll be busting a nut—right before a big, fat nap.

➤ OPTION #3: *Flip the Switch*

Tell him you were sleeping because the work they expect you to do is so boring and tedious it would put anyone to sleep. Tell him you took this job expecting to be challenged only to find your potential being wasted. You might end up getting a promotion. Or fired.

IN THE FUTURE . . .

Learn how to sleep with your eyes open. Or better yet, wear sunglasses and say the florescent lights are hurting your eyes. Sure you'll look like a douche bag, but this way you can grab a quick nap without getting caught.

Best Places to Fall Asleep

- Between two massive breasts

- Between two gorgeous ass cheeks

- Between . . . [insert your particular sexual perversion here]

Worst Places to Fall Asleep

- On a tightrope

- Woods where they shot *Deliverance*

- On a bed of nails

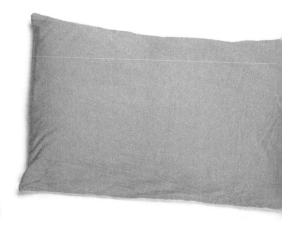

167. You Have *Way* Too Many Bosses

"Did you get the memo?" "Did you get the memo?" "Did you get the memo?" "Did you get the . . ."

"Yes, I got the fucking memo!"

It's one thing to get an update from your boss—*one* boss. It's quite another thing to get the same update from a hundred bosses throughout the day. You're going insane and you can't take it anymore.

The WTF Approach to Dealing with a F*#!-ing Boss Parade

➤ **OPTION #1:** *Become a Boss*

There are so many of them they might not even realize. Just start going around bothering people the way your "bosses" have pestered you for so long. If you can't beat 'em, join 'em.

➤ **OPTION #2:** *Divide and Conquer*

Play these so-called bosses against one another. Spread rumors, send incriminating e-mails from their computers, and spill coffee on one of their desks with a note that reads: "Fuck you. [sign another boss's name]" Sit back and watch them destroy each other one by one. It's like a Shakespeare play, but less interesting.

➤OPTION #3: *Embrace It*

This is your chance to shine . . . over and over and over again.

WTF Tip

Here are a few common phrases to get your bosses off your back . . .

- "I'm working on it, chief."

- "You'll have it by the end of the day"

- "Just putting the final touches on it."

- "You know me, I'm a perfectionist."

- "I got a hooker pregnant and I have to take her to the abortion clinic before my wife finds out."

for the ladies . . .

All you have to say is "I am bleeding profusely out of my vagina."

IN THE FUTURE . . .

Work for yourself. Then you only have one asshole to answer to.

Professions with Too Many Bosses

- Soldier

- Mafioso

- Plantation hand

168. Your Boss Keeps Calling You by the Wrong Name

It's been over a month since you started working and your boss still doesn't know your name. You feel like shouting out, "It's Greg, not Craig!" every time he calls for you. But there never seems to be the right moment to point it out and, considering your boss's quick temper, you don't want to push your luck. But enough is enough already. He should know who the hell you are by now. What to do, what to do . . .

The WTF Approach to Getting Some F*#!-ing Respect

► **OPTION #1: *Wear a Name Tag***

"Hello my name is . . ." At first people may make fun of you, but tell them that you feel that wearing name tags makes the work environment friendlier—as if you are all part of the same team. Not only will wearing a name tag make the boss start calling you by your real name, he might promote you if the name-tag thing catches on. He might even call a special meeting to strongly encourage everyone to wear name tags. Don't worry, though, he'll give you credit for starting the trend. "Craig had a great idea when he started this name tag thing." FUCK!

➤ OPTION #2: *Suck It Up*

Don't push your luck. Let him call you "asshole" for all you care—just as long as you get a paycheck.

➤ OPTION #3: *Change Your Name*

Legally change your name to match whatever he is calling you. This way you can be referred to by your correct name without confronting him.

➤ OPTION #4: *Flip the Switch*

Call him by the wrong name and see how he likes it. Some good names are "Jerk face," "Bozo," "Shit-for-Brains" and, of course, "Cock sucking, piece of fucking shit, mother-fucking asshole."

What's in a Name?

Certain names go with certain kinds of people. Here is a breakdown of some names and the kind of worker they usually correspond to.

- Seth: Skinny and wiry, like a snake that thinks he's hot shit. He was the bad kid in school, the troublemaker. Watch out for him—he'll stab you in the back to get ahead.

- Jennifer: Hot blonde receptionist with upturned nose and bitchy adolescent voice who used to play volleyball but now plays with the boss's balls instead.

- Chad: Short, blond former high school soccer player who realizes now that his glory days are long over. He's average in every way, and knows it.

- Ira: Smart, but also a whiny little bitch.

- Doris: A sweetheart, but *way* too old to screw.

- Bobby Jo: She's a total redneck chick, but hot as hell. She loves shooting guns almost as much as sucking cock . . . almost. She's the party girl who, after downing a bottle of Jack, tried to blow Santa at the annual Christmas party . . . twice.

- Boris: A fat Russian pig.

- Jodi: Hot, funny, lonely—probably has a cat but is still out of your league.

- Greg: Good-looking, funny, life of the party, good-looking, wonderful, good-looking . . . did we mention he is attractive?

169. Everyone Keeps Passing Their Work on to You

"Hey, buddy. How's it going? When you get a chance take a look at this would you? Thanks, pal." And that's it. You're now stuck doing someone else's work. While one or two extra assignments would be okay, ever since you started the job it seems like everyone is pushing off their work on you. It's too much. You just can't do it anymore. But you're the new guy and you don't want to make waves. WTF?

The WTF Approach to Dealing with the F*#!-ing Workflow

➤ OPTION #1: *Just Do It*

Suck it up and do everything everyone asks of you. You know that you're weak, so don't fight it. Embrace that weakness and convince yourself it's really a matter of being kind and helping others.

➤ OPTION #2: *Do Their Work Poorly*

Make sure your assignments shine, while theirs suck. As long as you do your job and please your supervisor, you should be fine. Your peers will think you're a moron, but it's better than being a slave.

➤ OPTION #3: *Just Say No*

You were hired to do a specific job, not as a random errand boy. Tell them you are swamped and that you can't do it. Make sure to tell them you have spoken to your superior and they agreed that you should focus on your own work.

➤ OPTION #4: *Make a Trade*

When someone gives you work, take it and thank them. Then hand them work of your own. Before they can speak, say "good trade" and walk away.

➤ OPTION #5: *Write a Stirring Mission Statement*

Be like Jerry Maguire and write a heart-wrenching mission statement about everyone doing their part to help the company. Make sure you take the goldfish and the overrated squinty mousey chick with you when you get canned. Don't worry; you'll love her little boy with the freakishly large head.

ARE PEOPLE TAKING ADVANTAGE OF YOU?

You might be doing more than your job description. A quick checklist to see if you're becoming the office lackey:

- ❑ The receptionist asks you to do her toenails.

- ❑ The mailroom asks for your help licking envelopes.

- ❑ The intern convinced you that running coffee was your responsibility, not hers.

- ❑ You get excited about the weekend because finally you can catch up on your work.

- ❑ Your boss asks you to squeeze his balls while he bangs his secretary.

170. No One Will Speak to You

It's been three weeks since you started and not a friggin' peep. No one will give you the time of day—even when you literally ask for the time of day. You like your work, but this is the loneliest job in history. Day after day, not even a glance from a coworker. And forget about Fridays; they're the worst. When everyone is going out for happy hour, you're going home in traffic, with only your tears to keep you company.

The WTF Approach to Being F*#!-ing Noticed

➤ STEP #1: *Get a Kleenex*

Stop crying and act like a goddamn man for once!

➤ STEP #2: *Change Your Appearance*

Whatever look you are going for obviously isn't working. Get a haircut and a new wardrobe— particularly something flashy or outrageous. This should get you some attention and may work as a conversation starter.

➤ STEP #3: *Ride a Motorcycle*

Motorcycles are cool, and everyone likes to talk about them. Trade in your Prius for a Harley and make believe you are too cool for school. Don't, however, use that expression, which is a dead give-away that you are not too cool for anything.

➤ STEP #4: *Learn the Art of Sword-swallowing*

Or juggling. Or knife throwing. Or anything that can make you stand out during company meetings. Surely that's got to get someone talking.

➤ STEP #5: *Get Really Sick*

If you get really, really sick—like to the point where you almost die—people will be forced to talk to you when you recover, at least to welcome you back. Ideally, you should get sick while you are at work so everyone can see you leave in an ambulance. This will guarantee enough sympathy points to open up some sort of dialogue.

➤ STEP #6: *Jerk Off*

Fuck it. Apparently no one is paying attention to you anyhow, you might as well enjoy yourself.

GREAT MASTURBATION QUOTES

"We have reason to believe that man first walked upright to free his hands for masturbation."—Lily Tomlin

"Intercourse with a woman is sometimes a satisfactory substitute for masturbation. But it takes a lot of imagination to make it work."—Karl Kraus

"Don't knock masturbation; it's sex with someone I love."—Woody Allen

"Philosophy is to the real world what masturbation is to sex."—Karl Marx

"The good thing about masturbation is that you don't have to dress up for it."—Truman Capote

171. You Don't Know How to Use the Copier

Load paper. Load paper. Load paper. What? But you just did load paper! It's there and you can see it with your own eyes! What the f*#! is this goddamn machine's problem? How come it works just fine when anyone else uses it? You have a college degree for God's sake. Is this devil machine out to get you? Or are you completely inept?

Yes to both answers, dipshit.

The WTF Approach to Dealing with a Demonic F*#!-ing Copier

➤ STEP #1: *Get Help*

Make sure to ask someone lower than you on the food chain—you don't want your peers or superiors to know you're incapable of doing something as simple as making copies. If you are the lowest on the food chain, your job is probably heavily dependent on mak-

ing copies. Move on to Step #2 or start looking for new employment ASAP.

➤ STEP #2: *Strike a Deal with It*

You know, the way you do when your car doesn't start. Tell the copy machine that you will be forever indebted to it if it works for you—just this once! Then feel silly about trying to negotiate with an inanimate object.

➤ STEP #3: *Use Positive Thought*

See it happening, and then make it a reality. Visualize the copy successfully going through, and then put that idea into the world. Read *The Secret* if you need further assistance, jerk off.

➤ STEP #4: *Destroy It*

When that bullshit doesn't work, show it who's boss. Who can forget the scene in *Office Space* where the three main characters take a baseball bat to the printer in a deserted field? Rape that friggin' thing until it squeals.

> **NOTE:** Raping office equipment is legal. Raping office personnel is not. Remember that.

for the ladies . . .

Just ask a man. Men are always willing to help a woman. You may have to sleep with them as a form of gratitude. No pain, no gain.

Also Difficult to Operate . . .

- Soundboards
- Bulldozers
- Vaginas

172. You Get Caught Making Personal Calls

You try and fake it like you are speaking to a client: "Um, okay. Right. Well, that sounds good then. Okay, well have a great day and we'll talk soon. I love you."

We said you *try*, but you don't get away with it. It seems like every time you make a personal call your boss just happens to pass by. And guess what, he doesn't care whether or not leftover spaghetti for dinner is okay with you.

The WTF Approach to Taking Personal F*#!-ing Calls

➤ OPTION #1: *Talk More Quietly*

Maybe you just have a loud voice that carries? Tone it down a notch and maybe no one will overhear your calls. However, make sure to maintain a consistent level of volume on all calls, business-related as well as personal. You don't want to arouse any suspicion when you're overheard speaking quietly.

➤ OPTION #2: *Stick to Yes or No Answers*

If your girlfriend calls you and asks if you want your balls drained after work, just say "yes" or "no" depending how you feel. Don't say "Yes, I would love to have my balls drained." Pretend you're being cross-examined on the stand and she's a really, really horny attorney.

►OPTION #3: *Make Up a Code*

Develop a code that you can use with your friends and girlfriend. Examples:

WHAT YOU SAY	WHAT YOU MEAN
I'm going to need that spread sheet.	Spread a clean sheet down on the bed before I get home, bitch.
You are my favorite client.	I love the way you look naked.
The numbers don't line up.	Let's order out. No, not Chinese. What about that little Thai place around the corner? Yeah, that one.

IN THE FUTURE . . .

Don't have a personal life at all. Work and success are all that matter in life. What are you a socialist?

WHAT THE F*#! IS UP WITH . . .

NOT BEING ABLE TO HANDLE PERSONAL SHIT AT WORK

If you work from 9 to 5, five days a week with a shitty half-hour lunch break which most of the time you spend at your desk because you are swamped, then when the fuck are you supposed to handle all the personal shit you need to if not at work? The annoying details of contemporary life require an exorbitant amount of time. Talking to your insurance carrier, your bank, or God forbid the DMV requires hours of time. Bosses must understand that their employees have lives outside of their shitty jobs. So let them make a couple phone calls at work because you goddamn well know that's the only time they can.

for the ladies . . .

Just give the boss that "Oh no you didn't!" look when he complains about your personal calls.

173. Your Coworker Takes Credit for Your Work

You worked long and hard on this important account and now you are ready to reap the rewards. This is probably your best work. Surely you'll get noticed now. But when you strut into your boss's office to show off the product of your labor you find your coworker's already there—presenting it as if it were his own!

The WTF Approach to Getting F*#!-ing Credit

➤ OPTION #1: *Tattle*

Tell your boss straight up that this asshole stole your work. You'll look like a big old cry baby but screw it, you did the work and you deserve the credit. If the coworker puts up a fight, beat the living shit out of him until he passes out in a pool of his own rotten blood.

➤ OPTION #2: *Challenge Him*

In front of your boss, congratulate him on a job well done, and then ask him how he came up with all of these amazing ideas. What inspired him? Then sit back and watch the pig sweat.

➤**OPTION #3:** *Kidnap His Little Girl*

Stealing is stealing. Two can play at that game.

➤**OPTION #4:** *Do Nothing*

Crawl back to your desk with your little tiny balls between your legs like the pathetic dog that you are.

Work Is No Laughing Matter

"The world is divided into people who do things—and people who get the credit."

—DWIGHT MORROW

Princes and Princesses of Thieves

Famous people who are accused of stealing others hard work

- Elizabeth Hasselbeck: Sued by another author who accused her of stealing ideas for her book *The G Free Diet: A Gluten-Free Survival Guide*.

- Poincaré: His ideas weren't publicly available when Einstein supposedly stole them.

- Milton Berle: Constantly accused of stealing jokes.

- Alexander Graham Bell: Allegedly took undeserved credit for the telephone.

- Helen Keller: She stole the spotlight from hardworking little girls who could see, hear, and speak. Selfish bitch!

174. Your Assistant Is After Your Job

At first, he seemed like the perfect assistant. He did everything you asked him to and more, going above and beyond the call of duty. He was ambitious, hardworking, and even reminded you of yourself when you were fifteen pounds lighter and still had dreams. But then you notice that he might be a little *too* ambitious, and not have your best interest at heart. He starts palling around with *your* boss, taking on assignments from other partners, and leaving work whenever he feels like it. Then you hear the unthinkable from a trusted colleague: This little prick is making a play for *your* job.

The WTF Approach to Keeping Him F*#!-ing Down

➤ **STEP #1: *Threaten Him***

Call him into your office and talk to him man to man—or rather man to little conniving prick. Tell him that you know what he is doing and that if he doesn't stop you will make his life a living hell. Men-

tion your time in Vietnam or Iraq, even if you never served and are a complete coward.

➤ **STEP #2: *Embarrass Him***

If he doesn't take your threat seriously, bring him into a meeting with the partners and then ask him to go get coffee and doughnuts for everyone. Make fun of him behind his back so when he returns everyone can't help but laugh at his expense.

➤ STEP #3: *Make Him Everyone's Enemy*

Burn his bridges. Send a nasty e-mail from his computer filled with derogatory comments about everyone in the office including the boss and CC all your other coworkers. Then we'll see how popular he is.

➤ STEP #4: *Get Him Fired*

He still hasn't wised up? Here are some creative ways to get him the boot:

- Put a banana in the exhaust pipe of his car and destroy his transmission before a critical early morning meeting.
- Take the CEO's family picture off his desk, ejaculate on it, and leave it in your assistant's cubicle.
- Pay a pregnant street hooker to come into the office and demand that he accept his love child.
- Leave a couple pieces of paper with swastikas doodled on them on his desk.

ALWAYS REMEMBER ...

Never socialize. He's your bitch, not your buddy.

IN THE FUTURE ...

Save yourself the trouble and just have him transferred. Make the case that your ambitious little self-starter would be even more useful to the satellite office in Anchorage.

175. You Get Turned Down for a Much Deserved Raise

There is nothing worse than not being acknowledged for a job well done. And for the last several months you have been busting your ass. Coming in early, staying late, and basically giving up on any chance at a social life. So when it's time for your review you're confident that you'll get a glowing report and a raise to go with it. But you only get the praise, not the raise. WTF?!

The WTF Approach to Getting F*#!-ing Paid

> **OPTION #1:** *Stand Tall*

Come from a position of strength. Explain to your boss that you've earned that raise and that you are extremely disappointed your work is not being appreciated. Hint that you've received better offers from other companies. Careful though, he might tell you to take them. Then you're totally screwed.

> **OPTION #2:** *Stand Short*

Invent a sob story and beg like a dog. You were counting on the raise to pay for a new liver for your wife who is dying of a terrible condition called liver, you know, um . . . well, liver *something* anyway.

➤OPTION #3: *Slack Off*

If you're not getting a raise, fuck praise. Stop putting in all that time and energy. Just do enough to get by as you look for another gig.

MY DYING WIFE

➤OPTION #4: *Shut Up and Take It*

Kids are starving in Newark. Be happy you have a job at all you inconsiderate piece of shit!

for the ladies . . .
Drop your pants and earn that promotion the old fashion way.

HEADHUNTER'S TIP

There's a right way and wrong way to ask for a raise.

Right Way: I believe that I have shown to be a critical asset to the company, proving time and time again that I can excel in any situation, and accomplish any task handed to me. Recently, as I have taken on additional work and responsibilities, I believe that I have earned and should receive a pay raise commensurate with these new duties.

Wrong Way: I need money or these guys are going to kill me!

176. You Pass Gas During a Pivotal Presentation

You've prepared all week for this friggin' thing, practicing in front of the mirror countless times. Finally, the day has come for you to shine, the day where you finally get the respect and the promotion you've been working toward for so long. You're not nervous, you're as solid as a rock, and everything is going as smoothly as possible. Your ideas are clear; your delivery is confident; you've got the whole boardroom in the palm of your hand. Then, just when things couldn't get better, you let out the biggest goddamn disgusting wet sloppy fart of your entire life. Fuck!

The WTF Approach to Covering Up Your Stinky F*#!-ing Fart

►OPTION #1: *Pretend Nothing Happened*

Keep going, and focus your eyes on a picture in the back of the room. Do not look these people in the eye. Stand tall and finish your presentation—squeezing your ass cheeks to prevent another slip. Who knows, maybe they'll be so captivated with your sales projections that they'll forget how disgusting you are.

➤ OPTION #2: *Laugh It Off*

Let out a laugh and look at everyone in the room. Connect with them. Everyone has farted before, so who the fuck are they to judge?

➤ OPTION #3: *Incorporate It*

Make the fart part of the presentation. Say that consumers are going to be so happy about the new widget that they'll fart or shit their pants. They'll be thankful that, as a show of good taste, you refrained from demonstrating the latter.

➤ OPTION #4: *Walk Out*

Do you really want to see these people again? It's over. You'll be a laughing stock forever. Walk out and let another one rip on your way to the door.

***WTF*FACT:** You are the only person disgusting enough to ever do this. You fucking freak!

HEADHUNTER'S TIP

Do not mention this event as a funny anecdote at your next big interview.

Different Kinds of Farts

Shart: A more polite way of saying you just shit your pants like a pig.

Silent killer: These farts make no noise, but rate a 10 on the stink scale. Remember the maxim that "whoever smelt it, dealt it." If you can't control your asshole, at least keep your mouth shut so you don't get blamed.

Whoopee cushion fart: This kind is loud and resembles the type of sound that a whoopee cushion makes. It might not stink, but it's impossible to hide the fact that you were indeed the farter.

Little dumb kid fart: It's the type let out by stupid little kids that laugh and think it's funny because they have yet to learn how to live in polite society.

Death fart: This fart is so powerful that it pushes all your internal organs outside of your asshole. Seriously, keep regular and eat your grapes so you don't end up dying this way.

177. You Have a Bad Case of Carpal Tunnel Syndrome

It was bound to happen. After years of toiling away in corporate America you are finally stricken by the Yuppie's most feared malady: the dreaded carpal tunnel syndrome. Now, with work piling up on your desk, you can't seem to type a letter without wincing in pain, holding your hand like a bitch.

The WTF Approach to Fixing Your F*#!-ing Hands

➤ OPTION #1: *Rub It Out*

Go to an Asian massage parlor and get a hand massage. In fact, it doesn't even have to be an Asian masseuse as long as the person is small, wiry, and has high cheekbones.

➤ OPTION #2: *Ice It*

Everyone says to just "put some ice on it" when you're in pain. Of course, it doesn't really do shit, but do it anyway since that's what every asshole suggests.

➤ OPTION #3: *Be Like Stephen Hawking*

Get a fancy voice synthesizer like the famous scientist, Stephen Hawking. If he can uncover the mysteries of the universe without typing, you can figure out how to finish your next mindless "project."

➤OPTION #4: *Get a Cheap Secretary*

Hire some recently homeless college graduate to type up your shit for gas money and a few beers.

➤OPTION #5: *Shut the Fuck Up*

Stop whining and be lucky that you have hands, let alone a job. Do you know how many young children become armless and legless every year in Cambodia and other war torn nations riddled with minefields? How can you be so fucking selfish and insensitive?

Other Bullshit Sounding Syndromes

- **Bra-strap headache syndrome:** Chronic pain in the back of the neck muscles that radiates to the top of the head. A result of a tight-fitting bra. Usually happens to women with *huge* tits.

- **Traumatic Masturbatory Syndrome:** This *weird* syndrome is a result of years of masturbation where your thrusts are controlled by hand grip and that makes it harder for you to carry on with the same rhythm and strength during actual sex. Sufferers usually lack sensitivity in their sexual organs and finally succumb to desensitization.

NOTE: Stop yanking it asshole!

- **Baddiel's Syndrome:** Fear of animatronic toys (vibrators in particular)

- **Syndrome Syndrome:** All modern doctors have been showing symptoms of this syndrome. It's where they can't stop making up syndromes and disorders to diagnose people with.

178. You Get Accused of Sexual Harassment

All you said was "nice shirt" and now everyone is treating you differently. The stares, the whispers, the evil looks. Then you get called into HR to find your boss, a lawyer, and that woman you complimented. Yep, you're getting accused of sexual harassment. WTF?

The WTF Approach to Being Really F*#!-ing Screwed

➤ **STEP #1: *Deny It***

Unless they have proof, deny it until you die. If they keep it up, sue their asses for slander and cash in.

➤ **STEP #2: *Bring Her Flowers***

Smooth things over with your accuser even if you didn't do anything, and even if she is a fucking bitch. Bring her flowers and all will be good. Flowers are a rem-edy for anything you do wrong with a woman. You can forget her birthday, cheat on her, even tell her how fat her ass is—once she opens the door to see you with a dozen roses all is forgiven.

➤STEP #3: *Start Harassing Everyone*

Better not let this happen again. If you are getting accused of treating a particular person a particular way, start treating everyone the same way. Grab asses, send perverted e-mails, and add "in bed" to anything you say. Example: "Can you with help me on this project . . . in bed?" Then sit back and watch the fireworks.

> **NOTE:** We are not responsible in any way if you do decide to sexually harass your coworkers. But we do envy how much fun you'll have.

What Not to Do

Yell out: "You know you want me bitch!"

for the ladies . . .

Even if you aren't guilty, let them fire you. Whatever you get sued for won't be close to the kind of money you'll make when you sell the rights of this sexy story to *Lifetime*. Everyone loves the idea of a female sexual harasser.

WTF ABOUT TOWN

We here at *WTF* have your best interest in mind. So we've decided to help you navigate that fine line between sexual harassment and harmless flirtation.

SEXUAL HARASSMENT

WTF: Wow, you look very nice today.

Employee: Thank you.

WTF: Show me your tits!

HARMLESS FLIRTATION

WTF: Wow, you look very nice today.

Employee: Thank you.

WTF: May I *please* see your tits?

179. You Get Caught Stealing Office Supplies

It starts out innocently enough. Couple of envelopes here, some Scotch tape there, maybe a box of pens. Then before you know it you're leaving the office with a chair, a desk, and the vending machine strapped to your back. Your closet at home looks like an aisle at Office Max and now you can't stop, until the day a coworker catches you red-handed.

The WTF Approach to Being Caught Red F*#!-ing Handed

➤ **STEP #1:** *Lie*

Tell your coworker you are donating all of these office supplies to a needy charity. The children in Rwanda desperately need staplers. You are a philanthropist and you should be rewarded, not punished.

➤ **STEP #2:** *Bribe Her*

If she doesn't buy your BS, offer her a Hershey bar from the vending machine to keep her mouth shut. Every chick likes chocolate.

➤ **STEP #3:** *Flip the Switch*

Tell her that you are working on a top-secret assignment and the boss knows about it. Make sure to tell the busybody that if she gets involved it could cost her a job. Then immediately report her to HR and accuse her of stealing. Make sure to plant the vending machine in her purse.

WTFACT: The most common things "lost" in the office:

- Pens and pencils
- Paper
- Post-its
- Calculators
- Staplers
- Hopes, dreams, and the like

Water Cooler Talk

"Office supplies are like a buffet. You take all you can because it is there for you."

—Janet Fields, receptionist/moron

What's in a Name?

Why is it that everyone feels the need to change his title to sound more important?

BEFORE	AFTER
Secretary	Administrative assistant
Stewardess	Flight attendant
Friendly uncle	Pedophile

180. Someone Keeps Taking Your Stapler

It happens just about every day and always when you need it the most. You have a stack of papers on your desk that need stapling but when you reach over to get your stapler it's gone. Fucking scumbags.

The WTF Approach to Keeping People's Hands Off Your F*#!-ing Shit

> **OPTION #1:** *Steal Someone Else's*

Make it some other chump's problem, just like you do with everything else in your life. Fair is fair, right? Well, not "fair" since the person you steal from didn't take your stapler, but there's no need to split hairs here. You have been wronged, so wrong someone else. Chaos or random chance is the only truly just and unprejudiced force in the world. Be its agent.

> **OPTION #2:** *Steal Everyone's*

Take all the staplers in the office and hide them in the basement. Who's laughing now?

> **OPTION #3:** *Smell Out the Thief*

Set up a web cam and catch that asshole red-handed. Then staple his hands together. Drastic maybe, but trust us, he will never steal anything again—or hold anything for that matter.

➤ OPTION #4: *Set Up a Booby Trap*

Rig small explosives to the stapler and blow the thief sky high, killing him instantly. When the boss complains that you've murdered a coworker, just explain that stealing is wrong, and God was watching.

➤ OPTION #5: *Set the Building on Fire*

Like the guy in *Office Space,* set the building ablaze and move to an island paradise. Make sure to grab a ton of cash (and staplers) before you light the flame.

Work Is No Laughing Matter

"Every day I get up and look through the *Forbes* list of the richest people in America. If I'm not there, I go to work."

—ROBERT ORBEN

IN THE FUTURE . . .

Glue it down to your desk. Hotels nail down the remote and lamps, so why not do it with your stapler? If your boss tells you to un-glue it, steal his stapler and see how he likes it.

181. Your Boss Eats Your Food

You do all the right things—you put a label on your lunch with your name on it; hide it in the fridge; retrieve it before the noon-time rush. But then one day you get called into your boss's office to find him chomping down on your food with no remorse. When you tell him it's yours he just winks and says, "Thanks. Now get back to work."

The WTF Approach to Losing Your F*#!-ing Lunch

➤ OPTION #1: *Beat the Shit Out of Him*

Then blame it on low blood sugar. You have to eat every three hours or else you blackout and do violent things. Sorry, but if he didn't eat your food this never would have happened.

➤ OPTION #2: *Appeal to His Gentler Side*

Explain to him, in great detail, the painstaking efforts your wife takes to make these sandwiches for you and how, considering you guys never sleep together anymore, this is the one thing that you share. He will feel so sorry for you, he might even buy *you* lunch—and get you a hooker to boot.

➤ OPTION #3: *Act Horrified*

Cover your mouth and gasp. When he asks what's wrong just tell him that "You might want to see a doctor immediately." Then turn around and go back to your desk. He'll be in the bathroom shoving his finger down his throat in no time. He'll never touch your food again.

HEADHUNTER'S TIP

Here are some foolproof labels that will ensure no one touches your sandwich:

CAUTION: HUMAN FECES SAMPLE

I MADE THIS WITH MY FEET

ROAD KILL ON RYE

VEGAN CHEESEBURGER

I HAVE HERPES . . .
AND SO DOES THIS SANDWICH

182. You Have to Work with the Boss's Son Who's a Complete Asshole

There's a new member of the team in your department with whom you will be working especially close. He isn't very bright. He isn't very hard working. And he isn't very pleasant to be around. In fact, he's a total asshole. But none of it matters: He is the big boss's son and he's fucking untouchable.

The WTF Approach to Working with the Boss's F*#!-ing Offspring

➤ **OPTION #1:** *Tattle*

Tell the boss that his son sucks. If everyone else thinks the kid is a total jackass, the dad probably does too. Maybe this is the kid's last chance to straighten up and stop being a dickwad. Who knows, you might find the boss more receptive to your complaints than you think.

➤ **OPTION #2:** *Get Him Arrested*

Leave a bag of cocaine on his desk, or slip something in his coffee to make him go insane before an important meeting. No matter how close he is with his daddy, the boss will have no choice but to get rid of him if he breaks the law.

➤ OPTION #3: *Befriend Him— Then Destroy Him*

Make friends with him no matter how much of an idiotic asshole he is. Then, once you have earned his trust, convince him that he is better than his father and should run the company. This should be easy since he probably has Daddy issues and a giant chip on his shoulder. Conspire with him to try to sabotage his father. Then, before the plan goes into action, tell his daddy what his son is up to. This will serve to get rid of the wayward asshole while simultaneously getting you in close with the boss. You could even suggest that the boss adopt you as his son to replace that backstabbing prick. Win-win for everyone . . . except for the shithead son.

Work Is No Laughing Matter

"I like work; it fascinates me. I can sit and look at it for hours."

—JEROME K. JEROME

for the ladies . . .

This shouldn't be a problem. You either date the stupid bastard yourself or set him up with your hot friend. Once he starts getting laid he should be easy to manipulate.

IN THE FUTURE . . .

Be born to a powerful man so that you can be the boss's prick son.

183. Someone Is Spreading Rumors About You

The stares, the snickers, the surreptitious whispers behind your back. Did you leave your fly down again? Is there something on your face? Maybe some toilet paper stuck to your shoe? You check yourself out: nothing. But you know something must be up, so what is it? Then your closest ally lets you in on the buzz: Someone is spreading terrible rumors about you throughout the office. But who?

The WTF Approach to Battling the F*#!-ing Office Gossip

➤ **OPTION #1:** *Fight Fire with Fire*

Spread rumors about everyone in the office. Terrible, vicious rumors. Before you know it everyone will have forgotten the rumors about you entirely.

➤ **OPTION #2:** *Investigate*

Find out who the culprit is and expose him. Bribe fellow coworkers with coffee and bagels—even offer to take on some of their work. Everyone has a price. Soon you'll discover the source of the rumors. Once exposed, now all you have to do is plan the perfect murder.

➤ OPTION #3: *Embrace Them*

At least people are talking about you. If you are used to being ignored you should embrace your new found infamy. Being so infamous might just get you laid— unless the rumor is that you have no dick.

Rumors: The Bad, the Worse, and the Worst

Some rumors are worse than others. Check out the chart and see how a rumor can go from bad to worst.

BAD	WORSE	WORST
You smell.	You smell like a serial killer—and probably are.	You make perfume out of your victims' blood.
You're addicted to doing drugs.	You're addicted to doing drug dealers.	You're addicted to doing drug dealers who are illegal aliens and have no right to be in our country.
You drank too much at the office Christmas Party.	You drank so much at the office Christmas Party that you tried to blow Santa.	Every lunch break you get gangbanged by a group of angry, well-endowed elves.
You have a small penis.	You have a small penis with a big wart on it.	You have a small penis with a big wart dipped in poop.

184. You Keep Getting Passed Up for a Promotion

Billy got one. Bobby got one. Hell, even that mongoloid, Tom got one. But you? Nothing. Nada. After wasting away most of your twenties in a cubicle all you have is the same paycheck every month—not a dime more than when you started. WTF?

The WTF Approach to Getting What's F*#!-ing Due

> **OPTION #1: Move On**

People tend to get stuck in a job and never get out. Don't let that happen to you. People who move up quickly on the corporate ladder seldom do it at the same company. Take a chance, and get the fuck out.

> **OPTION #2: Confront Your Boss**

You can do this politely (i.e. address him privately about your grievances) or less politely (i.e. take him by the neck and squeeze). The latter is more fun, but the former will probably yield the better result—unless he's a real hard ass and will appreciate you taking the initiative.

►OPTION #3: *Work Harder*

That's right, keep working. Move into your fucking cubicle if you have to. Prove that you deserve that promotion. If you still don't get one then maybe you really suck at your job. Ever think of that, dipshit?

HOW TO ASK FOR A PROMOTION

Should you ask forcefully, or should you appeal to your boss's gentler side? Here's a quiz:

1. When asking for a promotion you should:
   A. Bat your eyes and lick your lips.
   B. Smile like the Cheshire cat.
   C. Look the boss dead in the eye like you want to screw him and/or kill him.
   D. Write down the title and the money you want on a piece of paper and hand it to him so he can laugh in your face.

ANSWER: D. Fucking prick! God, don't you just hate him.

Reasons You're Not Getting Promoted

- You're a slacker.

- You're an asshole.

- You're fat and ugly.

- No one likes you.

for the ladies . . .

Become a man. As sad as it will be to give up benefits like menstruation, pregnancy, and bikini waxing, in a man's world like ours it's your best shot.

185. You Get Wasted and Make an Ass of Yourself at the Christmas Party

Unless you work for *Playboy* or Vivid Video, holiday office parties are usually pretty lame—a pathetic attempt to pretend that people at work actually like each other.

Inevitably this so-called "party" consists of people standing around a table of snacks sipping wine and talking about the only thing they know how to talk about: work.

As a fun-loving optimist, you make the best of a boring situation by doing the only thing you can at a dull event: drink. So you drink, and drink, and drink. The next thing you know you're passed out face down in the middle of the party wearing nothing but your underwear and a Santa hat. Merry Christmas!

The WTF Approach to Doing F*#!-ing Damage Control

➤ OPTION #1: *Make a Great Speech*

Get up, throw some water in your face and make an incredible, impromptu speech that knocks everyone's socks off. Speak about the company, the direction it needs to go to succeed in today's market, and a moving closing statement about the nature of teamwork. If you don't know shit about the company you work for and have nothing interesting to say, just use the word "synergy" a lot. Using that word always makes you sound like you know what the fuck you are talking about.

➤ OPTION #2: *Pack a Gat*

Take out a gun and stick a turkey in your shirt. If you have ever seen *Trading Places*, then you know what we are talking about here. If you haven't, then move on to Option #3 fuck-head.

➤ OPTION #3: *Quit and Get Help*

You'll never live down the embarrassment, no matter how hard you try. When you wake up, leave the building and check yourself into an alcohol rehab center even if you aren't an alcoholic. When you come out, everyone—including your boss—will take pity on you and hire you back. They'll forget all about that night and consider you a hero for taking charge of your life and doing what's best for yourself and the company.

***WTF*FACT:** At every company Christmas party there is one drunk asshole. At every company *WTF?* author Gregory Bergman has worked at *he* is that drunk asshole.

186. You Are Your Boss's Secret Santa

It's that time of year again. Snowflakes are falling, Christmas carols have taken over the radio, and militant soldiers from the Salvation Army incessantly ring a bell outside the supermarket in order to drive you insane. Yep, it's Christmas time, and this year it's your turn to give—to your boss.

The WTF Approach to Buying a Gift for the F*#!-ing Man

➤ OPTION #1: *Splurge*

Do not be cheap. If you have to get your kid a pogo stick instead of that red bicycle you promised or your girlfriend/wife a macaroni necklace instead of a tennis bracelet then that's what you are going to do. The last thing you want to do is give your boss yet another reason to can your dumb ass.

➤ OPTION #2: *Do Your Research*

Talk to his wife or girlfriend or boyfriend—whatever the case may be—and find out what he would really like. Don't take any chances. You don't want to get him a nice bottle of Scotch only to find out that he is a recovering alcoholic who has fought like hell to stay sober after that unfortunate accident three years ago when he ran over that woman, her daughter, and their three legged dog.

➤ OPTION #3: *Quit*

You are underpaid as it is and now the prick is demanding a gift? Get him a card that says "Screw you. I quit!"

Have You Been Naughty or Nice?

Santa is coming to town. Here's a checklist to see if you qualify for a gift or if you will end up empty-handed this Christmas and on your way to hell.

❑ You cheated on your wife with her sister but in your defense it "just happened."

❑ You hit your kid in the head with a shovel but in your defense "he deserved it."

❑ You masturbated to tranny porn but immediately felt awkward and guilty about it.

❑ You spent your family's rent money on crack cocaine but in your defense it totally "ruined your high."

❑ You voted Republican.

We were with you until the last one. But no fucking way are you getting *anything* this year—or ever!

BEST GIFTS FOR THE BOSS	WORST GIFTS FOR THE BOSS
Box of Cuban cigars	Box of Cubans
Bottle of 100-year-old Irish Whiskey	Bottle of 100-year-old Irish peasant piss
Pussy	Pussy cat
Nice watch	Sundial
Money donation to their favorite charity	Money to finance drug relapse

187. Your Assistant Is Screwing the Boss

You thought you hired the perfect assistant. She's hard working, compliant, and eager to please. But not anymore. Lately she's slacking off big time. Then you find out that she's not interested in pleasing you because she's too busy pleasing your boss . . . with her vagina. You are now walking a very thin line. The last thing you want to do is piss her off, but you need her to get back to work. She has your future in her hands, or should we say between her legs.

The WTF Approach to Handling a Slutty F*#!-ing Assistant

➤ OPTION #1: *Catch Her In The Act*

Tape it and blackmail your boss. You're missing out on what could be a perfect opportunity to not only create job security, but also advance in the company. Install a mini-camera in his office and tape them doing the deed. Better yet call his wife and have her come down to the office. Then right before she's about to go in and catch them, stop her. Make sure your boss knows you helped out in this sticky situation.

➤ **OPTION #2:** *Report it to HR*

Anonymously of course. Send a note to HR explaining what is going on and let them deal with it. Odds are they will both be let go. At least your assistant will, and maybe your boss will be transferred. Either way you will be in the clear and get a new assistant.

➤ **OPTION #3:** *Do Nothing*

Just because she can suck a dick, doesn't mean she's good enough with clients to take over your job. Unless, of course, she's *really good* at sucking dick.

➤ **OPTION #4:** *Follow Her Lead*

Fuck it, fight fire with fire. Start screwing the boss's assistant. Hopefully you can get some dirt on your boss while you're at it.

GILF (Grandmother I'd Like to F*#!) Alert

Careful, usually the boss's assistant has been with him for years. She's likely some sixty-year-old grandma you wouldn't want to bang . . . would you?

Hottest GILFs

- Sarah Palin

- Goldie Hawn

- Sophia Loren

- Helen Mirren

- That old white-haired woman who's at the Santa Monica Boulevard bus stop every morning with that cane and those tits . . . you know who you are.

188. You Sleep with the Client and Lose the Account

Well, now you've really gone and done it. While we're proud that you finally got laid, did you really have to screw your client? Screwing a client metaphorically is one thing (it's expected), but *literally*? This can only lead to trouble. Now you've lost the account, and maybe even your job.

The WTF Approach to Saving Your F*#!-ing Ass

➤ **OPTION #1: *Reason with Her***

Tell your client that you are sorry for whatever you did to offend her and that you promise it will be just business from now on.

➤ **OPTION #2: *Pass Her Off***

Get her assigned to another agent. You may not be able to save your pride, but you can still save your job. Just because you suck in bed, doesn't mean there isn't someone at Moron & Moron, LLP who can handle her properly. When in doubt, approach the black guy in the office. You know, the one with the really, really big desk.

➤ **OPTION #3: *Become a Eunuch***

You're obviously unfit for polite society and have to be stopped. Screwing your own client? You animal! You monster! Castrate yourself and end your sexual cravings. The safety of the civilized world depends on it.

Top Five Professions Where Screwing Clients Is Expected

1. Porn star

2. Prostitute

3. Masseuse

4. Sex therapist

5. Attorney

Top Ten Worst Things to Hear During Sex

1. "What's your name?"

2. "Do you smell something really, really bad?"

3. "I have something to confess: I am your real mother."

4. "Faster, slower, harder, to the left, no scratch that, to the right . . ."

5. "Mind if I shit on you now?"

6. "If a train is leaving from Boston headed West and another train is leaving from San Francisco headed East . . ."

7. "Look at me. Please, baby, look at me."

8. "Is it in yet?"

9. "Ha, ha. Oh my God, really? It is in? No way!"

10. "I love you."

IN THE FUTURE . . .

Get better in bed. Obviously you need to up your game. Read *Cosmo* to find out how to make a woman swoon, start taking penile enhancement pills, and strengthen your tongue by trying to touch the tip to your nose.

189. You Have to Fire Someone You Like

Firing someone is tough—but even tougher when it's a friend. You know his sad little story and don't want to be the one to crush his hopes and his dreams. And no matter how you go about canning him, he's going to blame and resent you. Remember the time you banged his mom? This is just like that—but less gross.

The WTF Approach to Firing a F*#!-ing Friend

> **OPTION #1:** *Distract and Deflect*

Fire him and take him to Vegas. It's the cure for the blues. Break the news Friday afternoon and, after he starts to cry, tell him you've booked a hotel and several escorts at Caesar's. A Jacuzzi party with prostitutes can make anyone forget about anything.

> **OPTION #2:** *Make Him Quit*

If you are too cowardly to do the deed, start piling on the work and blame it on the guys at the top. Say your hands are tied and if he wants to keep his job he'll will have to stay late and work weekends, even work on Christmas Day. We give it a month. Then when he threatens to quit tell him, as a friend, if you fire him he'll get a severance package. Now it's on him.

➤ OPTION #3: *Inflate His Ego*

Convince him that this job is preventing him from living up to his full potential. "You're better than this," tell him. Explain to him you always thought he deserved much more out of life, and that he should follow his dreams. Remind him of that funny drawing he did of the teacher in junior high. Then tell him that drawing comics is where the money is.

➤ OPTION #4: *Just Do It*

Pack up his shit and leave it at the front door. Then make sure security knows not to let him in. He'll get the hint. Cruel maybe, but at least you won't have to do it face to face, pussy!

Think Before You Fire

The best way to fire a friend:

Boss: Sorry to do this but I am going to have to let you go.

Employee Friend: Oh, my God! How will I get by?!

Boss: Not my problem, loser. Vegas on me?

The worst way to fire a friend:

Boss: Beat it.

Employee Friend: What?

Boss: Pack your shit and get the fuck out of here before I call security. And by the way, I fucked your wife.

(*Door Slam*)

190. You Have to Lay Off the Whole Division

It's good to be the boss. You make more money, people constantly kiss your ass, and you can basically do as you please. But, unless you are a sadistic animal, there is one time when being a boss sucks balls: When you have to can someone and put them out on the street.

Letting someone go is tough enough, but when you hear you have to lay off an entire division, you can barely catch your breath. Have fun, boss man!

The WTF Approach to Firing a Lot of F*#!-ing People

> **OPTION #1: Sugarcoat It**

Send them all to a baseball game. Don't spend a lot on the walking dead, so maybe something in the nose bleed section. Then, during the seventh inning stretch, pay to have the words "YOU'RE ALL FIRED" on the JumboTron screen. At first they might start laughing, feeling sorry for whoever that was directed to. But they'll get the hint when they see the next message with your company logo and the words, "THAT MEANS YOU, MORON!" Grab a hot dog and a beer to cheer yourself up. You had an emotional day, after all.

➤ OPTION #2: *Move the Rest of Your Company*

Pick up and move the rest of your people to another office building without telling that division. Change your name and number.

> **NOTE:** If this happens to you, see "Your Company Suddenly Relocates without Telling You" (Entry #202).

➤ OPTION #3: *Shift the Blame*

Call them in one by one and explain that you have to let the division go because of one of their coworkers. Tell Steven it's because of Bob. Then call Bob in and blame it on Paula. Then call in Paula and blame it on Steven. You get the point. They'll be so pissed at each other they won't have any energy to blame you.

191. You Crash the Company Car

Work life, even at the top, has very few perks: a membership to a country club, a parking spot right in the front, a sexy secretary willing to start off your mornings with a customary hand job, or, for the really lucky, a company car that you don't have to pay for.

After years of slaving away for the company, you are finally given a company car. For months now you've been living like a fat cat, driving the pimped out new Mercedes on the company's dime. Life could not get any better. That is, until you wreck the fucking thing and tear it in half. Shit, your boss is going to kill you.

The WTF Approach to Covering Up Your F*#!-ing Crash

➤ **OPTION #1:** *Hide the Evidence*

Sell the car for scrap and then call in to work and say that you were carjacked. Tell a harrowing story about a guy dressed in black with a gun. They'll just be happy that you're alive.

➤ **OPTION #2:** *Set the Car on Fire*

Set the car on fire and dance around it like a complete lunatic, laughing maniacally. Then get a paid leave of absence for a mental breakdown. It's better than working, anyway.

> **OPTION #3: *Flip the Switch***

Tell them that there was something wrong with the brakes and that they didn't work when you tried to stop. Scream and carry on to your bosses that they put your life in danger by giving you this crappy car. Make enough of a fuss and they'll end up apologizing to *you*.

WTFACT: The first automobile-related fatality occurred in London in 1896. After that the coroner said: "This must never happen again." It did.

IN THE FUTURE . . .

Take your eyes off your BlackBerry and look at the fucking road, asshole.

Things You Should Never Do While Driving

- Get a manicure
- Get a pedicure
- Read the paper
- Floss
- Cook

WHAT THE F*#! IS UP WITH . . .

TEXTING AND DRIVING

It's one thing to be on the phone and driving, but quite another to be texting and going 60 mph in that hunk of metal filled with gas called an automobile. What are you, a fucking idiot? How can you drive if you can't see? Newsflash for all you texting drivers out there: Messaging back "K" to a text from your girlfriend about having chicken and rice for dinner (again) isn't exactly worth dying for.

192. Your Parking Spot Is Given to Someone Else

There are a few little things that keep all of us going to work, things that make life at the office just a little less horrible. Things like free coffee and bagels in the morning, a cubicle or office we can decorate as we see fit, and, of course, a parking space to call your own. Take away one of these perks and the full scale of your miserable life hits you smack in the face. So the day you drive into the lot and realize they've taken your parking spot away and given it to someone else, you're ready to lose your shit.

The WTF Approach to Dealing with Losing Your F*#!-ing Space

➤ OPTION #1: *Fuck It*

Just keep parking there. Get in early every day and park your car in your old spot before the prick gets to work. Who knows, the bosses might even give it back to you for working so hard and coming in early. Maybe all they wanted from you was a renewed commitment to the job, the same gusto and tenacity that you brought to the position years ago.

➤ OPTION #2: *Go Gangster*

Throw the prick that got your spot down the stairs. Hopefully, he'll break his neck. This way you'll get your spot back because when he eventually gets released from the hospital and goes back to work, he'll get a handicapped spot right in the front. Win-win for everyone!

➤ OPTION #3: *Break Your Own Neck*

Fuck it. That handicapped spot really is *right* in front. It's worth it.

What Your Car Says About You

Cars make a statement about the driver. Here are some examples on what the car says about the driver.

Volkswagen Bug: Old hippy if it's the old version; young chick or gay man if it's the new one

Cadillac Escalade: Violent gang member

New Volvo: Yuppie scumbag who can't afford a BMW or Mercedes

Old Volvo: Pervert and/or kindergarten teacher

Bentley: Basketball player, movie star, or financial criminal

Maserati: Asshole who can't afford a Bentley

BMW: Asshole who can't afford a Maserati

Land Rover: British dickhead

Van: Plumber and/or rapist

Harley Davidson: Genuine scumbag or Yuppie pretending to be a genuine scumbag

Hummer: Man born without a penis

Mitsubishi Eclipse: Hot young co-ed with tits so big that she almost looks deformed—in a good way

Chrysler 300: Middle-class professional who wants to fool you into thinking it's a Bentley if you look really, really fast

---

IN THE FUTURE . . .

Ride a motorcycle so you never have to worry about parking. It might make a nerdy douche bag like you look cooler, too.

---

193. You Spread a Disease Throughout Your Office

You wake up one morning feeling like shit. Sore throat, sneezing, coughing, fever, but you used up all of your sick days last week when you went to Vegas . . . fuck! And it turns out the old adage "What happens in Vegas stays in Vegas" isn't always true. Looks like you came back with a new strain of flu—the dog flu. (Guess you shouldn't have screwed that golden retriever behind the dumpster next to the souvenir shop.)

Though you feel terrible, you *have* to go to work. Somehow you make it through the day without passing out at your desk, or crying. And then within a week you're feeling better. But as you get better, your coworkers get sicker and sicker. Looks like they all have the dog flu because some asshole spread the virus throughout the whole company.

The WTF Approach to Handling a F*#!-ing Office Epidemic

➤ OPTION #1: *Benefit from It*

Since most of the employees are out sick, take this opportunity to show your strength. Work double time, take on more responsibilities, and who knows, you might just wind up with a promotion out of it.

➤ OPTION #2: *Own It*

Take the credit for all the damage and don't apologize. Fuck them and their weak immune systems.

➤ OPTION #3: *Make It Worse*

Give them something to really complain about. Go out and find someone with leprosy whose skin is hanging off and show all of your coworkers what a real disease can do. They should be lucky it's just the dog flu and quite their bitching. At least their flesh is still on their bones.

IN THE FUTURE . . .

Don't have sex with dogs . . . no matter how good that golden coat looks at 5 A.M. after a three-night binge.

WTF HEALTH TIPS

In order to keep your office environment clean of germs and infections, here are a few pointers on what's okay to spread—and what isn't.

Things You Should Spread

- Love
- Goodwill
- The Word of God
- Peanut butter on your dick

Things You Should *Never* Spread

- Rumors (unless you hate that person)
- Herpes
- Ebola
- Peanut butter on someone else's dick

194. You're a Cop and Can't Remember the Codes

You made it through the academy. Somehow managed to pass the physical and psychological exam, and just slipped by on the written. Now your childhood dream of being able to shoot and kill gang members has finally come true. You can't wait to get your feet wet—and shoot a Crip in the face. But there is one problem: You can't seem to remember the codes. You're the dumbest cop on the beat—and that's saying something.

The WTF Approach to Remembering those F*#!-ing Codes

➤ OPTION #1: *Watch* Cops

Sit down and watch a marathon of the show *Cops*. They rattle off codes every thirty seconds. Just fake it 'til you make it.

➤ OPTION #2: *Carry a Cheat Sheet*

That's probably how you passed most of your tests in school. Just write the codes down on a piece of paper and pull it out when you need it. But be careful. No one is going to wait for you to find the correct code before they blow you away.

➤ OPTION #3: *Get Shot*

Not somewhere fatal, try the leg or the shoulder. This way you will get a paid leave while you recuperate, giving you ample time to learn those codes. If you still can't remember any codes after this ordeal and your paid leave, tell your superior you have post-traumatic stress syndrome from the shooting and you want to be transferred to a desk job. This would be called A-19. Translation: I am a fucking pussy.

➤ OPTION #4: *Make Up Your Own*

So what if you call in a high-speed chase when there's just a cat in a tree? To those poor cat-loving kids, it's just as urgent.

CODES *NOT* USED BY LAW ENFORCEMENT

Here are a few codes that are too complicated to be used by law enforcement professionals:

- DaVinci Code
- The Code of Hammurabi
- The Bro Code

IN THE FUTURE . . .

Don't be a cop. The pay sucks and you only get to kill people once in a while.

195. You Fall Off the Scaffold

When you told your friends and family you would be working on a scaffold they had some concerns. Namely, why the fuck are you working on a scaffold when you graduated at the top of your class? Not to mention you're a notorious klutz and you're afraid of heights. It was only a matter of time before the inevitable happened. What a jerk.

The WTF Approach to Surviving as a F*#!-ing Klutz

➤ OPTION #1: *Sue*

We smell a hefty law suit. Even though it was your fault, blame it on the scaffold manufacturer. They'll probably settle out of court and you could make millions and never have to work again. True you'll miss scaffolding, but you'll find other, equally fun things to do with your free time and big money—like screw supermodels in a pile of cash.

➤ OPTION #2: *Become Religious*

If you survived the fall, God must really like you. So get on your knees and start praying, asshole. This is your second chance to be a good person and stop being such a jackass.

NOTE: We are assuming that you are a jackass because only a fucking jackass would fall off a scaffold.

➤ OPTION #3: *Shake It Off*

You don't want everyone to think you're a pussy do you? Pick up your mangled body and what's left of your dignity and get back to work!

Most Dangerous Jobs

- Firefighter
- Police officer
- Convenience store clerk
- Commercial fisherman
- First Black president

Creepiest Jobs

- Mortician
- Grave digger
- Taxidermist
- Mickey Rourke's makeup artist
- Michael Jackson's dermatologist
  . . . especially now

WTF: UP CLOSE AND PERSONAL

I used to have rock fights with my friends after school as a kid. One day, like the idiot I was, I stood on top of a roof that I was supposed to be sweeping (little after school gig), and started a rock fight with a couple kids. Standing on the edge, I reveled in sadistic delight as I pummeled them with rocks, like an Arab throwing a stone at an adulterer. And then, as quickly as it began, the fun stopped. Hit in the knee cap with a sharp rock, I tumbled to the ground, smashing my head onto the cement. Good times.

—GB

MOST UNNECESSARY JOBS

- Adult film screenwriter
- Bathroom attendant
- Congressman
- The Pope
- Bum with dirty windshield wiper who you keep telling to "get the fuck off my car!"

196. You're the Only English-Speaking Person in the Kitchen

You finally got your dream job as a cook in the back of some smelly diner. You love it. After all, who wouldn't? But there is only one problem: No one understands you and you have no idea what the hell anyone else is saying. Hello— does anyone here speak *American*?! WTF?

The WTF Approach to Siendo el único Que Habla F*#!-ing Inglés
(Being the Only One Who Speaks F*#!-ing Inglés)

➤ **OPTION #1:** *Use Sign Language*

Maybe not the official sign language, like in the deaf community but the kind that even a moron can understand to cover the important things like, "you wash dish," "you cook food," "you suck cock."

➤ **OPTION #2:** *Learn Their Language*

Odds are it's probably Spanish, and that shit is pretty easy to learn. If you can't beat 'em, join 'em.

➤ OPTION #3: *Call INS*

Get all your cooking coworkers deported. Now you are not the only the English-speaking person in the kitchen. You're the only person in the kitchen. Looks like you'll be getting a raise.

for the ladies . . .

Doesn't really matter if you can't communicate with anyone in the kitchen. Everyone is staring at your tits anyway.

WHAT THE F*#! IS UP WITH . . .

AMERICANS BEING THREATENED BY ILLEGAL ALIENS

Illegals are taking our jobs away! Illegals are taking our jobs away! Illegals are taking our jobs away! You hear this all the time on certain cable news networks. Yes, illegal aliens—many of whom come from Mexico and other Central American countries—are taking our jobs away. But they're the shitty ones. The kind of jobs "real" Americans won't do—like pick strawberries or mow a lawn all day. You know, there's a word for grown American men who need to wash dishes for a living, it's called "loser." Look it up. Oh wait, redneck moron, that would require the ability to read.

197. You Drive a School Bus but Hate Kids

The children sing the entire ride to school. One day, you've had enough: "The wheels on the bus go round and round, round and round, round and round. The wheels on the bus go round and round all . . ."

"Shut the fuck up!" you scream at the little animals, whose downright childish stupidity has finally, after months of torture, driven you totally and completely insane. One little pussy, Billy, cries, while the others just stare quietly, scared out of their wits. For the rest of the drive they actually shut up.

But the next day it's back to normal. That's right, no matter how terrible and mean you are, these kids just will not get the message and act like adults. Bastards!

The WTF Approach to Dealing with F*#!-ing Kids

➤ **OPTION #1: *Invest in an iPod***

Listen to your favorite, upbeat songs to help drown out the sound of the children's horrible voices and put a smile on your face. Natu-rally, you'll have to still look at them once in a while to make sure they are safe and you don't get sued, but at least you won't have to hear every inane comment they make.

➤ OPTION #2: *Throw Them Under the Bus*

Literally. Just toss the troublemakers under the bus and run over them. Not enough to kill them, but enough to show them who's boss.

➤ OPTION #3: *Ditch 'em*

Leave them stranded in the middle of nowhere. If Option #2 is a little too harsh, just drive them out to an open field, park the bus, take the keys, and leave the little fuckers. Maybe hide out and watch them lose their shit, just for fun. Eventually one of them will take the lead, à la *Lord of the Flies* . . . that would be better than any reality show on television.

for the ladies . . .

You should never be in this position. You're genetically designed to *love* children no matter what. If for some reason you can't stand kids, you should go to your doctor immediately because you probably have a brain tumor . . . or a very, very small dick.

WHAT THE F*#! IS UP WITH . . . WORKING WITH KIDS YOU HATE

Why do many people who choose to work with kids hate them? The mean schoolmaster, the uptight bus driver, the fascist gym teacher—the only staff member in school who likes kids is the typically avuncular kind-hearted guidance counselor. The reason? He is a sexual deviant steps away from prosecution.

WTF: UP CLOSE AND PERSONAL

I had a bus driver in grammar school that I hated. She was a total bitch. Then one day she surprised me by agreeing to play my George Michael tape, particularly the song "I Want Your Sex," which I found to be very, very cool since it kept repeating the word "sex." Luckily, she did not actually want my sex, since, to be honest, overweight middle-age bus drivers with bad skin and hair like red wool were not (and are still not) my type. Three cheers for Ms. Whatever-the-fuck-her-name-was.

—GB

198. You Knock Out a Customer with a Bottle

You should have realized this wasn't *Cocktail*. And that you are no Tom Cruise. The two of you have nothing in common. He looks good playing air guitar in his underwear, you don't. He is rich and famous, you're not. He is a clinically insane idiot, you're . . . well, you might have *that* in common.

Nonetheless, part of your job as a bartender is being able to show what a prodigious juggler you are, tossing glasses in the air like a sideshow attraction. And you were doing pretty well too, until you got cocky and tossed a bottle of Grey Goose in the air while spinning around to catch it. That didn't work out so well. In fact, the bottle fell on a customer so hard you nearly killed him. WTF?

The WTF Approach to Handling a F*#!-ing Bleeding Customer

➤ OPTION #1: *Buy the Guy a Drink*

It's the least you can do. Give him a few shots on the house for the pain. Assuming he does not have to be rushed to the hospital, that is.

➤ OPTION #2: *Get Drunk*

Before the guy wakes up and sues the shit out of you, take a few bottles and leave the premises. It might not help him any, but at least you'll feel better about the whole thing.

➤ OPTION #3: *Join the Crowd*

Laugh along with everyone else at this poor schmuck lying on the floor in a pool of his own blood.

➤ OPTION #4: *Ignore It*

That's right; he's not the only person in the bar. Odds are nobody even saw it—or gives a shit if they did. All those losers in the bar care about is getting *their* drink, so get back to work. Let his friends deal with him.

for the ladies . . .

Just giggle and say, "Sorry." Push your tits out too when you say this. Works every time.

IN THE FUTURE . . .

Practice makes perfect. Study Cruise's moves at home. Practice throwing bottles in the air like a jackass while watching *Cocktail*.

199. You Crash into Your Boss's Car

There you are late for work again. You cruise down the freeway at 100 mph and fly into the company lot. You look at your watch. Whew, just in time. You'll be able to get to your desk without anyone noticing you're late. You turn the corner and then—*wham*—you slam into the rear end of your boss's Mercedes. WTF?

The WTF Approach to Getting Away with Wrecking Your Boss's F*#!-ing Car

> ➤ **OPTION #1:** *Pass the Blame*

Park your car very far away and start running. Then when you're good and sweaty run into the office and tell your boss you just saw some asshole hit his car and take off. You, being a good citizen, chased after the car, but it got away. You'll look like a hero for chasing after the car. You might even get a raise. Use the extra funds to fix your car.

> ➤ **OPTION #2:** *Start Crying*

Walk into the office crying like a baby. Tell him you are very sorry and that you will take care of it. Pussy.

> ➤ **OPTION #3:** *Drug Him*

Drop some sleeping pills in his coffee. When he passes out take him to his car and drive him somewhere out of the lot. When he wakes up he'll think he blacked out while driving and hit something. He'll probably be in a panic, thinking he has a brain tumor or some shit like that, but fuck it, not your problem.

> **OPTION #4:** *Flip the Switch*

Blame that pompous ass for the crappy parking job. What did he expect leaving his car parked like that? It was only a matter of time before someone hit it.

Get to Work on Time

If you are constantly late for work, we suggest the following changes to your routine:

- Use a jet to get to work, not a beaten down Pinto that doesn't start.

- Wake up earlier. If you have trouble waking up, stay up all night drinking Red Bull.

- Carpool with people who are not lazy morons like yourself—you'll be forced to get up in time.

- Pluck your eyebrows at night, rather than in the morning. And by the way, any dude that plucks his eyebrows is gay.

- Jerk off at night. Yes, a good jerk in the morning is splendid; we'll give you that. But there is a time and place for everything—including ejaculating all over yourself.

Water Cooler Talk

"I once hit into my boss's car, but I never told him. He passed me up for a raise two years in a row. Now that's fuckin' karma!"

—Kevin Tahl, accountant

200. You Spill Coffee on Your Computer

Fuck! Shit! Goddammit! Son of a bitch! Oh, for Christ Sake! Motherfucker! Not again! Jesus!

Yep, you've done it again, jackass. You spilled coffee all over your keyboard, monitor, and some even dripped into the processor. And forget about your pants, your penis hasn't been this hot since what's her name gave you your first—and her first—painfully inadequate hand job in the seventh grade. While you can probably save the computer, your work from today including that important assignment is now kaput. FUCK!

The WTF Approach to Dealing with a F*#!-ing Coffee-Soaked Computer

➤ **OPTION #1: *Start a Witch Hunt***

Go to your boss and complain that some idiot came into your cubicle and knocked over your coffee, and didn't have the damn decency to fess up to it. By the end of the day he'll be interrogating everyone, and will have long forgotten about that pressing assignment, buying you a couple more days.

➤ OPTION #2: *Clean It Up*

What the fuck are you doing just sitting there with your hands on your head, rocking back and forth and lamenting over your stupid mistake and your lost work? Clean it up, dipshit!

➤ OPTION #3: *Suck It Up*

Literally. It is wrong to soak it up with a paper towel when there are starving people in China who would love a cup of coffee to fill up their empty stomach. Get on all fours and slurp it up.

WTF: UP CLOSE AND PERSONAL

I have spilled coffee on my work computer and personal laptop over 7,000 times in my life. To tell you the truth, I like it.
—GB

WTFACT: Over 99 percent of the working population has spilled coffee or another liquid on their computers. The remaining 1 percent is made up of camels and people who are so fucking anal they make you sick.

WTF ABOUT TOWN

WTF: Excuse me. What would you do if you spilled that cup of coffee on your . . . (*WTF* loses footing and knocks into the schmuck, causing his coffee to spill onto his lap and all over his computer.)

Random dickhead worker: AAAHHH!! What the fuck?!

WTF: Well, that answers my question.

Things You Should Never Spill Hot Coffee On

- Your crotch . . . unless you're into pain

- Your car dashboard

- Crack

- Small children

- Your wife's tits . . . unless she's also into pain

201. You Want to Quit but Need Unemployment

It's official. You hate your job. Every *fucking* thing about it. You hate your boss. You hate your coworkers. You hate your desk. And you really hate that stupid inspirational picture on the wall of a rock with a caption that reads "Perseverance." Fuck perseverance. But you can't just quit and forgo unemployment benefits. WTF?

The WTF Approach to Getting F*#!-ing Canned

➤ **OPTION #1:** *Do Nothing*

If you stop showing up, the company might be able to rightfully deny you unemployment. But if you just sit there like a fucking dunce, you should be safe. Just stare at the computer and zone out all day, every day until they can't take it anymore.

➤ **OPTION #2:** *Fake a Mental Breakdown*

You're on the verge of a real one anyway. Start flipping out screaming and then hold your head and rock quietly at your desk. Who knows, before they let you go they might even suggest some paid time off. A vacation could do you some good. True, the vacation will probably be in an institution, not the Bahamas, but it still beats sit-

ting in that fuck-
ing cubicle all
day surrounded
by people you wish
were dead.

> ➤ OPTION #3: *Fall
Down the Stairs*

Break a leg or
another useless
bone (when was
the last time you
went running,
anyway?), then
take some paid
time off and get
some workman's
compensation.
It's better than
unemployment
and eventually
could lead to
disability—the
American
dream.

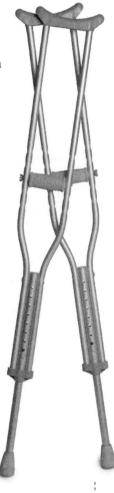

You Might Be Getting Fired If . . .

❑ Your boss is watching every move you make.

❑ Your coworkers start to avoid you.

❑ Your password doesn't work.

❑ You hear rumors about the company merging.

❑ You're a moron and it was just a matter of time.

Top Reasons Someone Gets Fired

Dishonesty and/or a bad attitude

Employer: This is great work.

Employee: Go fuck yourself!

Refusing to follow directions and orders.

Employer: I want this report by Friday

Employee: I want a lot of things in life. What's your point?

Lying on a resume.

Employer: It says on your resume you speak the Southern African tribal tonal language of Xhosa fluently.

Employee: Yes I do.

Employer: So do I.

Employee: Shit.

Talking too much and conducting personal business at work.

Employer: Is that report done yet?

Employee: Not yet, sorry 'bout that.

Employer: Why not?

Employee: I've been updating my Facebook status all day. It's very time consuming. Hey, why didn't you add me as a friend?

Inability to actually do assigned job tasks.

Employer: I need you to staple these presentations together.

Employee: Not a problem. How do I work the stapler?

202. Your Company Suddenly Relocates Without Telling You

At first when you show up at the office and the lights are off you think everyone is throwing you a belated surprise birthday party. But after fifteen minutes you realize not only is no one there at all but all the offices have been locked. The phones are dead; the computers are gone. Then it hits you, your company has vanished, just like in that movie *The Game*. But, unlike Michael Douglas's character, you're a broke loser and you're now out of a job. And by the way, if it took you fifteen minutes to realize that there were no desks, offices, or people, then it's no wonder they left your stupid ass behind.

The WTF Approach to Picking Up the F*#!-ing Pieces

➤ OPTION #1: *Collect Unemployment*

Technically you have been fired, but without the notice and severance pay. So drag your ass over to the unemployment office and start getting some cash. Then go get drunk. On second thought, get drunk first then go to unemployment—just like most of the pigs in line.

> **OPTION #2:** *Burn the Building Down*

Start the fire, then call 911. Tell them you came to work and found it like that. The authorities will find those bastards for you.

> **OPTION #3:** *Start Your Own Company*

You have the space, now fill it. Get a bunch of investors, hire a bunch of people, and promise them equity, and then split, leaving everyone with their balls in their hands. What goes around comes around.

COMPANIES THAT SHOULD VANISH

It would be a better world if these companies simply disappeared suddenly.

- ShamWOW
- Wal-Mart
- AIG (before we gave them trillions of dollars)
- Halliburton
- The Olive Garden

Water Cooler Talk

"I came to work one day and found that the whole office and everyone had vanished. I thought I was on like 'shrooms or getting punked for a second but they actually did disappear. Luckily I work for my father and I hate him with all my heart. Fuck you, dad! Free at last!"

—Ted Johnson, unemployed with serious daddy issues

203. Your Coworker Gets You Fired

Thanks a lot, asshole. And to think you bought this bitch lunch one day, remember that? Now this little piggy returned the favor by getting you fired! You knew you shouldn't have told her that you weren't actually sick last week, but instead decided to take a much needed vacation from your boss, whom you hate. Well, the gig is up and your boss knows that you weren't home in bed after all. Why? Because bitch-face told him, that's why!

The WTF Approach to Life After Getting F*#!-ing Fired

➤ STEP #1: *Ask Why*

Like a dying man in a movie killed by his best friend, confront her and ask, "*Whyyyy?!*" This will probably only make you look insane and weak but who cares? You'll never see these assholes again anyway.

➤ STEP #2: *Get Revenge*

Get your coworker fired. Call in the office using different voices every day asking for her and, if she isn't there, tell the reception-ist to tell her that she is a whore. Order a ton of pizzas for delivery to the office under her name, slash her tires in the morning so she's late for work, and find any other creative way you can to make her life miserable and put her in the spotlight at work. Eventually, whether it's her fault or not, the bosses will can her for being a nuisance.

➤ STEP #3: *Join a Cult*

Since you'll likely lose your house now that you're worthless and unemployed, you need to get a roof over your head. Most cults give you a place to live as well as three squares a day. Cults offer better conditions than prison or a homeless shelter—though you'll be surrounded by really dangerous people.

➤ STEP #4: *Become a Stand-up Comedian*

Start hitting the clubs and talk about how this asshat at work got you fired. Tragedy + Time = Comedy . . . this shit will be funny. Then publicly name this person every time you get on stage. Eventually it will get back to your coworker.

for the ladies . . .

If this happens to you, find that coworker's husband/boyfriend and sleep with him. If she's not dating anyone, go find her father and screw him.

WHAT *NOT* TO DO

• Kill her

Everything else is fair game.

204. You Are Denied Unemployment

Getting fired is bad enough, but getting fired and then being denied unemployment—the one thing to keep you going—is just about the worst thing that can happen to a person, except perhaps a vicious herpes outbreak. Then again, if you have ever been given the boot and then denied unemployment benefits, you might take ass herpes over it any day—though employers never give you that choice. In all seriousness, not being able to make ends meet is a scary fucking prospect.

The WTF Approach to Getting Some F*#!-ing Money

> **OPTION #1:** *Fight It*

Go to the appropriate agency that handles unemployment benefits in your state. Just Google "unfairly denied unemployment benefits" and you should be directed to all the relevant info. If you cannot Google "unfairly denied unemployment benefits," then you prob-

ably were not "unfairly" denied anything, moron.

> **OPTION #2:** *Beg*

Listen, the fact that you were fired for jerking off at your desk wearing nothing but a pinwheel hat and flippers does not exactly bode well for you in that unemployment hearing. The state won't side with you—no matter how liberal it is. You're best just calling your boss and begging him for the benefits. Make sure to promise to pay him back later when you get another gig.

➤ **OPTION #3:** *Threaten Sexual Harassment*

No matter what you did to get fired, legal or illegal, you can always threaten to sue for sexual harassment—even after you worked there. If you won't win the unemployment hearing, you might as well make some cash at your former employer's expense some other way.

WTF: UP CLOSE AND PERSONAL

I was once denied unemployment after I purposely got myself canned from one of most horrible jobs in the history of work as an editor of a financial magazine. The bastards I worked for then denied me unemployment without any basis other than their misplaced adolescent anger.

Without a dollar to my name and a wife to support, I needed this unemployment to survive. So I fought it—and won. I was not only granted unemployment but also an additional settlement the specifics of which I cannot discuss. But I can say that I did not get that blowjob I asked for in the initial agreement. Fucking lawyers; they ruin everything!

—GB

WTF? Work *Quiz*

1. In most states, which of the following is *not* a valid reason to deny a terminated employee unemployment benefits?

   A. Caught performing sexual acts with the boss's stapler

   B. Never showed up for work

   C. Set the warehouse on fire

   D. Because the boss is a scumbag

2. What is the best thing about receiving unemployment benefits?

   A. You don't have to get up to go to work.

   B. You don't have to stay late at work since you are never at work.

   C. You get paid to smoke pot and watch *Star Wars* all day.

   D. All of the above

3. What is the worst thing about being unemployed?

   A. When you hear on the news about the unemployment rate, you know you are part of it.

   B. Filling out that questionnaire every week or so about the jobs you supposedly queried.

   C. Friday nights and Happy Hour lose their meaning and appeal.

ANSWER KEY

1. D
2. D
3. B (Really, those things are just too time consuming.)

Chapter 4

WTF?

WOMEN

How to **S**urvive 44 of the **W**orst
F*#!-ing Situations with the Ladies

205. You're Too Shy to Approach Girls

Your eyes lock from across the room. She smiles. You smile. Now all you have to do is go over there and say something clever, like "Hey." But even the thought of that makes your heart race, your palms sweat, and your dick shrivel to the size of a toddler's. God might have blessed you with good looks, but he forgot to give you a set of balls. Pussy!

The WTF Approach to Working Up the F*#!-ing Nerve

➤ **OPTION #1:** *Send a Note*

Write down something witty and attach it to a drink. Have the bartender or server give it to your girl. Hopefully, she will return the favor by coming to you. Or better yet, by coming on you.

➤ **OPTION #2:** *Take a Class*

They have classes for everything. Learn the basics of how to start a conversation and get over your social anxiety. Then practice on women with whom you're comfortable, like your mom or your sister. Just remember to keep from going too far. Or else you might fall for a family member.

➤ OPTION #3: *Get Wasted*

Nothing cures the nerves like a pint of whisky. That's why it's called liquid courage. Soon you'll be talking to girls, dancing with girls, maybe even dancing with boys (don't ask; don't tell). Careful, though—if you drink too much, you might go home with a fat Persian clown covered in body hair. Yum.

WOMEN ARE NO LAUGHING MATTER

"I'm dating a woman now who, evidently, is unaware of it."

—Garry Shandling

MOST EFFECTIVE PICK-UP LINES

- Is your last name Gillette? 'Cause you're the best a man can get.

- Are you a parking ticket? You've got fine written all over you.

- I have never had a dream come true until the day that I met you.

- I lost my number. Can I have yours?

- If I could rearrange the alphabet, I'd put U and I together.

- 'Sup? (accompanied by a head nod)

LEAST EFFECTIVE PICK-UP LINE

- You want to get a pizza and bang? What's the matter, you don't like pizza?

206. You Always Say the Strangest Things When You Meet a Girl

"Hello." "Hey." "How are you?" These are a few common things men say to women when they first meet. You, however, say things like: "Does it smell like feet in here?" "I just cried a little in the bathroom." "I wish I was dead—what about you?" For some reason you can find the courage to walk up to a girl and talk to her, but you can't seem to control what comes out of your mouth.

The WTF Approach to Removing Your Foot from Your F*#!-ing Mouth

➤ **OPTION #1: *Don't Talk***

Women love the silent type anyway. This might really work to your benefit. Just smile, nod, and laugh once in a while. She'll be eating out of the palm of your hand in no time.

➤ **OPTION #2: *Bring a Translator***

Bring a friend to translate what you're saying. If you say something weird like. "I like your shirt," your translator will say something like: "He likes the way your shirt brings out the color in your eyes." Careful, though—she might end up boning your translator, so make sure you pick a friend who is gay.

The Do's and Don'ts of Flirting

Flirting is an art form. How good a flirt are you?

1. In a crowded room, what is the most effective subtle sign you can give that you like a woman?
A. Walk over, poke her, and say, "Hi, sexy!"
B. Look at her, and when she looks at you, you look away.
C. Walk over and grab her crotch.
D. Ignore her completely.
E. Throw a bottle at her head.

2. You see someone across the room who you think is attractive or who you would like to meet. You:
A. Wait until she leaves and ask a friend later who she was.
B. Try to make eye contact with her and smile.
C. Hold up a sign that reads "Let's bone."
D. Have a friend tell her you'd like to meet her.
E. Walk past her and accidentally bump into her.

3. Which of the following is the best way to flirt?
A. Stare at her until she looks away.
B. Lean into her with a hard-on.
C. Send Morse code messages that you like her.
D. Laugh at her stupid jokes.

Answer Key
D. Chicks love a challenge.
E. Works in '80s movies, so it must be true.
D. Chicks love to think they're clever and funny.

for the ladies . . .
It doesn't really matter what you say, he's probably not listening to you anyway.

207. You Can't Seal the Deal

You have no problem approaching girls at a bar or club. They are usually receptive, and you are pretty damn good at being charming. You almost always get their number, but for some reason, despite the fact that things go well, you never actually close the deal right there—you can never seem to get them to come home with you.

The WTF Approach to Sliding into F*#!-ing Home

➤ OPTION #1: *Work on Your Game*

Pay attention to other guys who take girls home. Listen to them and observe them closely as if you were writing a novel about them. What is it that they do differently? Try that.

➤ OPTION #2: *Do It in the Bathroom*

The nice guy routine works for numbers, but not for spontaneous sex sessions in the bar bathroom. Tell her you are going to take a leak and ask her if she could hold your dick for you. She might go for it. After all, what girl wouldn't?

DATING IS NO LAUGHING MATTER

"A man on a date wonders if he'll get lucky. The woman already knows."

—Monica Piper

WTF: UP CLOSE AND PERSONAL

This is about a friend of mine. He's tall, good looking, and relatively charming. Unsurprisingly, he has little trouble approaching women. In fact, many approach him. He does a good job of flirting with them throughout the night, giving them all the attention they need. Then, after spending all night with the same fucking chick, he walks her out of the bar and tries to get her to come home with him. No dice. They always decline, leaving him with a phone number, a raging hard-on, and thoughts of murder and malice on his mind. You know who you are out there. Loser!

—JM

208. Girls Never Notice You at the Bar

Maybe you are *too* good looking. Are the girls too scared to even look at you for fear of ruining their new panties? Okay, probably not. But it doesn't necessarily mean you're totally ugly if girls never seem to look in your direction when you are out on the town. It could just mean that, like your *WTF?* author Gregory Bergman's penis, you are just average. But average sometimes doesn't cut it (just ask his wife). Here's how to go from being ignored to getting all eyes on you.

The WTF Approach to Getting F*#!-ing Seen

> ➤ OPTION #1: *Wear Something Outrageous*

Become a character and wear something that forces girls to take notice of you. Pickup artists call this "peacocking" because, like a peacock, you are showing off your bright colors to get the attention of a female. You don't have to dress like a total lunatic; a very bright shirt or a weird hat will do. Anything so that you stand out in the crowd. This projects confidence.

And it's better to be a confident guy in a stupid outfit than a well-dressed anonymous guy that no one talks to.

➤ OPTION #2: *One Word: Wheelchair*

I know it's morally wrong, but so is being at a bar looking for chicks, according to some religions. So, since you are going to hell, go out in style. Get a motorized wheelchair and chicks can't help but notice you. Not to mention you will never, ever be treated so well in your life! VIP all the way. Girls will be hitting on you left and right because they pity you and they think you are harmless. Plus, girls are more like guys than you think. And what guy do you know that never thought about banging a cripple?

➤ OPTION #3: *Get Really Smashed*

Even if you are a plain-looking unnoticeable dude, if you drink enough, you'll get noticed somehow. Maybe not in a good way, but noticed nonetheless.

for the ladies . . .

If guys never seem to notice you, whip out your tits. Then they'll see you!

209. You Get Sabotaged by a Hot Girl's Bitchy Friend

In every group of girls at a bar there is that one friend who is a total bitch. Maybe she's just been dumped. Maybe it's that time of the month. Or maybe she's just in such dire need of dick she doesn't know what to do about it. Whatever the reason, the miserable bitch is intent on spoiling the fun for everyone else. Now, after investing all night and a ton of cash, your chances of banging the hot chick are slipping away—right through the fingers of her evil bitch friend.

The WTF Approach to Dealing with a F*#!-ing Saboteur

> **OPTION #1:** *Divide and Conquer*

Bring one of your friends to take the bullet. Some people call him the wingman or the grenade blocker. Have him flirt with Bitchzilla and clear the path for you.

> **OPTION #2:** *Get Her Wasted . . . Really Wasted*

Like almost dead wasted. If she is passed out or dead somewhere, she can't be a problem.

WTFACT: Every thirty seconds another poor schmuck's chances of getting laid are sabotaged by some fat bitchy friend.

➤ **OPTION #3:** *Flirt with Her . . .*
Carefully

Not enough so the object of
your affection thinks you're not
interested, but enough to get the
uptight bitch to loosen up and be
your pal. Once she lets down her
guard, grab her friend and split.

WTF: UP CLOSE AND PERSONAL

I cannot tell you how many times
I was minutes away from taking a hot chick home only to be
sabotaged by the hot girl's bitchy
friend.

—GB

I cannot tell you how many times I
would have gone home with some
creep like GB had it not been for a
bitchy friend of mine stopping me
at the last second.

—JM

A GUIDE TO FEMALE BODY LANGUAGE

As humans, we speak with our bodies,
not just our words. Women, being technically human, do the same. Under-
standing their body language can come
in handy. Here are some examples.

GESTURE: Slightly tilted head.
MEANING: Inquisitive. Thinking about
cock and/or shoes.

GESTURE: Standing with hands on hips.
MEANING: Aggressive. Angrily in
search of cock, ovulating.

GESTURE: Walking.
MEANING: Mode of transport from one
physical space to another—for cock.

WTF ABOUT TOWN

Some women can't get over being
bitches. In those cases, it's best to give
it right back to them.

WTF: Excuse me, would you like to
dance?

Bitch: No!

WTF: I'm sorry you misunderstood me;
I said you look fat in those pants.

210. Your One-Night Stand Refuses to Leave the Next Morning

There is a reason it is called a "one-night stand"—it lasts for one night, ladies! (Okay, two if there are hardcore drugs involved.) But it isn't a marriage, hence the whole having sex part. But unfortunately the girl who stumbled home with you last night just doesn't share this philosophy. She stares at you with puppy dog eyes when you tell her you are leaving for work. "Well, I'll see you when you get back, honey." WTF do you do when she just won't leave?

The WTF Approach to Handling a F*#!-ing Squatter

> **OPTION #1:** *Ask Her to Marry You*

Maybe she is trying to stay because she feels unwanted. Try some reverse psychology. Shower her with attention and affection. After all, maybe she feels she wouldn't want to belong to any club that would have someone like her as a member.

> **OPTION #2:** *Cry and Say You're Gay*

You just slept with her to prove to yourself—and to God—that you could live as a straight man. But the urge to do guys in the butthole is just too strong. Tell her that you can still be friends. Girls love gays as friends.

➤OPTION #3: *Call the Cops*

Make sure to get rid of your pot plant before the boys in blue show up. Of course you will look like a pussy that can't get a girl out of his house, but better to call the cops than to wind up on the show *Cops* after you throw her ass out by force.

➤OPTION #4: *Become Really, Really Undesirable*

Piss on the floor, offer her doodie for breakfast, or just keep telling inappropriate black jokes until she sees what a scumbag you really are and bolts.

IN THE FUTURE

BANg iN yOuR CAR. ThAt wAy shE hAs to lEAve oR gEt pushed out of A movINg vehicle. HER choice.

➤OPTION #5: *Move*

Drastic times calls for drastic measures. If the bitch won't leave, you might have to.

for the ladies . . .

If your one-night stand won't leave, start screaming rape. Watch him run.

211. You Get Caught Trying to Sneak Out after a Hook-Up

Who the hell does she thinks she is? Did you sign a contract stating you would stay with her in the morning and hold her like a lost little kitten? Well, in a word: yes. At least, according to her. Women have this strange concept that an agreement to be civil is implicit in the act of shoving your dick inside their mouths. God, where do they come up with this shit? Anyway, you try to sneak out, but the girl wakes up and glares at you with a look that says, you ain't going anywhere, motherfucker. Fuck!

The WTF Approach to Getting F*#!-ing Out of There

➤ **OPTION #1:** *Run for It*

You've already pissed her off and if you liked her you'd have stayed a while and not been a dick. So run, she can't be that fast—not if you nailed her right the night before, that is.

➤ **OPTION #2:** *Make a Joke out of It*

Say you were just kidding and then sit back down on the bed like the bitch you are.

➤ OPTION #3: *Lie*

Tell her you were going to get some bagels and coffee to surprise her. Then ask her what she wants from the bagel place and leave. Don't return. Stupid girl.

➤ OPTION #4: *Be a Man*

Tell her that you are under no moral or legal obligation to stay with her. Tell her she should be ashamed to even expect you to stay. Tell her you are not her BFF, but just a stranger with a sore cock.

WTFACT: Coyote Ugly: The man wakes the next morning in a strange bed with a sexual partner from the previous evening who is completely physically undesirable. The man must gnaw off his arm to avoid waking the sleeping beast. The "double coyote ugly" is where the man gnaws off his other arm because he knows she'll be looking for a one-armed man.—*Urban Dictionary*

WTF: UP CLOSE AND PERSONAL

You know what's worse than a woman who expects you to hold her all night long? A guy who can't take a hint. Truth is, fellas, a lot of women don't want you to spend the night, we want you to screw us and go bye-bye. So when we say, "Wow, it's so late. I have such a big day tomorrow." That means "Grab your dick and get the hell out of here, I want to cuddle with my cat." Maybe that's why I'm still single.

—JM

for the ladies . . .

This is easy—guys never wake up. You could light off fireworks in his naked ass and he wouldn't move. The only way you can wake a guy up is by blowing him. So let him sleep, grab your stuff, steal some cash from his wallet, and take off!

212. You've Been Dating Online for Months and No One Is Interested

Y ou finally gave in and signed up for online dating. You've seen the commercials. All those sickening, loving couples who swear by this shit. So you figured, screw it, lets give it a try. You spend hours on your profile and use the best possible profile picture you could find. You're all set. Now all you have to do is wait for your matches to get in touch. You check every day only to find that you have *no* winks, flirts, e-mails . . . nothing! Turns out even in dating cyberspace you're a loser!

The WTF Approach to Dealing with No F*#!-ing Matches

➤ **OPTION #1:** *Widen Your Net*

Maybe your dating radius is too small. Extend it to 100 miles, 200 miles, 300 miles . . . fuck it—Earth.

➤ OPTION #2: *Change Your Profile*

If you're like most guys, you probably put some sappy bullshit like "Loves to have romantic candlelight dinners and walks along the beach." While on paper that seems like what women want to hear, the truth is that women love assholes. So why not give them what they want? Try something like "I like sports, beer, football, and sex, and if you don't like it, then go find yourself a mama's boy!" What woman in her right mind could turn that down?

➤ OPTION #3: *Change Yourself*

Maybe it isn't Match.com; maybe it's you. Reinvent yourself. Get to the gym, highlight your hair, shave your back and balls, and get a penile implant. No one wants to date Quasimodo with a hairy back and no dick.

Online Profile Tips

When filling out your online dating profile remember these simple steps:

- Be honest: Tell her you like sex.

- Talk about what you're looking for: Explain what kind of sex you would like to have.

- Talk about what you're not looking for: You aren't looking for anyone who doesn't like sex.

- Add a picture: of you having sex.

DATING WEBSITES TO AVOID

- OnlyWantYourMoney.com

- NeedAGreenCard.com

- MailOrderTrannies.com

213. Your Match.com Date Looks Nothing Like Her Picture

So you finally found the perfect girl. You're so excited as you wait for her to arrive. You patiently stare at the door, when all of a sudden this thing starts moving toward you. At first you think nothing of it; it must be meeting someone else here, but when the faceless blob approaches you, you panic. This can't be your date! Your girl is thin, blonde, with piercing blue eyes and a rack that could melt a cheese sandwich from across the room. But this monster standing before you barely resembles a human being, let alone a former Miss Texas. WTF?

The WTF Approach to Dealing with a F*#!-ing Liar

➤ **OPTION #1:** *Fake an Emergency*

Text your friend when She-Beast isn't looking and have him call you. Then use whatever lame emergency excuse you can: Left the stove on, friend's car broke down, dog died, friend died, etc. Just get out of Dodge, stat!

➤ OPTION #2: *Confront Her*

When actors show up for auditions and don't look like their picture, the casting director has the right to ask them to leave. So why should this be any different? Call her out and then spit in her face for dramatic effect.

➤ OPTION #3: *Get Wasted*

See if this beast looks any better through beer goggles. If so, screw her. Just make sure to get out before the morning light.

WTF? ABOUT TOWN

Let's listen in on a great first encounter . . .

Woman: Hi.

Man: You look nothing like your photo.

Woman: Well I just gained five pounds.

Man: That's five too many. Now get the hell out of here!

Woman: I thought you'd be taller, anyway.

for the ladies . . .

Who cares about his picture? It's what's in his jeans that matters. The back of his jeans. You know, his wallet.

DATING DRAMAS

"I've never thought I was someone who only cared about looks. And then I met her. When my blind date walked into the coffee shop I threw up in my mouth. You know what I mean? When you almost throw up, but you don't, so you like swallow it or whatever? Anyway, that's what I did when I saw her/it/monster pig. But I said hello, being the gentleman that I am, trying to avoid eye contact as if she were Medusa. Then I excused myself to the restroom, and left town for good."
—James Tunnel, 36, Seattle, Washington. Previously, Spokane.

214. She Calls You Every Day after Your First Date

At first you thought it was very thoughtful of her to call you and thank you again for such a great date. After all, you did take her to an expensive romantic dinner at Olive Garden. But then she calls you again the next day to see what your plans are for the weekend. Has this girl never heard of playing hard to get? She's calling you every day and you've only been out once. Thank God you didn't screw her; you'd probably have to get a restraining order.

The WTF Approach to Dealing with a F*#!-ing Needy Chick

➤ OPTION #1: *Be Honest*

Tell her that you had a nice time on the date and *you* will give her a call soon. If she calls you again after that, call the cops and get a restraining order. This bitch is crazy.

➤ OPTION #2: *Change Your Number*

This is as good a time as any to upgrade your phone. Get a new iPhone with the stalker app. That way you'll never have to deal with girls like this again.

➤ OPTION #3: *Do Nothing*

Hey maybe this girl is the one? She apparently already *loves* you. Do a check of your options and if she's the best you can get, marry her.

THINGS YOU SHOULD DO AFTER A FIRST DATE

- Call once

- Send a text

- Send an e-mail

THINGS YOU SHOULD *NOT* DO AFTER A FIRST DATE

- Send flowers

- Make a mix tape

- Send a cell phone picture— of your cock

215. You Can't Get Out of the Friend Zone with the Girl You Really Like

When she broke up with her boyfriend, you were there for her. When her mother died, you were there for her. When she had that herpes scare, you were there for her. The consummate friend, you have always been her shoulder to cry on. And what do you get in return? A hug and that "you're such a great friend" bullshit. But you want more. You love this girl, but you can't seem to get out of the friend zone.

The WTF Approach to Getting Out of the F*#!-ing Friend Penalty Box

► OPTION #1: *Tell Her*

Sit her down with some wine and come out with it. You never know, she might have the same feeling but was afraid you didn't think of her that way. Probably not, but at least you'll get it off your chest.

WOMEN ARE NO LAUGHING MATTER

"I was never in the friend zone with a chick. Then I got married."

—GB

➤ OPTION #2: *Be a Dick*

You know how she always falls for the bad boys who don't treat her well? Well, become one of those assholes. Start by telling her she is gaining weight and her skin is looking weird lately. Get a bad boy makeover, and start being a total prick. You'll be screwing her in no time.

➤ OPTION #3: *Sleep with Her Friends*

It's the closest thing you're ever gonna get to having her, so you might as well. Then hopefully they'll talk about how great you are in the sack and she'll see you in a different light. Like her-ankles-around-your-neck light.

➤ OPTION #4: *Write a Movie About It*

Hollywood loves these stories of unrequited love. Write it, sell it, make it become the next big Hollywood thing. She'll want you then. Of course, you won't want her.

➤ OPTION #5: *Tell Her You're Dying*

You only have a month to live and this is your dying wish. Then after you have sex with her, tell her it was her love that cured you. She can't leave you now.

F*#! "JUST FRIENDS"

How can you tell if you're in the friend zone?

- She tries to set you up with other girls.
- She calls you her "brother."
- She screws other guys in front of you while taunting you and telling you "You know you want this shit but you can never get this shit! Hahaha!"

216. Your Girl Is Out of Your League

She's hot. You're not. She's successful. You're out of a job. She plays the classical piano. You play guitar hero . . . badly. She's athletic. Your body looks like it's made out of Play-doh. Every day you scratch your head and wonder why she'd even consider a schmuck like you. Then you look down at your penis. Nope, that's not it either. Your girl is way out of your league and you know it. How long before she drops you like a sack of rotten potatoes covered in human feces?

The WTF Approach to Dating Outside of Your F*#!-ing Class

➤ **OPTION #1:** *Grow Some Balls*

Literally. If you grow really big ones, then no woman will be out of your league. Chicks dig big balls.

➤ **OPTION #2:** *Cheat on Her*

It is only a matter of time before she listens to everyone and dumps your dumb ass for someone better. However, if you cheat on her and then tell her about it, she'll feel so damaged and worthless that it just might draw her to you even more.

➤ OPTION #3: *Bring Her to Your Level*

Find out what's wrong with her. There has to be something if she's with you, so dig and dig deep. Call her friends, family, hire a private detective if you have to. Just get the dirt. This might be your only path to salvation. Once you find out that she ran over a small child or used to be a man, you'll feel like she is less deserving of you and isn't that the way it should be?

WTFACT: Television shows have encouraged this sort of thing for years. It's the classic tale of the big fat loser guy with a hot wife. Don't believe us, just look at these examples.

The Honeymooners

According to Jim

The King of Queens

The Flintstones
(Wilma was a hot piece of ass!)

WHAT THE F*#! WAS SHE THINKING?

- Julia Roberts & Lyle Lovett

- Heidi Klum & Seal

- Marilyn Monroe & Joe DiMaggio

- Beyoncé & Jay-Z

- Christina Aguilera & Jordan Bratman

- Larry King & All Seven Wives

217. She Keeps Mentioning That Her Ex Has a Huge Penis

You've been dating for a few weeks now and things seem to be going pretty well. You get along great, you have similar interests, and the sex is pretty good. But lately she's been talking about her ex-boyfriend, which usually doesn't really bother you accept all she keeps talking about is what a big dick he has. Ahhhhh!

The WTF Approach to Battling F*#!-ing Penis Envy

➤ OPTION #1: *See for Yourself*

Don't pretend you aren't curious. Look, if it's *that* huge you need to go check it out for yourself. Find out what gym he goes to and join up. Wait in the locker room for the monster to be exposed.

➤ OPTION #2: *Cut It Off and Give It to Her*

Find this guy, drug him, chop off his enormous penis, and give it to her as a present. You want it, you got it.

➤ OPTION #3: *Make Yours Bigger*

Try Enzyte, or ExtenZe, and grow your dick. Maybe try the pump if you have to. Whatever it takes, pencil dick.

WTF: UP CLOSE AND PERSONAL

As a woman who has had a lot of sex (sorry, Dad), I can tell you bigger is not always better. Yes of course we want to be able to feel you; if a woman asks, "Are you in?" then you know you have a problem. But if a guy is too big, there is a whole other set of problems. I was once with a guy whose nickname was "Meat" and let me tell you, I couldn't move at all during sex. I was pinned in one position, not enjoyable at all. So to all you medium-sized guys out there, keep up the good work. And for all those ladies who insist they need a huge dick in order to "feel it," you're all whores with stretched-out vaginas.

—JM

WTFACT: Jodi Miller just gained thousands of new male fans.

> **IN THE FUTURE . . .**
>
> Date a virgin midget from Thailand. If your dick still doesn't look big, the time has come to take your own life.

218. You Find Out She's Slept with Way More People

There comes a time in every relationship when you both disclose how many sex partners you've had. You're nervous 'cause you don't want your girl to think you are a man-whore when you tell her the number. But you're the one who ends up being shocked. Turns out your lady has played hide the salami with ten times the number of partners that you have. WTF?

The WTF Approach to Dating a F*#!-ing Slut

➤ **OPTION #1: *Break Up with Her***

No matter how liberal you are, you will never be able to deal with the fact that you are her 150th lay.

➤ **OPTION #2: *Start Boning!***

That's right; you can't be outdone by a woman. Start screwing every woman who will have you—pay for it if you have to. Then come back with a bigger number than hers . . . and a scorching case of herpes as proof!

➤ **OPTION #3: *Get Tested***

Godspeed and good luck.

SHE MIGHT BE A HO IF . . .

❏ There's a sexual position named after her.

❏ She has a counter by the bed.

❏ Everywhere you go, random guys wave at her and yell, "Thank you!"

❏ There are mirrors on her ceiling.

❏ When you tell her how many sexual partners you have had, she laughs and says, "You mean in one week, right?"

COUNT IT!

Why do some girls think if they let the tip in, it doesn't count as having sex? It does. The minute any portion of the penis is inserted into the vagina, it counts as intercourse. And if you're gonna put the tip in, why not put the whole damn thing in? Seems very unsatisfying. It's like having a pile of cocaine on the table and just licking it a little.

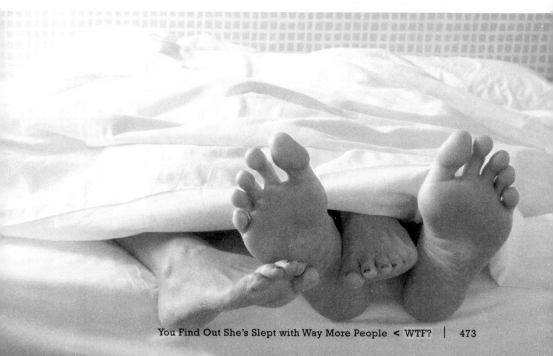

219. Your Sex Tape Winds Up on the Net

You told her it would only be for your personal use, no one would ever see it. You even joked when she was a little reluctant: "It's not like it's going to be broadcast over the Internet or something." Then, somehow, someway, it was. WTF?!

The WTF Approach to Being a F*#!-ing Internet Porn Star

➤ OPTION # 1: *Apologize*

Tell her you're sorry you turned her into a notorious slut. Then ask her if she wants to do it again, now that her dream of being the first woman president is probably over. See if she can have any of her remaining friends join in as well.

➤ OPTION #2: *Don't Sweat It*

So what if your wiener is all over the Net? It's not like your boss is going to see your nasty little movie. Plus, it's not likely that you'll be running for public office anytime soon—unless you happen to be a Bush.

➤OPTION #3: *Start a Porn Website*

If your little video seems to be gaining some popularity on the web, maybe you should think about doing some more of these little films.

➤OPTION #4: *Hide*

Lay low for a while in case your little starlet's father comes looking for you. Then again, she wouldn't be such a little slut if she had a daddy who cared. Put some time in at the gym just in case.

Our POV on POV Porn

POV—point of view—porn is really big now on the Internet (so we hear). POV porn is filmed from the perspective of the guy. The idea here is that it is apparently more erotic because it looks like you, the viewer, is the one receiving a blowjob. But can you really suspend reality enough to believe that you have a ten-inch black penis? And how come POV porn is only filmed from the perspective of the guy, what about POV porn for girls filmed from *their* perspective. Can you imagine? Just a big dick coming right for your eye . . . ahh!!!

IN THE FUTURE . . .

NEVER mind. No mAtteR how this ends, mAkin9 A porno with A fRESHMAN WAS definitely worth it.

YOU MIGHT BE ADDICTED TO PORN IF . . .

❏ You spend more time looking for the "perfect" video to whack off to than you do looking for a girl to have sex with.

❏ The minute you cum, you check and see if there was a better video to jerk off to, which invariably leads to another in a series of masturbatory sessions.

❏ You argued with your Intro to Film professor that *Citizen Cum* was a better film than *Citizen Kane*.

❏ You actually pay for any type of porn.

❏ In your school papers, you keep misspelling "come" as "cum."

❏ When you cum come across a long, free clip that buffers quickly, you know that your day just reached its peak.

❏ On a first date, you ask your new lady friend if she wants to have a threesome with the waitress.

❏ You take your girl to the petting zoo—and ask her to bang a goat.

❏ You believe the average penis length is a little over a foot.

❏ Every time your friend tells you about another great free porn site, you immediately cancel your weekend plans.

IF YOU CHECKED . . .

3–4: get a girlfriend
5–6: get a psychiatrist
7–10: get a priest

220. Your Girl Gives You Herpes

Ah, love. It fills your heart with unbridled joy, gives you that tingling sensation on your skin, makes your balls itch nonstop . . . wait, what? That's right, just months after you and your girl start dating, your girl gives you herpes. Sonofabitch!

The WTF Approach to Getting the F*#!-ing Gift That Keeps on Giving

➤ **OPTION #1:** *Dump Her Ass*

Drop her as fast as she dropped that cute little STD on your dick. Then sue her for the medical bills, medication, and emotional pain.

➤ **OPTION #2:** *Marry Her*

Look, now that you have herpes your dating pool just got a lot smaller . . . and more disgusting. What girl is going to knowingly go into a relationship with a guy who gets outbreaks on his dick every few months? She will have to be the one. Now you can sit back and enjoy a little game together called "connect the dots."

➤ **OPTION #3:** *Become a Skydiving, Windsurfing Kayaker*

Just like the people in the herpes medication commercial. Apparently, contracting herpes is a natural step in becoming a happy and rugged (very rugged) outdoorsman.

➤ OPTION #4: *Pay It Forward*

Now that you have this nasty little STD, you might as well get some good old-fashioned revenge. Call up that one special tramp who left you high and dry; convince her to give you one last roll in the sack for old times' sake. This time she won't forget you.

➤ OPTION #5: *Resent Her*

Say that you understand and forgive her, but secretly resent her for the rest of your life. You know you're going to anyway.

WTF ABOUT TOWN

The following is a partial transcript from Case #675435: Herpes vs. Jane Doe.

WTF: Please state your name for the record.

Herpes: Herpes Simplex 2

WTF: Is it true that on June 18, at approximately 3:12 A.M., you made a commitment to the plaintiff, Jane Doe, to stay with her for the rest of her life?

Herpes: It is.

WTF: And do you deny the fact that, since that commitment, you have not been faithful?

Herpes: Look, I wanted to be faithful but the temptation was just too great. I admit I had indiscretions.

WTF: With over 40 million people?

[*The crowd in the courtroom gasps.*]

Herpes: Okay, that number hasn't been proven yet.

WTF: I would like to submit as evidence 10,000 sex tapes where you can clearly see the defendant is present.

Herpes: Look, I'm sorry. I really am. To be honest, I think I have a problem. I believe I'm a sex and love addict and I need help.

WTF: Please. Whenever someone cheats, they use the "I have a sex addiction" defense. We're not buying it Mr. Simplex 2.

[*The courtroom breaks out in chaos and oozing genital warts. It's a nasty situation.*]

221. She Thinks Blowjobs Are Gross

So far your relationship has been going great. You have fun together, your friends like her and she loves to have sex. But she doesn't like giving head. In fact, every time you gently push her head in that general direction she pops up and gets mad. WTF?

The WTF Approach to Selling a F*#!-ing BJ

➤ OPTION #1: *Dip It in Chocolate*

Who doesn't love chocolate? If you don't want to cover the entire dick, just dip the tip in creamy sweetness and let your lady go to town. She might even start to enjoy it. Careful, though—you don't want her to start getting fat. No one likes getting BJs from a fatty.

➤ OPTION #2: *Flip the Switch*

Make a rule, no oral sex for anyone! She doesn't like putting your dick in her mouth, then you won't stick your tongue on her pusshole either. Fair is fair.

➤ OPTION #3: *Dress It Up*

Like a puppy. Put a little blanket around it and make it look cute and cuddly. Women love puppies.

➤ OPTION #4: *Guilt Her*

Tell her that she doesn't love you because she won't give you pleasure. Make her feel terrible about it. After all, what shows love more than taking your piss-topped cock in her mouth?

WTF: UP CLOSE AND PERSONAL

Guys always say if they could suck their own dick they would never leave the house. I say if you could suck your own dick I'd marry you. Then I'd never have to do it.

—JM

for the ladies . . .

Wax. Maybe he won't go down because you look like a porn star from the '70s. Get a Brazilian and you should be good.

IS ORAL SEX, SEX?

Some say it is (like Oprah), some say it isn't (like thirteen-year-olds). I think it depends on a few factors. Oral sex should be considered sex if the following conditions are met:

1. The orgasm is swallowed, and not spit out

2. You smoke a cigarette afterward

3. Neither one of you is a licensed dentist

4. The neighbors complain about the noise

5. At least one of the two participants is under eleven years old

IN THE FUTURE . . .

Join the popular dating website lovetosuckdick .com. You shouldn't have a problem meeting an open-minded lady there.

222. She Makes You Go Down on Her for Hours

Cunnilingus. It's one of the words that just rolls off the tongue. And it's fun, too! But enough is enough. Your neck is aching, your back is breaking, and your tongue feels like . . . well, like you've been eating pussy for two hours. "I'm almost there!" she cries out every ten minutes or so to encourage you. Will you cum already, for Christ's sake?

The WTF Approach to F*#!-ing Chowing Down

> **OPTION #1: *Strengthen Your Tongue***

Exercise it daily, morning and night. If you are going to be doing this a lot, you might as well make it as painless as possible.

> **OPTION #2: *Up Your Game***

Get a couple lesbian pornos and study them. Nobody knows how to please a woman better than a woman—except a black guy.

> **OPTION #3: *Buy a Toy***

There are so many to choose from, all of which are better than anything you can do. Dildos, vibrators, sex machines, suck machines— technology at its best. But be careful, she might just realize she doesn't need you at all anymore and dump your ass.

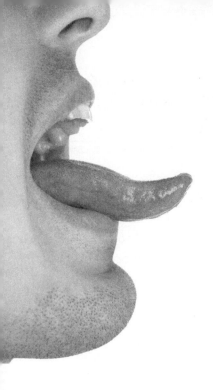

➤ OPTION #4: *Hire Someone to Pleasure Her*

If she needs the feel of the real thing and toys just don't cut it, hire a day laborer to go down on your wife for a couple bucks an hour. It shouldn't be hard. Just go to Home Depot, there are plenty of Mexicans outside who need work. And trust us, they'll be happy to oblige. Eating pussy beats the hell out of landscaping any day of the week.

➤ OPTION #5: *Get Better at It*

Obviously you're doing something wrong. Practice until you get it in less than five minutes. Trust us, she'll be as happy as you.

WOMEN ARE NO LAUGHING MATTER

"Cunnilingus is next to godliness."

—Kali Nichta

---

for the ladies . . .

If your guy is having a hard time finding the spot, show him. Unless you want to get a tongue rash.

---

223. She Wants to Have a Threesome with Your Best Friend

Finally, you met a chick that you like that wants to have a threesome. Awesome! Imagine the possibilities! All the comfort and solace of true companionship without the sexual monotony that comes along with it. Then she tells you just what kind of threesome she wants: She wants another guy. And more than that, she wants your best friend. WTF?

The WTF Approach to Having a F*#!-ing Threesome

> **OPTION #1: _Size Him Up_**

Find out how big your friend's dick is. If it's smaller than yours, then let him screw your girl if you think it will turn you on. If it is bigger than yours, then feel envious just like you always do when someone has a big dick.

> **OPTION #2: _Just Say No_**

It's not worth it. Sure it might be fun to watch your best friend shove his penis in your girlfriend's mouth, but who knows how you'll feel afterward? And equally important, who knows how she'll feel afterward? Emotionally, that is. (Obviously, physically she will experience some slight soreness and discomfort.)

> **OPTION #3:** *Just Say Goodbye*

Don't ever talk to her again. Filthy whore!

> **OPTION #4:** *Make a Deal*

She can sleep with your best friend, if you can bone her best friend. No, not the fat redhead, the other one with the big tits, what's her name?

THREE'S A CROWD

Wee! Yay! Wow! Is that my foot? These are the things commonly said when you are banging away in a threesome or an orgy. But all good things must come to an end. Many a couple know that often the feeling of elation during a threesome is immediately followed by jealousy, existential woe, and—once in and a while—chlamydia.

REVELATIONS BETWEEN THE SHEETS

My girlfriend and I had a threesome with one of my college buddies. The night started off innocently enough. We met up with my friend at a local bar for some drinks, then back to her place for more drinks. Then all of a sudden my girl, who was totally wasted, said, "We should screw. All of us." At first I thought she was kidding but when I realized she wasn't, I was so excited it felt like fucking Christmas. My friend was also totally game. So there we are, rolling around on the bed. Then my friend starts banging her from behind while she's blowing me. This was awesome until I heard her say, "Yeah that's it. Do that thing you did last time." Last time? What the hell? This tramp has already screwed my friend. I pretended not to hear so I could finish. We broke up the next day. Lesson here is that if something seems too good to be true, it usually is. Bitch!
—Jason Crosby, Massachusetts

THREESOME ETIQUETTE

There are certain rules to follow when you're getting it on with multiple partners.

Do . . .	Don't . . .
Videotape it.	Look down.
Get drunk.	Feel around in the dark.
Jerk off while they're going at it.	Jerk off in the corner crying.

224. You Can't Find Your Girl's G-Spot

You can find her vagina (good for you, genius), but you just can't seem to find the sweet spot. She is getting frustrated, and you don't know what to do. Turns out you'd probably be able to find Bin Laden before you found your girl's G-spot.

The WTF Approach to Hitting the F*#!-ing Spot

➤ OPTION #1: *Ask for Directions*

We all know the saying "men don't ask for directions." Well, this time you should. Shit, have your girl draw a map. Trust us, once you get there, it will be worth it.

➤ OPTION #2: *Do Nothing*

Who cares if you can find it or not, as long as you're bustin' a nut, that's all that matters right?

➤ OPTION #3: *Hire a Better Cock*

Get a guy with a bigger, better penis to screw her and give her the earth-shattering orgasms that you cannot. Then move slowly to the balcony and throw yourself off.

> **OPTION #4:** *Get a G-Spot Vibrator*

Fake cocks are better than real ones nowadays for women. Choose one of a thousand different kinds of vibrators specifically curved to stimulate the G-spot. Then kiss her goodbye, for she'll need you no more.

WTFACT: The G-spot is a term used to describe an erogenous zone of the vagina. It's named after Ernst Gräfenberg, who was the first guy to supposedly find it. If you're going on the hunt, it's typically one to three inches up the front vaginal wall. Another fact: Ernst Gräfenberg was a pimp.

225. She Hates All Your Stuff

It starts slow. First, your favorite *Playboy* Playmate poster ends up in the trash. Then your football lamp mysteriously disappears. You go to sit in your beat-up beanbag chair and that, too, is gone. Finally, you confront your girl, who doesn't even try to hide it. "I threw it out," she says, without an ounce of regret. "Because you live with me now and you have no taste." WTF?

The WTF Approach to Dealing with Your Bad F*#!-ing Taste

➤ OPTION #1: *Store It*

Take what's left and stick it in a storage facility. You might think you will always be with her, but odds are you won't. Save your stupid ugly shit for when you inevitably become a bachelor again. Maybe the next girl will have that same shit taste as you.

➤ OPTION #2: *Flip the Switch*

Who is she, Martha Stewart? So maybe two naked girls on a tractor isn't everyone's idea of "art," but you like it. Insist on a compromise, and make her get rid of some of her shit. If she says no, tell her she can take her opinion and shove it up her tight Crate & Barrel ass! Then consider yourself single.

WTF Matching Game

Sometimes she's right. Your crap sucks. But at least it doesn't suck as bad as other people's crap. Match the crap with the sucker who owns it.

1. Lava lamp	A. Persian
2. Lava lamp with cum stains	B. Douchebag
3. Wagon wheel table	C. College student that doesn't get laid
4. Leather couch	D. College student
5. Original Picasso	E. Surfer dude
6. Bob Marley poster	F. White trash pig
7. Framed Ed Hardy T-shirt	G. Rich, old guy, soon to be robbed
8. Persian rug	H. Typical dumb white guy
9. Confederate flag	I. Bachelor desperate for play
10. Fabergé egg	J. Lesbian
11. Football phone	K. Republican

Answer Key

1. D	7. B
2. C	8. A
3. H	9. F
4. I	10. K
5. G	11. J
6. E	

COMPROMISE

If you're going to live together, you better start compromising now. Give a little to get a little. For each item you get rid of, she has to bring another girl home. Before you know it, you'll be hosting orgies in a very well-decorated apartment.

226. She's a Total Slob

irty girl. Sloppy slut. Messy mama. It's one thing to say this when you are having sex, it's quite another to say this when you're not. But you just can't take it anymore! Crumbs in the bed, dirty underwear all over the bathroom floor, and a sink piled high with dishes. At first when you started dating this woman, you liked the fact that she wasn't a neat freak, but this is disgusting. Now that you're living together, you realize that your girl is a pig.

The WTF Approach to Dating a F*#!-ing Pig

➤ OPTION #1: *Try to Tame Her*

Even the wildest of beasts can be domesticated. Make her clean and then, as a reward, buy her some jewelry to reinforce the positive behavior. Girls like bright shiny objects.

➤ OPTION #2: *Hire a Professional*

Like Cesar Milan, the Dog Whisperer. He's turned even the most untrained bitches around.

> **OPTION #3:** *Hire a Maid*

If you love this woman and it doesn't look like she's ever going to clean anything and cannot be trained, hire a maid. Sure, it might cost you a little extra dough, but so would going to the doctor because of all the infections you keep getting from living like a pig.

Driven Away

Inspect a girl's car when you meet her. Typically, a woman's car is a good indication of how clean she is. If there are bags of garbage, clothes, and other crap in her vehicle, she probably lives in a pigsty. If she actually lives in her car, however, cut her a break for it being messy; there are other reasons besides her messiness to avoid a relationship with her. Namely, the fact that she lives in her car.

WTF ABOUT TOWN

At WTF we keep up with popular culture. Meaning we watch a lot of TV. One show, *Hoarding: Buried Alive* on TLC, focuses on people who suffer from the compulsion to hoard everything they buy. We talked to one such hoarder and the following conversation ensued:

WTF: Wow, you have a lot of shit.

Hoarder: I know, I have a problem.

WTF: What's that guy doing over there in the corner?

Hoarder: I have no idea. I slept with him three years ago and now he's eating cat food in the corner.

WTF: Damn.

Hoarder: But I alphabetized him.

WTF: Oh, okay then.

Never date a hoarder. There's a chance you will become part of her property.

227. She Takes Up the Entire Closet

When you moved in together you knew there would be compromises—like you not being able to screw everything you see, for instance. And you know she needs more space in the house because she has breasts. But does she really need to take up the whole closet with her handbags and shoes? Who does she think she is, Carrie Bradshaw? And by the way, if you know who Carrie Bradshaw is, then you're officially gay—and need way more closet space.

The WTF Approach to Living with a F*#!-ing Closet Whore

➤ OPTION #1: *Get Another Closet*

No apartment or house only has one closet, so move your shit to another one. If there isn't another closet in your place, then you are a total loser and probably don't have anything worth storing anyway. Throw it out.

►OPTION #2: *Use Another Room*

If she won't share, then hang your clothes in the bathroom or kitchen. When she complains—and she will—tell her you have nowhere to put your clothes and if she doesn't like moving your underwear to get the cereal, then she can make some room in the closet!

►OPTION #3: *Become a Nudist*

Stop wearing clothes. If you have nowhere to put your clothes, then throw them out and go the way nature intended. You'll probably lose your friends, your job, and your girl, but you and your cock will finally be free!

TOP FIVE THINGS HIDDEN IN CLOSETS

1. Clothes

2. Shoes

3. Socks

4. Coats

5. Your homosexual lifestyle

WTF: UP CLOSE AND PERSONAL

When I was a wee lad, we used to play a game called "five minutes in the closet." Like spin the bottle, it's a co-ed sex game, but with a twist. A boy and a girl would have five minutes to do whatever they wanted in the closet. Knowing there was little time, I always tried to get as much done as possible. The first time I played it, I immediately dropped my shorts and exposed my penis to the girl. She shouted. "We only have five minutes!" I told her, "We don't have time to fight about what to do." That was the first and last time Sherry ever played five minutes in the closet—at least with me.

—GB

228. She Leaves You a Chore Chart Every Morning

Monday: Take out the trash. Tuesday: Clean the gutters. Wednesday: Eat her out. Chores. Chores. Chores. It never stops. You knew your girl was a little controlling, but this is ridiculous. Every morning you wake up with another damn to-do list. What are you, five years old? This relationship is supposed to be a partnership, but it's more like a dictatorship. And that would be fine if you were the dictator. But you're not. It's time to face it, you are your girl's little bitch. Shame on you!

The WTF Approach to Dating a F*#!-ing Control Freak

➤ **OPTION #1: *Revolt!***

Pull those tiny little things you call balls out from in between your ass and stand up for yourself. Tell her you have no problem helping out and doing your share of stuff around the house, but the next time she leaves a chore chart for you, it's going up her vagina. Take that!

NOTE: This could backfire. Don't be surprised if she wraps tomorrow's chore chart around a big fat dildo.

➤ OPTION #2: *Just Do It*

If this keeps the peace around the house, just do it and be done with it.

➤ OPTION #3: *Flip the Switch*

If she's gonna leave you a chore chart, you leave a *whore* chart for her. Each day she must do at least one whorish thing to prove her love.

> **DATING IN AMERICA**
>
> "My ex-girlfriend used to leave a chore chart for me every morning. Eventually, it really started to bother me. Annoyed, I killed her one night in cold blood."
> —Robert Benson, somewhere in North America

229. Every Night Is Netflix Night

Every once in a while it's nice to order in, open a bottle of wine, and rent a movie. You'll even let her pick out the movie as long as there's a chance you'll be getting some action after. But lately, these Netflix nights seem to be getting more and more frequent. You can't remember the last time you went to dinner, a bar with friends, or even saw a movie in the theater. Every night is movie night. And as for sex afterward? Not lately. Cuddle up, because that's as good as it's going to get. And guess what tonight is? That's right, it's *Twilight* movie marathon night.

The WTF Approach to Battling Bad F*#!-ing Movies

➤ **OPTION #1:** *Take Action*

Make dinner reservations somewhere or make plans with friends. So before she can jump into those unattractive sweats and grab the popcorn, you tell her to get dressed because she is going out. She might just get excited that you took the reins.

➤ **OPTION #2:** *You Pick the Flick*

If she wants to watch a movie every night, when it's your turn to pick, make it *A Midsummer's Night Cream* followed by *A Tale of Two Titties*. After a week of hardcore porn she won't want to see another movie again. And if she does, it will probably be more porn.

Get rid of your DVD player and television. Can't watch a movie if there's no television, right? Tell her you think watching television and movies are rotting your brain.

NOTE: Keep a spare television at your office. I mean, seriously, you can't live without television. What are you, a caveman?

NO TV? F*#! YOU!

Why do people like to make a big deal out of the fact that they don't own a TV? We get it, you're so cultured that you don't rot your brain with mindless TV shows. You're reading all the time. Yeah, it would be one thing if that were true, but half the people who don't watch TV are just sitting around smoking pot and staring at a Jimi Hendrix poster. Not exactly an intellectual exercise.

WTF: UP CLOSE AND PERSONAL

As a thirty-year-old semimasculine and semisophisticated man, the whole *Twilight* phenomenon was laughable to me. For years I didn't get the obsession with the movie and the douchebags in them—all this talk of Team Jacob and Team Edward. Ridiculous. Then on one of our many movie nights, my wife made me watch *Twilight*. Instantly, I was hooked. I have now been a struggling Twihard for over one year. —GB

TEAM EDWARD VERSUS TEAM JACOB	Edward	Jacob
Looks	Tall, pale, and mysterious	Blends in more on a Caribbean cruise
Life Expectancy	Will live forever	Will live forever—but as a dog
Special Powers	Can turn into a bat and fly away	Might get pulled over in Arizona for being an illegal

230. Your Free Time's Now Spent at IKEA and Target

You love doing things with your wife. Dinner, movies, and even sometimes shopping—for lingerie. But there are two places that make every man immediately sick to his stomach: IKEA and Target. These stores are like kryptonite for anyone with a dick.

The WTF Approach to Getting Out of F*#!-ing Shopping Trips

➤ OPTION #1: *Show Her Your Penis*

Take it out right now in the middle of the aisle and remind her that you are not one of her girlfriends, and that you do not give a fuck which toilet seat cover would look best in the bathroom. You have a dick, and therefore you are bio-logically conditioned not to care about shit like this.

➤ OPTION #2: *Make a Scene*

If taking out your cock and waving it around was too subtle, make a huge embarrassing scene. Start screaming and pulling out your hair, crying and kicking in the aisle like a two-year-old. Keep yelling: "I wanna go home! I hate you!"

➤ OPTION #3: *Organize an Escape*

Get with other equally annoyed men shopping with their girl-friends. Take them aside and whisper to them to meet you in the bedding section. Then, have a secret meeting and plan your escape. Bored boyfriends of the world, unite!

➤ OPTION #4: *Fake a Seizure*

Between being in the back of an ambulance and being in Target looking at kitchenware, take the ambulance any day of the week.

WHAT THE F*#! IS UP WITH . . .
GUYS NEVER HAVING FUN

If you really observe couples doing anything together, be it shopping, traveling, going to the movies, you'll notice something. The guy is not really having fun. *Ever!* This is our little secret that we need to let out of the bag and tell women. We don't really *like* being around you. Not really. Sure we don't mind going to a good restaurant or seeing a movie, but if you think that we are having a good time walking around afterward, getting some ice cream, stopping to look at some clothes in a window, you are dead fucking wrong. We do it because we have to. But all things considered, no matter how interesting and pretty you are, no matter how much we love you, between walking around with you and doing *anything*—like working on a septic tank—with one of our buddies, we'll choose the latter.

231. Her Parents Have to Move In with You

Your wife comes in and tells you her parents are coming to visit. Okay, how bad can that be? You'll get drunk with her father and talk politics; she and her mom can go shopping. All good. You ask how long they plan on staying and your wife says vaguely "a while." A while? Turns out her father lost his job of thirty years and all their savings in the stock market. And now they've lost their home. Now "a while" your wife confesses, is really "until they get back on their feet." Back on their feet? You'll be lucky to get them out of the house before they're dead.

The WTF Approach to Dealing with F*#!-ing Unexpected Roommates

➤ OPTION #1: *Put Them to Work*

Make them earn their keep. Think positive. You'll now have a live-in maid/cook and your own personal driver. If they want to live there, they're gonna have to work for it.

> **WOMEN ARE NO LAUGHING MATTER**
>
> "My mother-in-law broke up my marriage. My wife came home and found us in bed together."
>
> —Lenny Bruce

➤ OPTION #2: *Take It Out on Her*

Remember that you are screwing his daughter. If the old man becomes a pain in the ass, make sure he can hear you give it to his daughter every night. If that doesn't spice things up in the bedroom for you and make you feel at peace, nothing will.

➤ OPTION #3: *Buy Them a Trailer*

Make it a double-wide. Then tell them to take a nice long cross-country trip. In other words, here's a moving house, now get the hell out of here!

WTF: UP CLOSE AND PERSONAL

"My in-laws moved in with us for a short time. At first I was dreading it. I tried to stay at the office as much as I could. But as it turns out, I really got to know her parents. Like for instance, turns out my father-in law loves Internet porn. I caught him watching it in my office. He was so mortified he now bribes me to keep my mouth shut. Which, to be honest, I would have done anyway, considering I have four unlimited memberships to various porn sites."

—Dr. Burgess, Maine

232. You Lose Your Job and Have to Hit Up Your Father-in-Law

It happens every day: people lose their jobs. You think you'll find another one right away, but the joke's on you: there are *no* jobs. And that savings account you kept promising to start has a total of twenty dollars in it. You've filed for unemployment but you still can't make ends meet. Time to tuck that tail between your legs.

The WTF Approach to Begging for F*#!-ing Cash

➤ OPTION #1: *Knock Her Up*

Get your wife pregnant, fast. Before you beg her father for some cash, get his little girl knocked up so you have good news before the bad. He'll be so happy, he will write you a check, no questions asked.

➤ OPTION #2: *Steal from Him*

If you can't bring yourself to ask him, then break into his house when you know he's not home and steal that priceless Babe Ruth rookie baseball card. Desperate times call for really fucked-up measures.

➤ OPTION #3: *Start to Cry*

No one likes to see a grown man cry. Sure he'll probably think less of you as a man, but you are less of a man anyway if you are hitting your father-in-law up for cash.

➤ OPTION #4: *Make Your Wife Ask*

It's always better to have a woman ask for money, especially from her daddy. Go out and get drunk while your wife saves your ass again!

The Right Way and the Wrong Way

Don't be an idiot when it comes to hitting up the old man. Take a look at these guidelines so you know what *not* to do.

➤ THE WRONG WAY

WTF: Hey, I need some money.

Father-in-law: How much?

WTF: A lot, asshole. Do you know how much your daughter spends? The bitch has bankrupted my ass.

Father-in-law: When do you think you'll be able to pay me back?

WTF: (Laughing uncontrollably) Good one!

➤ THE RIGHT WAY

WTF: I could really use a loan.

Father-in-law: (sigh) How much?

WTF: Whatever you can spare. These times are tough and it makes me feel sick to think I won't be able to take care of my precious wife (your daughter) in the way she deserves.

Father-in-law: Just this once.

WTF: Thanks, Dad.

Father-in-law: Don't push it, asshole.

233. She Won't Let You Hang Out with Your Friends

et's go to IKEA. Let's go to the movies. Let's do yard work. Let's rent a movie and wait to pass away. Fun. Every free moment you have, you spend with your girl. Whenever you try to make plans with your friends, she vetoes it and tells you she has already made plans. WTF?

The WTF Approach to Getting Some F*#!-ing Guy Time

➤ OPTION #1: *Grow a Pair*

Look, tell her that you are spending time with the guys, like it or not. If she starts bitching, just walk out. Unless you stand up for yourself now, you are never going to get out of her grip.

➤ OPTION #2: *Flip the Switch*

You can't hang with your buds, fine; she is no longer allowed to get together with the "girls." No more wine and whine parties. No more brunches. No more *Sex and the City* marathons. Nothing. It will just be you and her *forever*. Then immediately regret you just said that.

➤ OPTION #3: *Invite Her Along*

Sometimes a woman doesn't want you to hang with your friends because she's afraid you'll get into some trouble. So bring her to your fantasy football draft night. Poker night, Guitar Hero, bowling. Once she gets a taste of your boring, nerd-filled life she will give her blessing. Then once she's out of the picture, go to a strip club with the boys and grab yourself some titties.

Role Models

These classic films continue to encourage this behavior.

- *The Hangover*
- *Very Bad Things*
- *The Pianist*

for the ladies . . .

If your man won't let you hang out with your friends, he's a controlling, possibly abusive man. Or he just knows that your friends are all slutty drunk whores. Remember, he met you on Facebook, so he isn't an idiot.

234. Her Best Friend Is Always Over

The best thing about living with your woman is that you get to spend time together alone. It's nice to be able to have sex any time of day, hang out in your boxers and chill. Except you're never alone because her best friend is always there. And she is always crying about some random hook-up, or bitching about her work, or whining about the fact that she just can't lose that extra fifteen pounds. The two of them are always watching *Gossip Girl* and painting their toenails. Instead of a quiet place for you and your girl to share, your apartment has become a fucking sorority.

The WTF Approach to Tolerating her F*#!-ing BFF

➤ OPTION #1: *Lay Down the Law*

Tell your girl that when you come home you want to see her, not her annoying friends. That's why you moved in with her. If you wanted to see her friends, then you would be living with (and banging) them.

If she wants to consider some sort of arrangement like that, be more than willing to listen.

➤OPTION #2: *Find Her Friend a Man*

Invite your single buddy over and fix them up. Then at least when she comes over, you'll have a friend to play with too.

IN THE FUTURE . . .

DATE A girl with no friends. With nothing to do, All she can do is have sex to entertain herself.

➤OPTION #3: *Hit on Her*

Make a pass and tell her that it's so hard to see her when she comes over. Tell her you've had a secret crush on her and for the sake of your relationship with your girlfriend, you need her to stop coming by so much. She'll be flattered and you'll have some peace!

➤OPTION #4: *Charge Her Rent*

If her BFF is gonna eat your food, sit on your couch and breathe your air, she needs to pay for it. Make a little extra money, then head over to the strip club whenever the friend comes over.

235. Her Friends Are Trying to Break You Up

It's hard enough to convince a woman you are not a scumbag, let alone all her friends. Navigating the critical world of your girlfriend's girlfriends takes a special skill. You've got to be friendly, but not too friendly. (Do not try to bone them, for instance.) You have to be a good guy, but not disgustingly good or they might get jealous. Most importantly, talk about your girl incessantly; about how lucky you are to be with her.

The WTF Approach to Surviving F*#!-ing Sabotage

►OPTION #1: *Have Them Killed*

All of them. Sure your girl will be sad, but there is always Facebook. She'll make new friends in no time.

►OPTION #2: *Flip the Switch*

Try to take away something they care about. Like their boyfriend, their job, or their newly born son. LOL. Newly born son! Get it? Leave a note saying that it is in the son's best interest to have a new mom.

►OPTION #3: *Show Them*

All of them. Yes, even the fat red-head. Once they see that you can't perform, they'll pity you.

for the ladies . . .

If your boyfriend's friends want to break you up, it's because they miss playing video games with him and/or they want to bang you.

WAYS TO WIN OVER YOUR GIRLFRIEND'S GIRLFRIENDS

- Compliment each of them on their looks every time you see them.

- Go out to dinner with them all and pick up the check.

236. Your Girl Leaves a Dear John Letter on Your Bed

You wake up one morning and your girl isn't beside you. Maybe she left early for work? Then you find a note next to the bed. Sweet, she probably ran out to get you some breakfast in bed! As you start to read the letter, you realize that she isn't coming back with breakfast—or at all for that matter.

The WTF Approach to Getting Over Being F*#!-ing Dumped

➤ **OPTION #1: *Move On***

Doesn't look like you have a choice, dipshit.

➤ **OPTION #2: *Find Her***

Track her down at work, at a friend's place, anywhere, and demand she explain herself. Then take that apple she left you and shove it up her ass. Maybe that's what she really wanted: a man that takes control—and knows how to use an apple.

➤ **OPTION #3: *Get Even***

Not with her, since it is impossible, but with the world. Take all your frustration out on other women unfairly and leave them high and dry, like she left you.

➤ OPTION #4: *Go Public*

Post the letter on Facebook or another social network explaining how this was the love of your life and how devastated you are that someone you cared so much for left you so abruptly. Trust us; you'll get a ton of sympathy pussy!

WHAT THE F*#! IS UP WITH . . . DEAR JOHN LETTERS

Why is it called a Dear John letter and who the hell is John, anyway? WTF did our research and according to legend, the term "Dear John" letter was popularized during World War II when, after a long separation from her husband overseas, a woman wrote a letter to her man on the battlefield informing him that she was leaving him in search of available dick. Luckily, most of the men probably got killed before they received the letters. Otherwise, they would have seriously hurt morale.

Love Songs for the Loveless

Most of the most popular songs are about love. The songwriters must have been in love when they wrote them. Here are some titles that might have ended up differently if the songwriter weren't in love.

- Gloria Estefan's "Anything for You" would become "Nothing Ever Again"

- Jewel's "Because I Love You" would become "Because I Loved You (Until You Cheated on Me with My Best Friend)"

- Celine Dion's "Because You Loved Me" would become "Because You Loved You and Only You"

- Britney Spears' "Born to Make You Happy" would become "Born to Make You Wish You Were Dead"

- Madonna's "Crazy for You" would become "Crazy Because of You"

237. You Have to Split Up Your Crap after the Breakup

The breakup. It's one of the most devastating and liberating experiences in a man's life. Sad about being alone and missing her, yet thrilled at the prospect of anonymous intercourse with strange vaginas—during the breakup, all our conflicting emotions are in high gear. Needless to say, it is a very difficult time, and one through which you must try to navigate amicably like the mature adults that you are. Oh, and by the way, whore, is this my copy of *Catcher in the Rye* or yours?

The WTF Approach to Dividing Up the F*#!-ing Stuff

➤ OPTION #1: *Take It*

She took your heart out of your chest, stepped and spat on it, shat on it, and then vomited on it and threw it in the trash. The least she can do is give you the benefit of the doubt and let you keep the book. Tell her it is a guy's book anyway and, you hate women, just like Holden Caulfield, and can relate.

➤ **OPTION #2:** *Stop Reading*

Reading is for girls. Boning is for men. Now that you are single, less reading, more boning. Only read about boning . . . unless it's about war. Killing and boning. LOL.

➤ **OPTION #3:** *Give It to Her*

You got chlamydia; she gets *Catcher in the Rye*. Fair trade.

for the ladies . . .

Just do what you always do—take whatever the hell you want.

IN THE FUTURE . . .

DATE A girl who doesn't READ. GiRls who READ ARE ugly.

WOMEN ARE NO LAUGHING MATTER

"A relationship, I think, is like a shark. You know? It has to constantly move forward or it dies. And I think what we got on our hands is a dead shark."

—Woody Allen in *Annie Hall*

238. You're Both on the Lease and You Both Want the Place

Finally you can agree on something: You both want to end this toxic relationship. But there's one problem: both of you are on the lease and both of you are claiming the right to stay in the apartment. If this were an episode of *The Brady Bunch* you could just tape a yellow strip down the center of the apartment and share it, but guess what? It's not. And she's no Marcia Brady!

The WTF Approach to Keeping Your F*#!-ing Home

➤ **OPTION #1:** *Never Give Up*

Fight to the death and never give up. You are not just fighting this fight for yourself, but you are fighting it for all men who are bullied by their women and who walk away with their tail between their legs, giving up for convenience sake rather than sticking with the fight.

➤ **OPTION #2:** *Give Up*

All right, it looks like she isn't going to give in. Just seeing her face is not worth all this hassle. Let her take her victory, and just move on. Would you rather be fighting with a girl you hate in a beautiful apartment or banging a beautiful girl in an apartment that you hate? Now you're thinking, kid.

➤ **OPTION #3:** *Play for It*

That's what they'd do in *The Brady Bunch*. Win it. Build a house of cards and the first person to make it fall loses and moves out.

➤ **OPTION #4:** *Beg*

Tell her she has broken your heart and this is the only thing you have left of your shattered relationship. Throw in some tears for dramatic effect. Sure, she'll probably tell all her friends what a pussy you are, but you'll be laughing while you're chilling in *your* apartment!

➤ **OPTION #5:** *Burn It Down*

Now no one can live there. Problem solved.

WTF ABOUT TOWN

Girl: It's over.

Guy: You're damn right, it's over.

Girl: Now get out!

Guy: What?

Girl: Get the hell out of here!

Guy: Me? Why should I be the one to go? What about you?

Girl: Me? No, you need to leave and you need to leave right this minute.

Guy: But I pay rent and I am on the lease.

Girl: Ha! And I have a vagina. Do *you* have a vagina

Guy: Well, no but . . .

Girl: I rest my case. Now get your vagina-less ass out of here!

Guy: You make a good point. Sorry to have bothered you. I will now be on my way.

IN THE FUTURE . . .

Never let a woman on a lease unless your credit sucks and you have no other choice.

239. She Wants to Get Married but You're Like, "F*#! That!"

Time is running out and you know it. It's been a couple years, and her biological clock is ticking so loud it wakes you up at night. There is no more wiggle room to procrastinate. She wants a ring on that finger and she wants it now.

The WTF Approach to Getting Out of Popping the F*#!-ing Question

➤ **OPTION #1: *Just Say No***

Ever met a happily married couple? Exactly! Just say no and hang on.

➤ **OPTION #2: *Refuse on Principle***

Tell her you don't believe in marriage. You don't need to get a marriage certificate to prove you are in love. Tell her marriage is a dying institution. For Christ's sake, even homosexuals can do it in some places.

➤ **OPTION #3: *Give In***

It's inevitable. We as men are lonely and weak and although we really don't like being with one woman, the thought of dying alone is marginally worse.

➤ **OPTION #4: *Join Netflix***

Because the rest of your life is going to be one long fucking movie night. Enjoy the show!

How to Pop the Question

Asking a woman to marry you is a big deal. Don't choke.

➤ **THE WRONG WAY**

Girl: When are you going to marry me?

Guy: Where is this coming from?

Girl: We've been together for a while and we're happy.

Guy: Exactly, we're happy.

Girl: (crying) Don't you love me?

Guy: (Sigh) Oh, for Christ sake. Pick out a ring under $1,000, plan the damn thing, and get that cheapskate father of yours to chip in. Okay? Text me later, hon, I have to meet the guys . . . it's poker night.

➤ **THE RIGHT WAY**

Girl: When are you going to marry me?

Guy: If I tell you, then it won't be a surprise. Sex?

GREAT PROPOSAL IDEAS	NOT SO GREAT PROPOSAL IDEAS
• Write it in the sand	
• Message in a bottle	• Write it in the sand—with your piss
• Set her screensaver to read: "Will you marry me?"	• Message on her voice mail
	• Carve "Will you marry me?" into your chest

HAPPILY *UN*MARRIED COUPLES

If it's good enough for Hollywood . . .

- Goldie Hawn and Kurt Russell
- Angelina Jolie and Brad Pitt
- Kermit the Frog and Miss Piggy
- Bert and Ernie

240. You Don't Know How to Date Anymore

The divorce is final and you're on your own again. You've got your own pad and you're getting back out there. But boy, have things changed. You met a hot girl who wants to go out with you—at Starbucks. But first you have to find her on Facebook then text her to see when she's available. You try the old-fashioned way and call her, but she doesn't answer. She texts you back and tells you to meet her at her gym. Hold on, this is so confusing . . .

The WTF Approach to Getting Back in the F*#!-ing Game

➤ OPTION #1: *Turn On the TV*

Watch the CW channel. All it has are shows with hot young people who are dating and screwing. Just do what they do. Make sure to buy an Ed Hardy T-shirt, pump up at the gym, get a fake tan, and act like total fucking douchebag.

➤ OPTION #2: *Go Online*

This seems to be the easiest way to get back out there. Most likely, you'll find a woman who is also newly single after a long period of time. Follow her lead and you'll be in another shitty relationship before you know it. You're welcome.

►OPTION #3: *Go to a Twelve-Step Meeting*

Broken women are far more receptive than chicks that have their shit together. AA, NA, SAA (sex addicts anonymous)—you really can't go wrong. These women are so desperate for companionship that going home empty-handed is really not an option.

►OPTION #4: *Do Nothing*

Dating sucks. The uncomfortable first date conversations. You have to pay for dinner without a promise of any action. Stay single and use the money you would have spent on the dinners and movies on hookers and drugs. Much more fun and far less expensive.

YOU MIGHT BE RUSTY IF . . .

❏ When you ask a girl out, you say, "Pick you up at eight" without asking her address or waiting for an answer.

❏ When she tells you to put on a condom, you ask "Why?"

❏ The last girl you slept with before your ex was named Gertrude.

❏ A hand job is "scoring" in your book.

❏ You act like a gracious gentleman and not a selfish asshole.

241. You Run into Your Ex— and Her Handsome, Rich New Boyfriend

The last thing she said to you was that she deserves better. Maybe, you thought, but not *that* much better. She might be a little out of your league but she's no supermodel. So when you run into her at a restaurant and meet her new boyfriend, Dr. whatever-the-fuck his name was, you realize that she wasn't kidding. Objectively, this man has you beat. He's taller, better looking, more educated, richer, and it might just be the way his pants fit, but it looks as though he's hiding a mongoose in his jeans. Alone and twenty pounds heavier, you feel as though you might just have a heart attack right there—and the double bacon cheeseburger and French fries in your stomach aren't helping. WTF?

The WTF Approach to Seeing Your F*#!-ing Ex

➤ OPTION #1: *Flip the Switch*

Tell her that you are also dating a tall, handsome doctor. Then thank her and tell her that being with her made you realize that you were gay.

➤ OPTION #2: *Run*

Screw the bill. Just run and pay later. Get the hell out of there, stat!

➤ OPTION #3: *Use It*

Use the thought of them banging to motivate you. Stop being a loser and get your shit together. Lose some weight, start your own company, and score yourself a hot model. Then shoot a sex tape with your new smoking hot girl and send it to your ex.

for the ladies . . .

Smile and laugh as if you know something he doesn't. Then say something vague like, "Well, birds of a feather." He won't know what the hell you're talking about. This will haunt him for weeks.

HE MIGHT BE BETTER THAN YOU IF . . .

❏ He has a big dick. You have what looks like a deformed outtie bellybutton.

❏ He can bench 300 pounds. You weigh 300 pounds.

❏ He spends his days off helping out at a soup kitchen. You spend your days waiting in line at a soup kitchen.

242. You Just Can't Get Over Her No Matter What You Do

It's been months. You've tried drinking. You've tried therapy. You've tried drinking before therapy. And you've tried—God knows you've tried—to forget about her by humping anything that crosses your path. But the fact is you can't get over her. The way she smelled. The way she felt. The way she smiled. The way she dumped your ass and kicked you while you were down. How in God's name will you ever move on?

The WTF Approach to Dealing with a Broken F*#!-ing Heart

➤ **OPTION #1: *Try Hypnosis***

If it can help people quit smoking and block the pain of childbirth, it should be potent enough to help you forget about your ex-girlfriend's rack.

➤ **OPTION #2: *Be a Man***

Whoops, too late for that. Go to Option #3.

➤ **OPTION #3: *Be a Woman***

You've already been acting like it for the last few months, so you might as well live your life as a chick, real pussy and all.

➤ OPTION #4: *Vegas Baby, Vegas!*

Go to Las Vegas with your friends. If you still think about her while you are there, then please put down this book right now and return it to the shelf if you have not purchased it. We don't want your business, lameass.

MEN WHO WENT NUTS OVER A WOMAN

- Romeo Montague

- O.J. Simpson

- Every guy who's ever caught a glimpse of *WTF?* author Jodi Miller—even from a distance

for the ladies . . .

You can't get over your ex? Buy a vibrator . . . a really, really big one and name it for your ex. Remember, Tom Hanks in *Cast Away* managed to substitute real human contact for a volleyball, and he didn't even get to screw it. (Although we never saw the director's cut.)

Get Over It

Are you still pining for your ex? Take this quiz:

It's been three months since you broke up and you still . . .

A. Carry a picture of her vagina in your wallet.

B. Cry out her name while you masturbate.

C. Walk up to girls who look like her and spit in their face.

D. All of the above.

A: You're fine. After all, let's be honest, it was a good pussy.

B: You really need to get laid.

C: You might want to relocate someplace where the girls don't look like your ex—like Eskimo country.

D: You are still pining for her, and should seek help.

Answer Key

243. She Wants a Big, Expensive Wedding You Can't Afford

She has dreamed about her wedding since she was a little girl. On a hilltop, in a long flowing dress, 500 of her closest friends and family members. Beautiful, ornate fountains overflowing with champagne. When she accepted your proposal, you figured that her father would have to find a way to pay for it. Problem is, her father is a loser. He was laid off from his job over a year ago and lost all his family's savings gambling. And no matter how much you put away, your KFC wages are just not going to cut it.

The WTF Approach to Planning a Budget F*#!-ing Wedding

➤ OPTION #1: *Distract and Deflect*

Convince her that eloping is far more romantic. Tell her that you want to share this experience with only her. Tell her that you don't need a bunch of people witnessing you profess your love: God and Jesus will suffice. If she really loves you and you sell it right, she might give in.

➤ OPTION #2: *Win a Big Wedding*

Many television shows and radio programs give away dream weddings. Enter yourself in one of those. When you inevitably lose, go to Option #3.

➤ OPTION #3: *Tell Her the Truth*

She already knows it. Tell her you would love it if she could have her dream wedding but there's no money. Then tell her you could start saving now and wait five years or have a good old-fashioned keg party and get a friend to marry you in your backyard.

EXPENSIVE WEDDINGS DON'T BUY HAPPINESS

Couple	Cost	Outcome
Mariah Carey & Tommy Mottola	$500,000	Divorced (He probably paid that much to distract her from the fact that he was as old as her father.)
Brad Pitt & Jennifer Aniston	$1 million	Divorced
Tori Spelling & Charlie Shanian	$1 million	Divorced (She went on to break up another marriage. You go, girl!)
Madonna & Guy Ritchie	$1.5 million	Divorced (Because he realized she wasn't really British.)
Paul McCartney & Heather Mills	$3 million	Divorced
Liza Minnelli & David Gest	$3.5 million	Divorced (Because he's gay—why else would he marry Liza Minnelli?)

244. Your Wife Wants Children, but You Hate Kids

A job, a wife, a house in the suburbs, two kids, and a dog. That *was* your American Dream. But other than a few minutes with your nephew or you best friend's kids, you never really spent a whole lot of time with children. Then one day you do. And OMG, do you hate those little bastards! But your wife now wants kids even more. Shit!

The WTF Approach to Remaining F*#!-ing Childless

> ➤ OPTION #1: *Fake Your Orgasms*

This is hard to do for a guy, but you'll just have to find a way to make it happen.

> ➤ OPTION #2: *Cite Overpopulation*

This planet's population is growing at an alarming and unsustainable rate. Convince your wife that by having kids, she is just adding to the problem for the next generations, not contributing to society in a positive way. If you know your shit, you might just convince her.

➤ OPTION #3: *Get a Vasectomy*

This is a drastic thing to do, but it ensures that you'll be safe from kids. Even if you tell her you don't want kids and she agrees to respect your wishes, you never know if she is punching a hole in her diaphragm or skipping a day on the pill. Women, like the children they birth, cannot be fully trusted.

NOTE: Remember, vasectomies do not protect against HIV or any other venereal disease.

➤ OPTION #4: *Rent a Kid*

Adopt a kid from China. If you don't like it, you can always sell it to someone else or something. People are used to buying things from China, so you shouldn't have trouble getting rid of it.

PARENTS WHO HATED THEIR KIDS

- Marvin Gay, Sr.

- Emperor Nero

- Sue and Willie Coleman (Gary Coleman's parents, who stole all his money)

- God (he killed his only son, for Christ's sake!)

WOMEN ARE NO LAUGHING MATTER

"I have good-looking kids. Thank goodness my wife cheats on me."

—Rodney Dangerfield

245. She Wants a "Real" Man Around the House but You Can't Do Sh*t

She thought it was cute when you couldn't fix the broken fuse box. She thought it was adorable that you had no idea how to install track lighting. And she thought it was just a riot when you couldn't unclog the sink. But not anymore. Now every time you can't fix something she rolls her eyes and starts complaining. The honeymoon is over, and if you thought she loved you unconditionally, you better think again.

The WTF Approach to Being F*#!-ing Handy

➤ **OPTION #1: Become a Millionaire**

There's one thing a woman likes even more than a man who can fix anything, and that's a man who can *buy* anything. So make a shitload of cash and pay some slave to do all that bullshit around the house.

➤ **OPTION #2: Flip the Switch**

Tell her to fix it. You want to be treated equally? You got it. Hand her a wrench and tell her to take care of business.

WHAT THE F*#! IS UP WITH . . . HANDY BEING ATTRACTIVE

No matter what they say, women get turned on when you actually do something around the house. They like to play the damsel in distress, no matter how sophisticated they think they are. It is a biological fact that fixing a leak in the kitchen causes an immediate leak in a woman's vagina.

➤ **OPTION #3:** *Learn*

Look, you do have a dick right? Right? Okay, then you should be able to learn to do this shit. Take a class, buy a book, go online.

My wife used to think it was hysterical that her Jewish husband could not do anything around the house. She used to call her parents all the time and laugh about my incompetence. Fast forward a year, and all of a sudden this incapacity to perform even the most basic household tasks is far less charming. "I need a real man!" she shouts when I fail miserably at some fix-it job.

Women. You can't live with them, and being gay is really, really gross.

—GB

for the ladies . . .

You might want everything, but you can't have everything. If you wanted a handyman you should have married a plumber, not an accountant.

246. You Show Up Late to the Valentine's Day Dinner She Planned

You come home and smell the scented candles. The lights are dim and there's soft music playing in the background. You turn the corner and notice the table is set up for a romantic dinner. Oh shit, Valentine's dinner! You look over and there's your girl sitting in the corner with an open bottle of wine. You're too late and shit is about to hit the fan.

The WTF Approach to Dealing with One Pissed Off F*#!-ing Valentine

➤ OPTION #1: *Think Fast*

"Traffic, horrible traffic. Wait, no—flat tire, yeah! AAA took forever. Why didn't I call? Lost my phone, no, battery dead, yeah, just enough juice to call AAA. So happy that I'm home, had the worst day. You look beautiful. And skinny. So damn skinny. Like an Ethiopian. Except, you know, like hot."

➤OPTION #2: *Come Clean*

Just be honest. You screwed up plain and simple. Hopefully, she'll admire your honesty and let you off the hook. Offer to wash the dishes and go down on her for a few days.

➤OPTION #3: *Break Up with Her*

If she is really pissed, tell her you don't think this relationship is going to last and you want out. Soon she'll forget about the dinner and just be devastated about the breakup. Come back a day later and tell her you changed your mind. She'll be so happy that you are back it will be the best post–Valentine's Day sex ever!

247. You Throw Her a Surprise Party and No One Comes

Everyone likes a surprise party. Coming home to find a group of your family and your closest friends all huddled in your apartment screaming "surprise" as you walk in unaware of the festivities. But what if no one shows up? You prepare a big surprise party for your girlfriend. She's going to love it, you think. You call all her friends, buy balloons and other dumb party shit, and spend hours preparing the place for a wild and crazy time. But after an hour or so no one has come. It's just you and a ton of damn food and balloons. She should be home any minute. You hear the door. She opens it and turns on the light . . . WTF do you do?

The WTF Approach to Saving Her F*#!-ing Party

> **OPTION #1:** *Surprise!*

Hey, maybe she'll think it's sweet that you did all this yourself—just for her. Why do you need a bunch of people for a surprise party? When she asks why there is all this food, just tell her that you wanted to make it special. Then rent a movie on demand and sit around not talking like any other night.

> **OPTION #2:** *Deny It*

Say that you just redecorated the apartment to be more "festive," but there is no surprise party here. Then tell her that you have something special planned for just the two of you. Then take her to a nice romantic dinner so she won't know that she doesn't have any friends.

> **OPTION #3:** *Tell the Truth*

Something like this: "Bitch, you got no friends, what you want me to do?"

for the ladies . . .

Quickly get naked; he won't notice anything else.

IN THE FUTURE . . .

DATE A WOMAN with friends.

248. Your Wife Wipes You Out in the Divorce

The house went to her. The car went to her. The kids went to her. By the time she and her prick lawyer were done with you, the only thing you did get to keep was the herpes. And you thought she would, what, go easy on you? The truth is you never know a woman until you've met her in court. Say goodbye to all your shit.

The WTF Approach to Avoid Getting F*#!-ing Screwed!

➤ OPTION #1: *Kiss and Make Up*

If she'll have you back, beg her to give your marriage another chance. We know you can't stand the sight of her, but can you stand the sight of all those zeroes disappearing from your bank account? Money rules all. Why do you think your WTF authors became standup comics . . . the money? Duh!

➤ OPTION #2: *Get Even—Kind Of*

Meet a rich woman, marry her, father three beautiful children and then take her for everything she's got—just like your wife did to you. Then spend the rest of your days at the pool in your new house screwing José the gardener at will—just like your ex. Two can play at that game, bitch!

➤ OPTION #3: *Travel Back in Time*

Remember when you first clicked on her Match.com profile because she had big tits? Well, this time relent, moron.

➤ OPTION #4: *Buy Her a Pony*

Just get her a pony like all little girls want and she'll give back all the money.

➤ OPTION #5: *Kill Yourself*

Seriously, bro. Do it!

WHAT THE F*#! IS UP WITH . . .
LOSING HALF IN DIVORCE

Okay, I get the argument that once you are used to a life of luxury, it's hard to go back to living like a schnook. So I do think that a spouse is entitled to get some cash in the settlement. But half? How can you be entitled to *half* of what someone else made? Take a quarter and shut the hell up.

WOMEN ARE NO LAUGHING MATTER

"The difference between a divorce and a legal separation is that a legal separation gives a husband time to hide his money."

—Johnny Carson

DIVORCE AROUND THE WORLD

Think the United States sticks it to you on the divorce? Check out the repercussions in these places . . .

- The U.K.: The family home, fifty percent of all assets, and spousal support.
- Canada: Spousal and child support.
- Japan: Up to half of the benefits from their ex-husband's employee's pension.
- Iran: They're allowed to live . . . if they behave.

IN THE FUTURE . . .
GET A PRE-NUP, idiot.

ART CREDITS

DAILY BENDER

Want Some More?

Hit up our humor blog, The Daily Bender, to get your fill of all things funny—be it subversive, odd, offbeat, or just plain mean. The Bender editors are there to get you through the day and on your way to happy hour. Whether we're linking to the latest video that made us laugh or calling out (or bullshit on) whatever's happening, we've got what you need for a good laugh.

If you like our book, you'll love our blog. (And if you hated it, "man up" and tell us why.) Visit The Daily Bender for a shot of humor that'll serve you until the bartender can.

Sign up for our newsletter at

www.adamsmedia.com/blog/humor

and download our Top Ten Maxims No Man Should Live Without.